Racial Theories in Social Science

Racial Theories in Social Science: A Systemic Racism Critique provides a critique of the white racial framing and lack of systemic racism analysis prevalent in past and present mainstream race theory. As this book demonstrates, mainstream racial analysis, and social analysis more generally, remain stunted and uncritical because of this unhealthy white framing of knowledge and evasion or downplaying of institutional, structural, and systemic racism. In response to ineffective social science analyses of racial matters, this book presents a counter-approach—systemic racism theory. The foundation of this theoretical perspective lies in the critical insights and perspectives of African Americans and other people of color who have long challenged biased white-framed perspectives and practices and the racially oppressive and exclusionary institutions and social systems created by whites over several centuries.

Sean Elias studies racial group divisions and epistemological color lines in social science, black cultural-intellectual traditions, particularly black social thought and Louisiana Creole culture, and perspectives and practices of elites. He has taught at Prairie View A&M University (an HBCU) and Southern Methodist University (an HWCU) and now teaches at Colorado Mountain College while completing fieldwork on the Aspen elite.

n, Ella McFadden Professor at Texas A&M University, has .des of research on racism and sexism issues. Among his major are *Systemic Racism* (Routledge, 2006); *The White Racial Frame* edn, Routledge, 2013); *Racist America* (3rd edn, Routledge, 2014); *atinos Facing Racism* (Paradigm, 2014, with José Cobas); and *The Myth of the Model Minority* (2nd edn, Paradigm, 2015, with Rosalind Chou). He is the recipient of the American Sociological Association's Du Bois Career of Distinguished Scholarship Award and was the 1999–2000 President of the American Sociological Association.

New Critical Viewpoints on Society Series
Edited by Joe R. Feagin

Racial Theories in Social Science: A Systemic Racism Critique
By Sean Elias and Joe R. Feagin

Raising Mixed Race: Multiracial Asian Children in a Post-Racial World
By Sharon Chang (2015)

Antiracist Teaching
By Robert P. Amico (2014)

What Don't Kill Us Makes Us Stronger: African American Women and Suicide
By Kamesha Spates (2014)

Latinos Facing Racism: Discrimination, Resistance, and Endurance
By Joe R. Feagin and José A. Cobas (2014)

Mythologizing Black Women: Unveiling White Men's Racist and Sexist Deep Frame
By Brittany C. Slatton (2014)

Diverse Administrators in Peril: The New Indentured Class in Higher Education
By Edna Chun and Alvin Evans (2011)

Racial Theories in Social Science

A Systemic Racism Critique

Sean Elias and Joe R. Feagin

NEW YORK AND LONDON

First published 2016
by Routledge
711 Third Avenue, New York, NY 10017

and by Routledge
2 Park Square, Milton Park, Abingdon, Oxon, OX14 4RN

Routledge is an imprint of the Taylor & Francis Group, an informa business

© 2016 Taylor & Francis

The right of Sean Elias and Joe R. Feagin to be identified as the authors of this work has been asserted by them in accordance with sections 77 and 78 of the Copyright, Designs and Patents Act 1988.

All rights reserved. No part of this book may be reprinted or reproduced or utilised in any form or by any electronic, mechanical, or other means, now known or hereafter invented, including photocopying and recording, or in any information storage or retrieval system, without permission in writing from the publishers.

Trademark notice: Product or corporate names may be trademarks or registered trademarks, and are used only for identification and explanation without intent to infringe.

Library of Congress Cataloging in Publication Data
Names: Elias, Sean, author. | Feagin, Joe R., author.
Title: Racial theories in social science : a systemic racism critique / Sean Elias and Joe R. Feagin.
Description: New York, NY : Routledge, 2016. | Series: New critical viewpoints on society series
Identifiers: LCCN 2015040292| ISBN 9781138645219 (hardback) | ISBN 9781138645226 (pbk.) | ISBN 9781315628288 (ebook)
Subjects: LCSH: Racism. | Race relations. | Social sciences.
Classification: LCC HT1521 .E455 2016 | DDC 305.8–dc23
LC record available at http://lccn.loc.gov/2015040292

ISBN: 978-1-138-64521-9 (hbk)
ISBN: 978-1-138-64522-6 (pbk)
ISBN: 978-1-315-62828-8 (ebk)

Typeset in Adobe Caslon Pro
by Out of House Publishing
Printed and bound by CPI Group (UK) Ltd, Croydon, CR0 4YY

CONTENTS

PREFACE	IX
ACKNOWLEDGMENTS	XII
INTRODUCTION: POST-RACIAL AMERICA AND SOCIAL SCIENCE: REALITY OR MYTH?	1
PART I SOCIAL SCIENCES' HISTORIC MISFRAMING OF "RACE"	15
CHAPTER 1 THE TWIN BIRTHS OF SOCIAL SCIENCE AND RACE THEORY	17
CHAPTER 2 RACE THEORY AND THE RISE OF MAINSTREAM SOCIAL SCIENCE	37
PART II CONTEMPORARY MAINSTREAM SOCIAL SCIENCE AND RACE THEORY	55
CHAPTER 3 CHANGES IN THE FIELD OF RACE STUDIES	57
CHAPTER 4 SUBVERTING RACIAL ANALYSIS: EMPHASIZING PRACTICE, GROUPNESS, BOUNDARIES, AND REFLEXIVITY	78

Chapter 5	Class, Culture, Ethnicity, and Nationality—Anything But "Race"	102
Chapter 6	Race and the Genome: Biosocial Theories of Race	130
Chapter 7	Assimilation Theory's Dominion in Social Science	150
Chapter 8	A Systemic Racism Critique of Racial Formation Theory	181
Part III	Systemic Racism Theory: Background and Overview	207
Chapter 9	Critical Black Theory: Foundations of Systemic Racism Theory	209
Chapter 10	Systemic Racism Theory	248
Conclusion	Persisting Systemic Racism, the Empirical Reality	281
Index		289

PREFACE

In this book we use a systemic racism perspective in making critical sense of social science race theories in the past and present history of the United States and certain other Western countries. Several unsettling realities in the epistemology and practices of the social sciences have triggered our analysis of a host of historical and contemporary racial issues. In the first place, dominant theories and methodologies, as well as the constructed social worlds and worldviews, of mainstream social science are often unreflectively white-framed. Second, because of this dominant and uncritical white racial frame in social science, critical black theoretical perspectives and critical knowledge of other people of color have long been silenced, marginalized, or attacked. Subsequently, due in large part to this interminable neglect of critical black thought and critical insights of other people of color, necessary and key subject matter is missing in mainstream social science analysis. Missing are necessary conceptual concerns such as institutional and systemic racism, related ideologies and practices of white oppression, and concerted ideas and actions of whites and white social pathologies historically embedded in Western societies for several centuries.

An awareness of the ways these societal realities above problematize dominant knowledge paradigms and practices in the social sciences, and the fact that too little is currently being done to offset these troubling realities, are the primary reasons we have written this book. Indeed, until mainstream social science addresses and corrects numerous major biases, dysfunctionalities, and omissions in the field of racial analysis, the study of race and development of racial theory will remain severely impeded and regularly marred with this array of problems. More broadly, social analysis of human beings, explanations of the social world, and social theory in general will remain stunted without recognizing the significant role that racial meanings, racial grouping, and systemic racism play in greatly shaping contemporary society and human relations.

Sean Elias dedicates this work to Patricia J. Elias

ACKNOWLEDGMENTS

We are especially indebted to Pinar Batur, Edna Chun, Jessie Daniels, Rutledge Dennis, Kimberley Ducey, Frank Ortega, John Stone, and Adia Harvey Wingfield for their invaluable comments, suggestions, and criticisms on various drafts of this book, most of which have made this a stronger and more lucid analysis. Additionally, we would like to thank our many other colleagues and students, most especially those of color, who over the years in discussions and in their own published work have shaped the analyses of racial theorizing in this book. Finally, we would like to thank Dean Birkenkamp, our editor and friend, for his suggestions, encouragement, and patience as we completed this long-term project.

INTRODUCTION

POST-RACIAL AMERICA AND SOCIAL SCIENCE: REALITY OR MYTH?

During the 2014 political campaigns, US Representative Mo Brooks (R-AL) criticized Democratic Party recruiting and emphasized a conventional colorblind perspective:

> We should not be dividing anybody based on national heritage or race. Rather, we should be bringing us all together. That's what the melting pot ideal of America is all about. A person's skin pigmentation is something acquired at birth that has absolutely nothing to do with the merits of the person of how one should vote... I'm one of those who does not believe in racism and I believe everyone should be treated equally as American citizens... Race is immaterial.[1]

With the election of Barack Obama as president in 2008, the United States symbolically entered what most whites and some others have considered a post-racial age wherein skin color and "race" are no longer important. The majority white public and many white academics have proclaimed victory over racism and viewed US society as a new post-race and post-racism world, where one's skin color no longer matters. If racism, race, or color do manifest here or there, these incidents can be explained as isolated actions of extremists or remnants of a bygone era, not really representative of the current character and zeitgeist of US society, its major institutions, or its dominant culture. Supposedly, the highly racialized societal world of the recent past has dissipated, the racial hierarchy has substantially dissolved, and the reality of serious racial discrimination has largely disappeared.

In similar fashion, critical studies of racial group relations and critical theoretical analyses of institutional and systemic racism in the social sciences have frequently been delegitimized or marginalized. Social scientists from a variety of different racial backgrounds have seized upon and decontextualized Dr. Martin Luther King's statement that "people should be judged by the content of their character, not by the color of their skin."[2] Over the past few decades, certain colorblind views have become "common sense," even hegemonic, in numerous areas of the mainstream social sciences. One primary goal of this book is to examine this prevailing colorblind and post-racial framing in social science and reveal its numerous guises as they weave in and out of major racial theories developed since the 1960s. In our view, the pervasiveness of these typically uncritical colorblind and post-racial perspectives is not only corrupting of contemporary social science, but generally serves to legitimate persisting US and other Western countries' systemic racism, as well as their continuing and racialized imperialism across the globe.

Considering the speed with which this shift to emphasizing a post-racial, colorblind US society has taken place, it is surprising that few people—average citizens and social scientists alike—want to understand how the United States could be transformed from one of the world's most racist, segregated, and color-conscious societies into a supposedly post-racial society espousing colorblindness in such a short period. After all, for more than 80 percent of this country's four centuries, one's freedom from extreme white oppression hinged on one's perceived skin color and associated physical characteristics—a system of sanctioned racial oppression that only officially ended with the last major Civil Rights Act in 1968. The long historical epoch of slavery and Jim Crow (near-slavery) segregation generated a racialized socioeconomic system that rigidly divided white and black Americans according to physical characteristics—and still socially positions and frames whites as socially superior and powerful, and blacks and other people of color as inferior and powerless.

During the Jim Crow period in southern and border states (c. 1880–1969), housing, schools, train cars, buses, water fountains, public restrooms, and other public spaces were forcibly segregated by whites along strict color lines. In many cases, the signs signaling blacks' assigned spaces referred to them as "colored." Racial segregation in society and human divisions (for example, bans on intermarriage) between whites and blacks were legally enforced until the late 1960s—and, informally, many continue until this day.[3] During this long Jim Crow period, whites, especially elites, extended the white racial framing of society on numerous fronts. For example, in addition to white-on-black oppression, this period witnesses the changing of certain Southern and Eastern European immigrant groups, initially viewed as not white and facing some discrimination, into "white Americans." During this time the country also saw white racial fear and action directed against the "yellow peril" of Asian immigration and whites' continued vast land theft from Native Americans, still racialized as "redskins." Along the southern US border, whites generated patterns of group classification and segregation of Mexican Americans along racialized color lines. Throughout the late nineteenth century and twentieth century, powerful whites extended the US system of racial oppression of black Americans and Native Americans to include numerous other non-European groups. White domination in economic, political, and cultural institutions remained intact and became more sophisticated during this long Jim Crow period. Vivid racial realities of the color line were unmistakably a central part of the US social landscape leading up to the civil rights movements and intellectual crises of the 1960s.[4]

So, how did "race"—that is, society's many racialized structures and color-coded human relationships—supposedly disintegrate rapidly? With particular regard to the social sciences, how did the field of race and racism studies often get replaced by "ethnic" or "diversity" studies? Why have the post-1960s developments of black studies and other critical-racism studies come to be discredited among a great many white social scientists? And why has the critical study of US racism substantially declined in numerous areas? White racial frames of colorblindness and post-raciality, and key critiques of this framing, can help us better understand and answer these important questions. In the following pages, we critically examine these more recent forms of white racial framing, present a broad critique of white racial framing in society and social science more generally, and identify and analytically develop central concerns of systemic racism theory.

Social Science Knowledge and Theories of Racial Matters

Certainly, the mainstream social sciences produce useful and informative knowledge about the social world and human relations. Yet, they also generate much misinformation and disinformation—that is, much incorrect, tainted, and biased knowledge about that social world. Indeed, the social sciences both advance and obscure knowledge about societies and social interaction among human beings. At times, what passes for esteemed social scientific knowledge is, in fact, off-track or stunted. More often than one might expect, valuable social scientific knowledge grows at the margins of the disciplines, away from the mainstream or establishment arenas. We should recognize this important tension in the social sciences between avenues of misinformation and those of social scientific enlightenment.

Social science knowledge relies on its particular methods of questioning the social world and human interaction. What social scientists observe in the social world is *not* society itself or human social interaction itself, but society and patterns of human interaction shaped by social science perspectives, framing, and methods of questioning. To be sure, some social scientists' methods of questioning have benefited social scientific knowledge more than the questioning of others. Some have asked more significant, pointed, and critically aware questions about the social environment, and human actions and interactions in that environment, than have others. More importantly, some have addressed key pressing questions about the social world and human beings' behaviors that others avoid or are unable to conceive. Competing and contradictory views of the social world and human relations are employed in the social sciences, and thus necessary questions arise about whose views or methods of questioning most influence scientific knowledge, and which best represent the actual realities of societies.

Most social scientific knowledge emanates from the establishment community of social scientists—where professionalized social scientists compete for prestige in a field shaped by societal power structures, and where mainstream methods are themselves regularly in need of critical questioning. In mainstream social science, for example, racial, ethnic, class, and gender hierarchies are evident, as are a variety of related exclusive group networks and organizational privileges. Patriarchy, class elitism, ethnocentrism, and institutional racism continue to shape social science disciplines and inform conventional methods of inquiry. Numerous marginalized groups of social scientists—for example, critical feminist, Marxist, and black social scientists—have documented the hierarchies of power and privilege inside and outside the academic sphere. They have demonstrated how group power structures and imbalanced power relations in mainstream social science often work to bias and limit the production of social scientific knowledge.

In the following pages, we critically address various problems associated with mainstream racial theories and methods that inhibit social scientific production of knowledge. In this analysis we articulate a systemic racism perspective. From this perspective we critique mainstream racial theories and methods of questioning racial matters, which we often find to be corrupted by a lingering Eurocentrism and powerful white racial framing—and especially lacking due to a historical disregard for the perspectives and insights of social scientists of color.[5] Even though systemic racism in the United States and US and other Western colonialism across the globe remain pressing subject matter for the social sciences, most mainstream social scientists continue to employ weak instruments for measuring matters of white racism and colonialism and instead utilize concepts and theories steeped in narrowly constructed Eurocentric frameworks. Ignored or obfuscated are the precise instruments of assessing realities of racism and colonialism often produced by social scientists of color, who frequently operate substantially outside the mainstream and in opposition to Eurocentric social scientific worldviews. Equally disconcerting, significant numbers of establishment social scientists have moved away from serious analyses of societal racism altogether. Far from the colorblind, post-racial vision of those social scientists who retreat from a systemic racism analysis, we regularly observe a persisting white racial framing that contorts much research and theory in mainstream social science today as in the past, negatively affecting the historical development and current state of knowledge-generation in social science disciplines.

A Brief Introduction to Systemic Racism Theory

The primary goals of this book are to provide an intellectual and historical critique of the field of this mainstream racial analysis, past and present, and then offer a more precise, useful, and critical theory or paradigm of racial matters that analyzes and illustrates the ubiquity of systemic racism in contemporary society and whites' role in the creation and maintenance, including the racial framing, of this systemic racism.

Because the important concepts of systemic racism theory are only assessed in detail in the last chapter of this book, we will now briefly introduce for the reader some of these key concepts. *Systemic racism, the white racial frame,* and *the counter-frames of people of color* are central analytical concepts and themes in systemic racism theory. *Systemic racism* is the manifestation of historically developed, societally embedded ways of white Eurocentric thinking, of the organization of social groups according to a racial hierarchy separating whites and people of color, and of an array of racially oppressive institutions devised by whites that target people of color. Systemic racism thus involves a racialized system of power relations embedded throughout the social fabric of contemporary societies with intimate historical connections to the social systems of slavery and colonialism. In other words, systemic racism is a product of colonialist and slavery societies created in the past by whites, and in many cases involves a more contemporary reworking of the racialized thinking and practices that made up the social systems of colonialism and slavery. Systemic racism is thus synonymous with *white* racism. Today, systemic racism is a highly developed, well-institutionalized, structurally embedded, historically deep, white-defined racism that significantly shapes virtually every facet of many contemporary societies. Systemic racism emphasizes macro-level institutional and structural features of racism, but realizes the importance of examining how racial oppression shapes and operates at the micro and meso levels of society.

A fundamental feature and underlying mechanism of systemic racism is *white racial framing*, the thought and actions that construct and support the *white racial frame*. White racial framing involves the explanation and construction of social reality from the perspective of dominant whites, one normally steeped in Eurocentrism, thereby creating a long-lasting *white racial frame*. This white racial frame is a meta-structure that develops and reinforces ideas, actions, networks, institutions, and social structures according to the views and practical racial-group interests of white people. In contrast, the *counter-frames of people of color* present different understandings, practices, visions of the socio-racial arrangements of society, and the innovative means of realizing that vision. In most cases, the *counter-framing of people of color* challenges the status quo and dominant narratives of white racial framing.

Systemic racism theory is social theory that focuses on and seeks to explain the structures and operations of systemic racism, including its powerful white racial framing. Systemic racism theory is a *counter-system perspective*, one opposed to many of the white-framed concepts, theories, and methods that emerge at the center of much mainstream social science. As we show in later chapters, it is much more focused on people of color's insights and ways of investigating racial matters that are discovered on the margins of academia and the larger society, where fertile counter-frames are frequently developed. In contrast to most mainstream race theory, systemic racism theory addresses *institutionalized racism* (not just racial attitudes and racial group comparisons), the extreme forms of dysfunctionality associated with racial oppression, and whites' role in establishing systemically racist social systems. Additionally, systemic racism theory emphasizes historical and contemporary empirical analyses of many kinds as necessary components of any adequate racial theorizing, is highly skeptical of hyper-scientism and outdated approaches of contemporary social science, and views many aspects of today's mainstream social sciences as largely uncritical and uninspiring.

Several other important concepts discussed in the following pages that are central to systemic racism theory include *racial hierarchy*, the *color* line, *whites*, *people of color*, the *dominant* or *mainstream*, and *Eurocentrism*. The *racial hierarchy* that places whites above people of color in intrinsic human worth and societal position is a central feature of systemic racism, created by whites over the past several centuries in an effort to impose and justify exploitation, subjugation, and segregation of people of color. The white-framed racial hierarchy, discovered in many discourses on human intelligence and in the societal organization of neighborhoods and nations, generally works to establish whites as superior in resources and power to people of color. A major result of the racial hierarchy is the *color line*, the shorthand term for the racialized social, economic, political, cultural, and psychological divide between people of color and whites, a divide that is centrally material but also operates in the arenas of ideas, values, and beliefs. For example, the color line is apparent in contemporary educational institutions—the persistence of historically black colleges and universities and historically white colleges and universities—and in the epistemological divisions between critical black social scientists and mainstream white social scientists (see Chapter 9).

Considering that US society still maintains some substantially separate educational and other social institutions for whites and blacks, it is difficult to argue against the fact that socially constructed racial divisions are ever-present social realities. *Whites* refer to people of mostly European descent and the group that historically produced systemic racism over several centuries. In this societal development and historical march, whites generally have been the racial group that has possessed the greatest racial power and, correspondingly, been the greatest racial oppressor in pursuit of that power. People of color have long been targets of white oppression and subject to white abuses of power. *People of color* refers to the assigned racially coded classifications of groups by whites in the white-framed racial hierarchy. In this well-institutionalized system, people of color have historically been crudely divided into "blacks" (African descent), "yellows" (Asian descent), "reds" (American indigenous descent), and "browns" (Middle Eastern, Pacific Island, Meso-American and South American descent), all of whom stand in relation to "whites" (European descent). While this white-imposed hierarchy divides racial groups into at least five distinct categories, the racialized color line that has developed in the United States and other contemporary societies tends to even more broadly divide people between whites and people of color.

Because of contemporary whites' position of power and top ranking in the racial hierarchy (a hierarchy both symbolic and real), whites are presently the *dominant* racial group, that is, the group with the most power, resources, and capital. Because of this dominant social position, the ideologies and social practices of whites represent the societal *mainstream*, which includes whites' socio-racial framing and cultural hegemony. The aforementioned racial hierarchy, division between whites and people of color, and notions of the dominant and mainstream are tied to *Eurocentrism*, the ethnocentric belief that whites (people of European descent) and their social inherited belief systems, social worlds, and other characteristics of "whiteness" are superior to those of other racial groups.

Throughout this book we expose the problems associated with the racial hierarchy and color line; reassess taken-for-granted understandings of whites and people of color; illustrate weaknesses of the dominant and mainstream social structures, intellectual perspectives, and cultural practices; and reveal how Eurocentrism continues to pollute much of social science and US society. Thus, we offer a *critical* take on society and human behavior, a position that challenges the often damaging mainstream understandings and narratives about people and the social world. This critical position demands engaging in the task of questioning many common-sense explanations of the social world and human beings that still retain legitimacy in the social sciences and larger societal universe.

Challenges and Limitations of this Book

We should be clear about our goals in a short book about an expansive subject area. We offer a systemic racism perspective that provides a probing critique of, and response to, important trends in the field of race theory in mainstream social science. We do not offer a full overview of all important aspects of this now extensive field of race theory and analysis. Here we are concerned primarily with presenting a critique of the mainstream tradition of racial analysis in social science that has been predominantly white, male, and/or elitist, a dominant and unbending reality up until the demographic transformations (specifically, addition of men and women of color, white women, and whites from less privileged backgrounds) in social science that began in earnest in the late 1960s. Race theorists of color (men and women) and white women who have developed race theory are largely absent in the first two sections of our analysis because we are critiquing the dominant white male racial framing in mainstream social science, which has reigned throughout most of the history of US and Western social sciences.

This analysis has several other limitations. This is a study of systemic racism and the associated processes of racialization in the Western world, most often in the United States, and is specifically focused on the subjugation, social conflict, and other realities of racial oppression stemming from European-imposed social systems that emanate from European colonialism and slavery. Whites' power in this Western context is unquestionably our focus. However, we are aware of the many significant examples of and challenges to white power in the international or global context. Many examples of that global social conflict, systems of oppression, and intergroup relations are absent here, yet our aim is to better explain the white-framed racial phenomena of systemic racism that has shaped large parts of the social world in the West, "settler" nations, and colonial outposts outside the West for centuries. While our work is US- and Western-centric, we hope that our analysis demonstrates that the systemic racism perspective can be used to critically assess racial realities in societies well beyond the borders of the United States and the Western world.

Our work frequently sacrifices in-depth analyses for a broad assessment of the field of race theorizing. As we see it, at this moment in the development and simultaneous critique of racial theories and analyses, social scientists need to step back and take a broader view of the field, a task to which we contribute in this study. Our work may also be judged by some as being overly pessimistic about the state of racial matters or as anti-American or anti-Western because of our severe criticisms of the problematical racialized history of the US and the West. Again, at this moment in the development of racial analysis, it is especially important, indeed necessary, that social scientists address the harsh, sobering realities of US and global systemic racism and challenge whites' long abuse of racialized power. Scholarly works that fail to address fully the social and human problems associated with systemic racism and the dysfunctionality of white supremacy, in particular, will continue to repeat the stale, unproductive, misguided, and indeed harmful analyses of past mainstream social science.

As one astute reviewer of a draft of this book noted, one significant challenge to, and irony associated with, our critique of white social scientists' misframing and weak analyses of racial realities is the fact that we, the two authors, are white social scientists, members of the dominant US racial group. It is true that we will never escape certain white privileges and inclinations in our own particular forms of white framing. However, we at least recognize some of our limitations and challenges in presenting our views of racial matters, and adopt a thoroughly critical stance. We realize that the Western social sciences are largely white-framed and that we are without question white social scientists who have been trained in, and who inadvertently reproduce aspects of, the white racial frame. However, for some decades now, we have actively sought important knowledge outside the white-controlled mainstream in the works of black social scientists and other social scientists of color, whose views often provide keener insights about social reality than those clouded by white-framed narratives routinely used to perpetuate white power and position in society. Along with facing the challenges of our own positionality, we recognize that as white men, we have numerous privileges of whiteness and do not face the same academic and societal distancing and severe consequences for dissent from mainstream racial analysis that social scientists of color commonly face. As whites, we generally have the privilege and leeway of voicing these critical opinions in public. It is important to stress that much of our analysis of systemic racism is an analysis long voiced by social scientists of color, yet smothered by the equally long history of dominant white framing in the Western social sciences.

A Brief Overview of Book Chapters
Considering the continuing importance of racial matters in the US and globally, as supported by overwhelming amounts of empirical data,

we feel it necessary to critically address the contemporary culture of ineffective, misguided, or shortsighted social scientific investigations of "race" that are anchored in a white racial framing and its associated Eurocentrism. Part I begins with several chapters that review early developments of social sciences' misframing of racial matters and the systemically racist social contexts surrounding that development.

Next, the chapters in Part II demonstrate the numerous serious fallacies and intellectual weaknesses of colorblindness and post-race/racism perspectives and of various class, culture, nationality, ethnicity, biosocial, and assimilationist perspectives that downplay or supplant a necessary focus on matters of systemic racism. As we document, systemic racism and other power-critical racial analyses are routinely marginalized in mainstream social science by both conservative and liberal traditions of racial analysis. Problematically, too, many social scientists operate according to Eurocentric social science frameworks and power networks that ignore or downplay the perspectives of critical social scientists of color. Our way of questioning racial matters and assessing and developing the counter-mainstream theories presented here is one termed, as noted previously, *systemic racism theory*.

Then, in Part III we provide a more developed review of critical black theory of institutional racism over many decades. We thought it best to show in Parts I and II the intellectual history of this white racial framing in social science before demonstrating how this way of thinking about the social world and human beings has, from the start, been challenged by critical black social thinkers, and is today countered by a systemic racism theoretical approach with deep and continuing roots in critical black thought, past and present. In this section we analyze the counter-frames developed against systemic racism, the marginalized and displaced perspectives and analyses of people of color that have long challenged systemic racism and its dominant white racial framing of society. Some key questions arise here. Why are so few white social scientists aware of or engaged with these valuable knowledge frameworks and analytical positions? Why do so many white social scientists bypass the central themes discovered in the critical thinking of people of color, especially knowledge emanating from the strong tradition of critical black thought? The first chapter in this section of the book responds to these questions and others in a more developed discussion of critical black theory.

Many central concepts and claims of contemporary *systemic racism theory* originate with the longstanding critical black tradition in the social sciences. We demonstrate in this section's chapters that critical black sociologists have long provided highly accurate and profound understandings of racial matters, exposed the inner workings and reasoning of asymmetrically structured racial patterns, and explained the history and current state of white-imposed racism that works to subjugate people of color in US society and other societies across the globe. Building on these deep insights of critical black social scientists and other critical sociologists of color, as well as white social scientists critically aware of Eurocentric-framing and their position in unjust racist systems, in the last chapter we provide a more detailed overview of contemporary systemic racism theory, an overview drawing heavily on the systemic racism theory and allied field research of Joe Feagin and his numerous students and colleagues over five decades as important navigating tools. Here we delineate in some detail the foundations, central tenets, and broad implications of systemic racism theory. In this process we again address and demonstrate major deficiencies in mainstream sociology's methods of addressing current racial matters.

We then briefly conclude with a theoretical assessment of, and possible remedies for, the troubling state and future of racial meanings, unequal racial relations, and a deeply institutionalized, systemic white racism that negatively shape social worlds and relations among human beings in this and other societies.

Notes

1 Paul Gattis, "Rep. Mo Brooks: Democrats 'Dividing America by Race' in 'Waging a War on Whites,'" www.al.com/news/index.ssf/2014/08/rep_mo_brooks_democrats_dividi.html (accessed September 28, 2015).
2 For example, Shelby Steele, *The Content of Our Character: A New Vision of Race in America* (New York: Harper Perennial, 1998).

3 In 2013, Tennessee pastor Donny Reagan stated, "I don't believe in mixing marriages," and that if "you want to marry a black man, you girls don't ask me to do it…" See Lyndsey Price, "Preacher's Controversial Video Goes Viral," *WCYB.com*, February 20, 2014, www.wcyb.com/news/watercooler/ppreachers-controversial-video-goes-viral/24585838 (accessed September 30, 2015).
4 For details, see Joe R. Feagin and Clairece B. Feagin, *Racial and Ethnic Relations*, 9th edn (Upper Saddle River, NJ: Prentice Hall, 2011).
5 Eurocentrism is the view that European societies, culture, and knowledge are superior to the societies, cultures, and knowledge production of other racial-ethnic groups.

PART I
SOCIAL SCIENCES' HISTORIC MISFRAMING OF "RACE"

CHAPTER 1
THE TWIN BIRTHS OF SOCIAL SCIENCE AND RACE THEORY

"Race" is a foundational force in the development of the modern world and continues fundamentally to shape contemporary societies and interrelations among societies. More specifically, *racial matters* affect the lives of most human beings across the globe.[1] Thus, much is at stake in asking the right questions about contemporary racial meanings, framing, hierarchies, and power—that is, about the social-historical realities of systemic racism. Constructions of racial meanings and associated structures of racial relations, with their great power and privilege imbalances, continue to shape contemporary societal worlds and human beings' everyday interactions. Numerous contemporary societies are founded and/or grounded in racist systems that greatly and unjustly benefit whites and greatly and unjustly disadvantage people of color. The racially defined processes and structures of contemporary human relations and social worlds that we term *systemic racism* have generally evolved out of European-imposed slavery systems, historical imperialism and colonialism, and subsequent large-scale subjugations of peoples of color across the globe. As a result, systemic racism exists and persists as a *widespread* social reality of the modern age and our current societal worlds.

Yet, the mainstream social sciences largely operate as if white-imposed, well-institutionalized racism no longer exists or is a modest or disappearing problem in modern Western societies. This neglect of properly analyzing racially based social inequalities, stratification, and power structures—and the ways they affect the social opportunities and connectedness, life-chances, and life-worlds of differently racialized individuals and groups—is unconscionable and stymies the development and impact of social scientific knowledge as a whole.

Even contemporary mainstream social scientists who study racial matters often approach their analyses with weakly constructed research questions, unreflective theoretical positions, or conventionally limited methodological approaches. They are handicapped by the chains of professionalism and an inability to escape a long history, indeed tradition, of social scientific misframing of racial inequalities and hierarchies. Before we analyze the mainstream struggle to produce insightful scientific knowledge about racial matters and offer a detailed critique of trends in mainstream social science analysis, a review of some origins of social sciences' misframing of "race" is clearly in order. Many contemporary social scientists' failure to ask pertinent questions about systemic racism developed by whites, develop constructive theories about and methods for investigating racism, and challenge the pervasive white racial framing operating as a vehicle of misinformation throughout mainstream social science, is best understood by examining the founding of mainstream social sciences and their often problematical examinations of racial matters.

Unlike most mainstream analyses of the sociology of race that begin with Robert Ezra Park and the Chicago School of sociology, we extend our critical assessment back to the founding and early development of the mainstream social sciences, illustrated well in the social thought of Auguste Comte and Herbert Spencer, and their heirs: Karl Marx, Émile Durkheim, and Max Weber. Although their racial views have often been overlooked or downplayed, these famous social scientists have had a lasting influence not only on sociology and other social sciences in general, but also on their treatment of racial matters in particular. (Note that in Chapter 9 we also challenge the mainstream narrative that the US sociology of racial matters begins with the white male sociologists of the Chicago School.)

Reassessing Auguste Comte and Herbert Spencer

Not coincidentally, the mainstream social sciences were born about the same time that European and US imperialism and slavery systems were dramatically expanding throughout the nineteenth century. European analysts, including the new social scientists, helped to create systems of thought and knowledge that justified the human actions and social praxis of racial oppression necessary for colonization and enslavement across the globe. European colonialist empires and slavery systems, well-established by the eighteenth century, were formed through acts of massive oppression tied to major new knowledge claims, the latter by the nineteenth century involving full social scientific legitimization and rationalizing of these acts of extreme oppression. Newly formed European social sciences, along with Western religious doctrines and framing, played increasingly central roles in the material development and intellectual justifications for colonialism and slavery, and in the centuries-long subsequent post-slavery and post-colonial oppression of people of color.[2]

Europeans' global oppression of peoples of color—a central facet of colonialism and slavery systems—was sanctioned by social scientific arguments about the "racial superiority" of whites and "racial inferiority" of people of color living outside of Europe. The social sciences emerging in the nineteenth century were significantly influenced by previous European social philosophers such as David Hume and Immanuel Kant. In his writings, the still-influential Hume openly described "negroes" as inferior "breeds of men." Additionally, Europe's most celebrated philosopher, Immanuel Kant, actually taught courses on what would later be considered social science topics, in which he asserted that "humanity exists in its greatest perfection in the white race" and that there is a hierarchy of "races of mankind" with superior whites at the top.[3] Kant was among the very first Western thinkers to explicitly use the modern term and concept of "races" in a deterministically biological and hierarchical sense. About the same time, the prominent European anatomist Johann Blumenbach utilized "races" in the same biological sense in his influential "race" classification. He coined the term "Caucasians" (Europeans) for those at the top of his race hierarchy, with Mongolians (Asians), Ethiopians (Africans), Americans (Native Americans), and Malays (Polynesians) down the hierarchy.[4] Early white European and North American social scientists were influenced by these Enlightenment thinkers, whose racialized perspectives accented the biological and sociocultural supremacy of the European (white) "race."

One of the central activities of the newly forming social sciences was the further development of measures and questions about the differences among races and related theoretical arguments and research methods intended to demonstrate whites' racial superiority. Early European social scientists' preoccupation with racial matters centered on their theories and methods for understanding race, and this preoccupation had great impact on the development of the social science disciplines. Auguste Comte, the white European analyst who coined the term "sociology" and is often considered the "father" of the sociology discipline, developed the blueprint for sociology's early theoretical framework with his organicist theory of society, informed in part by European colonialist expansion and European-imposed social hierarchies. Comte's thought influenced numerous founders of mainstream sociology in Europe and the United States. Comte was not a racial analyst per se, but his sociological analyses such as *Cours de philosophie positive* (1830–42) delineated a Eurocentric view of society and a hierarchy of human beings.[5]

Underlying Comte's organicist societal model and human relations, and its subsequent development as "structural functionalism," are beliefs in the social supremacy and innate power of certain "advanced" individuals, groups, and nations. The model reflects beliefs in a naturally occurring social hierarchy and an unequal division of labor among individuals, groups, and nations. Additionally, built upon these beliefs is a view that some of these individuals and groups are *naturally destined* to rule over others. This theory of group superiority was easily adapted to justify group exploitation across racial, ethnic, class, religious, and gender lines. In the case of racial matters, versions of Comte's framework were used to justify colonialism and slavery systems—that is, to justify whites' colonizing, exploitation, and violence-enforced power over people of color.⁶ Eighteenth-century Christian beliefs that distinguished between God's chosen (whites and those who are civilized) and damned (those who possess the "mark of Cain" and who are primitive) also influenced Comte's view of human beings and the social realm.

Comte's influential sociological perspective clearly established a social theory of white or European supremacy. For Comte, "evolution at its highest point" is discovered in "the civilization of Europe."⁷ He endorses a sociological view of a racial hierarchy with whites at the top of the social pyramid, supported by people of color. According to Comte, whites are intellectually and morally superior to other races, and Europeans' societal organization is the most "civilized"—the model for a good society. He perceived the social organization of people of color as "primitive." By viewing non-Europeans as "underdeveloped" and "inferior," Comte further opened the door to the new social sciences' obsession with studying social pathologies of people of color and viewing white folkways as the norm to measure other racial groups. Additionally, by referencing shaky biological understandings of race popularized by the pseudo-sciences of "cerebral physiology" and "phrenology," Comte foreshadowed the future implementation by some social scientists of quack theories of race and quack methods for investigating racial group differences.⁸ More problematically, Comte formatively translated his ethnocentric social views about group differences and hierarchy into understandings of an organicist model of society and human relations, a general model that other European social analysts, such as Alexis de Tocqueville, Émile Durkheim, and Herbert Spencer, would develop into conventional forms of structural functionalism and social conflict theory, major frameworks in mainstream social sciences ever since.⁹

Alexis de Tocqueville, one of Comte's contemporaries, is often considered to be a founding sociologist whose analyses of US society in *Democracy in America* (1835) are routinely covered in social theory courses. De Tocqueville, a white French intellectual, forcefully spelled out Comte's and other early European and North American social scientists' views of "races," when he wrote: "If we reasoned from what passes in the world, we should almost say that the European is to the other races of mankind, what man is to the lower animals; he makes them subservient to his use; and when he cannot subdue, he destroys them."[10] While praised as a brilliant analyst and defender of democracy by most contemporary social scientists, de Tocqueville was in fact an early *white supremacist theorist* with an aggressively negative framing of African and Native Americans: "Among these widely differing families of men, the first that attracts attention, the superior in intelligence, in power, and in enjoyment, is the white, or European, the man preeminently so called; below him appear the Negro and the Indian." Later, he indicated in some detail his blatantly racist framing by insisting that a black man's "physiognomy is to our eyes hideous, his understanding weak, his tastes low; and we are almost inclined to look upon him as a being intermediate between man and the brutes."[11] The fact that mainstream social scientists have generally ignored de Tocqueville's white supremacist framing of US racial groups and society reveals as much about contemporary US social science as it does about the social science of de Tocqueville's era.

Much of Comte's thought, once translated and condensed by British social scientist Harriet Martineau, was imported into the US by the early white sociological thinkers George Fitzhugh and Henry Hughes.[12] In their influential books they utilized Comte's organicist thinking, evolutionary views of "races," and Eurocentrism to support a white-dominated US society that legitimized slavery and white oppression of black people and other people of color. Written in the 1850s run-up to the Civil War, Fitzhugh's *Sociology for the South* (1854) and Hughes' *Treatise on Sociology* (1854) formulated "sociological" theories, arguing forcefully that whites serve a more important function and necessarily occupy a higher position in the social structure than blacks and other people of color.[13] Because of this "natural" and "divinely ordained" division between superior and inferior races, a racialized society involving black enslavement and a social system controlled by whites was essential.

Hughes' *Treatise* envisioned a "societary" system labeled *warranteeism* that divided whites into a superordinate race of warrantors and blacks into a subordinate race of warrantees.[14] This social relationship with whites exerting complete power over black people reflected the "laws" of nature and the "ways of God." Fitzhugh's *Sociology for the South* and his later work, *Cannibals All! or Slaves without Masters* (1857), express the same racial views and sociological outlook as Hughes, arguing that black enslavement by whites was sanctioned by the Bible and that slavery and other blatant exploitation of people of color were part of the natural racial order.[15] Most white US social scientists of the late nineteenth century would try to bury these social science writings of Hughes and Fitzhugh in efforts to erase the link between the developing social sciences and earlier aggressive pro-slavery thought. However, many of the racial understandings of Hughes and Fitzhugh were not discarded but often reinvented with new terminology and theoretical reformulations that accompanied the growth of mainstream, professionalized social sciences in the early twentieth-century colleges and universities of the United States.

Along with utilizing Comte's thought, most early white social scientists embraced some of Herbert Spencer's ideas, specifically his social Darwinism that reworked Comtean notions of European social dominion. Spencer, a white English intellectual, borrowed Comte's views about race, but added a new dimension to understanding racial matters: a "natural" competition and conflict among races that leads to the social "survival of the fittest," a phrase he coined. Spencer examined the conflict among different societies. Drawing on the Comtean organicist metaphor, he discussed racial groups in diverse societies as organisms in "competition/conflict," organisms that are subject to different levels of adaptation and success. He claimed that superior racial groups adapt to changing social circumstances more quickly than inferior racial groups.[16] Equating skin color with intelligence and morality, and emphasizing the "more perfect intellectual vision" of Europeans, Spencer argued that whites possess inherent "traits"—social skills and technologies—that give them an advantage over people of color.[17] Additionally, he presented a hierarchy of races and societies ranked according to their level of "civilization." In this era, the sociological view of large social groups (i.e., races) as superior or inferior, primitive or advanced, was widely embraced by white social scientists across the globe, from Lester Ward, Franklin Giddings, and W.I. Thomas in the

United States to Gabriel Tarde, Ludwig Gumplowicz, and Houston Chamberlain in Europe. Moreover, Spencer's social Darwinism and Eurocentrism in general influenced the upper ranks of capitalists, including Andrew Carnegie, John D. Rockefeller, and Cornelius Vanderbilt, demonstrating the inseparable ties between white racism and Western capitalism.

Most white social scientists of the late nineteenth and early twentieth century embraced social Darwinist views about the social divisions among races. Spencer and subsequent social Darwinists posed questions concerning the coexistence of, and organic struggle among, biologically conceived races. They proposed the idea that if people of color (often termed "savages" and "natives") could not be civilized or exploited by whites, then they should be fully dominated or destroyed. This aggressively imperialist view of relations among racial groups, and the power dynamics of racial oppression inherent in whites' subjugation of people of color, were exemplified in Belgium's decimation of Congo's native population, "Kaffir" wars in South Africa, Australians' slaughter of "aborigines," and the significant reduction or extermination of Native American groups in the United States, Canada, and South and Central America. White social scientists' misframing of racial matters, especially social Darwinism, offered social science justifications for white domination over people of color. For the most part, this mainstream social science did not provide thoughtful critiques and accurate scientific knowledge to counter Europeans' racist aggression toward people of color and to advance critical understandings of this globally orchestrated racial oppression.

Spencer's undisguised racist views are further outlined in a letter to Mori Arinori, the Japanese minister serving in London in 1882. In the correspondence, Spencer's racial perspectives acknowledge whites' unbridled colonialist aggression and heightened fears of racial intermarriage. He writes that there is "abundant proof… by the inter-marriages of human races and inter-breeding of animals, that when the varieties mingled diverge beyond a certain slight degree the result is invariably a bad one."[18] Spencer believed in restricting the social interaction among racial groups, more specifically by actively segregating them. To this end, he proclaimed that immigration policies should eliminate or severely restrict cross-racial immigration, and that, if cross-racial immigration is allowed, the dominant racial groups in host countries should subdue minority racial groups allowed to immigrate. He emphasized that he

> entirely approved of the regulations which have been established in America for restraining Chinese immigration... If the Chinese are allowed to settle extensively in America, they must either, if they remain unmixed, form a subject race in the position, if not slaves, yet of a class approaching slaves, or if they mix they must form a bad hybrid.[19]

Both Spencer and Comte were instrumental in the growth of mainstream social science and especially in providing conceptual frameworks for mainstream analyses of racial matters in Europe and the United States. Considering that Comte is viewed as the father of sociology—the creator of a positivistic science that now emphasizes methods of quantitative analysis, and a forefather of structural functionalism—we find it surprising that his sociological thought and views about racial matters are largely erased from the current histories of sociology, studies of classical social theory, and accounts of "race" analysis in the social sciences. Comte's organicist framework, theories of the evolution of races, and arguments supporting white supremacy in societies were instrumental in helping to establish Eurocentrism and white racial framing in the social sciences. Comte helped to naturalize Europeans' oppressive treatment of people of color, thereby making it appear as if their racially subordinated conditions were normal or justified.

Building on Comte's white framing of the social world and Eurocentric worldview, Spencer further developed and refined a white-framed social scientific perspective of society. Like most social scientists of European descent in this era, he easily accepted the belief that national and global social worlds were fundamentally split between a well-structured white sphere and a dysfunctional, unstructured sphere largely inhabited by people of color. Like other European social scientists, Spencer certainly recognized racial conflict in the modern world, but evaded serious discussion of conflictual tensions among whites and people of color formed through brutally exploitative European colonialism and slavery. He failed to articulate the roots of the consequent "race problem": whites' extreme mistreatment and exploitation, with its accompanying racialized misperceptions and misrepresentations, of many peoples of color during the centuries-long periods of slavery and colonization. According to him, the racial *inferiority* of people of color was the cause of the so-called race problem, not global European and US colonialism and imperialism promoted by whites' unquestioned sense of racial superiority.

With the large-scale societal transformations of the late nineteenth and early twentieth centuries that accompanied unfettered industrialism and capitalist growth—much of it built on centuries of wealth and capital generation from highly exploitative colonialist and slavery systems—Spencer and his social science colleagues were experiencing more intensely shifting societal worlds than did their predecessors in the social sciences. The meanings of race and racial relations were shifting as well, but mostly not in a progressive manner. Spencer and his social science contemporaries, all elite white men, faced a new wave of societal issues—non-European immigration into "their" societies and the threat of significant challenges to whites' power, subjects inconceivable to most earlier European social analysts. As we noted, Spencer responded by condemning cross-racial immigration, interracial marriage, and people of color who vie for real societal power and resources.

Spencer, along with other white male social scientists of the day, sought to dissect what was viewed as the social dysfunctionality and pathologies of people of color, the racially oppressed, and not to reflect on the extraordinary social oppressions and dysfunctionality of whites, the global racial oppressors. One finds here one source of mainstream social sciences' tendency to blame the victims and ignore the victimizers in understanding societal problems and conflicts, a method still often employed in criminal justice studies, stratification analyses, international development studies, and mainstream racial relations studies. In addition to influencing the social sciences' focus on white-framed pathologies of people of color, Spencer helped to stimulate another trend in mainstream social sciences' approach to understanding cross-racial interaction—an unquestioned belief in the necessity of one-way "assimilation" for immigrants into white-controlled institutions and a one-way "civilizing" process (i.e., becoming like whites) for people of color. Knowingly and unknowingly, this type of thinking still undergirds much mainstream social scientific study of immigration, intergroup adaptation, and numerous other racial-ethnic matters, as we demonstrate in subsequent chapters.

Spencer's influence on the thinking of social scientists, other academics, and political and economic leaders was extensive in the late nineteenth century and first decades of the twentieth century. Most sociologists in newly established US sociology departments incorporated some of Spencer's ideas in their social theories and research.[20] Indeed, Spencer's views on the national and global organization of societies were passed to a new generation of increasingly influential white social scientists, and they in turn influenced yet more generations of scientists. Views about the grand racial superiority of whites, the necessary valorization of white civilization, and the inevitability of racial subordination and conflicts did not suddenly disappear with later generations of social scientists. They were often only modified, reworked, or toned down. Indeed, as demonstrated throughout this work, numerous examples of nineteenth-century social scientists' racial views can be found in contemporary academic investigations.

To take one important example, Spencer's focus on supposedly distinctive and lasting "traits" of racial groups has long been part of influential analyses in mainstream social science and other academic disciplines, including medical and other physical sciences. Problematically, mainstream sciences' conceptions of distinctive traits, genetic and physical characteristics, intelligence (IQ), and cultural behaviors of different racial groups are frequently white-biased. They tend to be built on numerous mischaracterizations of people of color from an age-old white racist framing. For example, the social science authors of a bestselling book called *The Bell Curve*, Richard Herrnstein and Charles Murray, have argued that "IQ test" data show that African and Hispanic Americans are genetically inferior in intelligence compared to European Americans. Although untrained in genetics and citing testing procedures that only measure *learned* skills, they still argued that supposed "IQ" inferiority flowed from inherited genetic differences between racial groups.²¹ With no or few egalitarian social interactions with people of color, and no field research experience on systemic racism issues, many past and present white social and physical scientists have been easily misinformed by this commonplace white racist framing about various groups they learned in all-white or mostly white social environments. Elements of this white racist framing still operate forcefully, covertly and overtly, throughout Western social worlds today, including throughout the worlds of the mainstream social sciences, physical sciences, and other academic disciplines.

Heirs of Comte and Spencer: Karl Marx, Émile Durkheim, Max Weber

While the purpose of this book is not to exhaustively review the past history of racialized analysis in social science, we should note briefly that other towering European figures in the history of sociology have operated out of a limited white racial framing of societies, including three influential "classical" theorists: Karl Marx, Émile Durkheim, and Max Weber. Marx, for all his brilliance as class analyst, failed to analyze in a substantial way the powerful racial dynamics shaping the human relations in societies with which he was familiar and to examine therein the numerous ways that race was deeply interlocked with class. His focus on white European working-class struggles with expanding capitalism ignored consequential, large-scale working-class rebellions in the Americas, including the rebellion of thousands of formerly enslaved black workers from 1791 to 1804 in what is now Haiti. Additionally, he overlooked the rebellion of tens of thousands of formerly enslaved African American workers who fled southern slavery and fought for the Union military in the US Civil War, thereby ensuring the Union's victory and their own freedom from enslavement. Both were black workers' revolts against the extreme racialized form of capitalistic exploitation ingrained in European-devised slavery systems. Although more aware than most

Europeans of racial exploitation in Western capitalistic development, his Eurocentric framing of Western class struggles missed seeing these enslaved black workers' rebellions as the first stages of the revolution against capitalism and its white elite. In addition, Marx's negative personal framing of blacks, seen in his letters, was likely a factor in his blindness to the importance of black working-class revolutions taking place before him.[22]

Considering his disdain for the subjugation of the worker and the power grip of capitalists, Marx offered surprisingly brief critiques of the racialization of Western colonialism and white capitalists' global exploitation of people of color and their lands. To his credit, he certainly analyzed the capitalistic aspects of imperialism and was one of the first Western analysts to see that advanced capitalism was based on whites' "primitive accumulation" of wealth from exploiting people of color and their lands, as in this passage from his book *Capital*:

> The discovery of gold and silver in America, the extirpation, enslavement and entombment in mines of the aboriginal population, the beginning of the conquest and looting of the East Indies, the turning of Africa into a warren for the commercial hunting of black-skins, signaled the rosy dawn of the era of capitalist production. These idyllic proceedings are the chief moments of primitive accumulation… [C]apital comes dripping from head to foot from every pore with blood and dirt.[23]

Marx was also well informed on issues of slavery and its economics, which he viewed as central to world trade and expanding capitalistic industrialization. As he expressed in one 1846 letter, "wipe North America off the map and you will get anarchy, the complete decay of trade and modern civilization. But to do away with slavery would be to wipe America off the map."[24]

However, Marx never deeply analyzed the powerful role of racialization that is evident in his comments on European colonialism and capitalism, and he was generally fatalistic and deterministic in his perceptions of indigenous peoples globally. In his view, they needed a capitalism stage in order to eventually be liberated by communist social systems, for the lands of the "backward" indigenous people of color were bound to be conquered by economically advanced Europeans. For example, Marx condoned Britain's colonization of India, believing that India was a "pre-destined prey of conquest" by a superior capitalistic country. Britain's colonization of India would bring non-European peoples "with no history" the advancements of Western capitalistic "progress," a step leading to the advanced societal stage of communism. In *Capital* and other works, Marx and his colleague Friedrich Engels perceived European colonialism rather narrowly as "a subsidiary of the stock exchange" and a capitalist venture, mostly ignoring the large-scale racial oppression dynamics of that colonization, genocide, and enslavement in overseas societies, as well as the systems of racial oppression later developed there by Europeans and their descendants.[25]

Like Marx, the leading French sociologist of the late nineteenth century, Émile Durkheim, failed to address seriously the racialized exploitation shaping the global social world around him and provided little critical analysis of colonialism, indigenous genocide, and slavery systems that enriched the European societies that he studied so well. Durkheim was significantly influenced by Comte. His theoretical model is substantially an expansion of the Comtean organicist model of society. He viewed European society's hierarchical and divided character as more or less normal, one where some individuals, groups, and institutions served a more important function than others. However, he did view the often inegalitarian division of labor in capitalistic societies such as France as unjust because the position of those in the upper and "lower classes" was often not based on individual merit and abilities, but on family socioeconomic inheritances. He did write of social "justice" and the need for individual merit to be the standard for mobility:

> If one class of society is obliged, in order to live, to take any price for its services, while another can abstain from such action thanks to the resources at its disposal which, however, are not necessarily

due to any social superiority, the second has an unjust advantage over the first at law.[26]

He argued that these unjust societal divisions should be made more equitable if there was to be healthy organic solidarity in society, and thus healthy societal development. Of Jewish background, Durkheim also spoke out against the anti-Semitism that exploded around the famous Dreyfus Affair in France in the 1890s, again signaling some significant concern with matters of social justice in European societies.[27]

However, Durkheim did not extend this underdeveloped discussion of internal societal justice to the global imperialistic operations of European countries. When he did write about global matters, he tended to divide human beings into the two groups of "primitive" non-Westerners and "modern" Europeans, the latter viewed as more developed culturally and intellectually in the human evolutionary scheme. Still, Durkheim also argued that the hereditary aspects of race then being emphasized by most social scientists, a perspective he generally accepted, were disappearing as societies moved from these "primitive" racial groupings to more complex cultural groups.[28]

Durkheim thus did embrace a *cultural* perspective on human group evolution and development, one that challenged pseudo-biological understandings of race and stressed sociocultural factors as major causes of differences in development among racial groups. Along with other dissenting social scientists of his time such as Franz Boas and Robert Park, he accented cultural explanations of racial matters. We address this shift in the white framing of racial meanings more thoroughly in the next section. For now, we should note that this shift—the cultural turn in racial theorizing—while a step forward, still remained steeped in Eurocentrism and much white racial framing. Cultural hierarchies replaced biologized racial hierarchies, and cultural explanations replaced biological explanations of white supremacy. However, what does not change are the influences of white European (male) authors and creators of these cultural hierarchies and explanations or the fact that these hierarchies remained white-imposed and white-framed, thereby demonstrating yet more Eurocentric knowledge generation. Durkheim's most noted concepts of "social solidarity" and "collective consciousness" paradoxically represent an elite white vision of societal cohesiveness and the ways of thinking and ethics of the dominant white racial group.[29] With regard to racial matters that shape and permeate industrialized societies, these sociological concepts are asserted to be examples of "neutral" and "value-free" social scientific language for what are actually white-framed understandings. For example, in the West, successful white dominance is often viewed as the greatest indicator of "healthy social solidarity," while Eurocentric thought and belief in racial entitlement, privilege, and superiority often define a "healthy collective consciousness."

Even the major German sociological analyst Max Weber, whose insightful analyses of power, the state, and nationality are frequently useful for understanding social stratification issues in industrialized societies, wrote unreflectively and in racist and ethnocentric ways about an array of racial matters—including the "hereditary hysteria" characterizing Asian-Indians, black Africans as genetically incapable of factory work, and the Chinese as slow in intelligence and other abilities. Weber viewed these racial traits as shaped fundamentally by the biological backgrounds of these groups. Moreover, like Comte, Spencer, Marx, and Durkheim, the often astute Weber unreflectively posits the premier status of Western "rationality" and advanced Western "modernization," which contrasted greatly in his view with the cultural "primitiveness" and mental "inferiority" of African and "Oriental" civilizations.[30] Nonetheless, despite his ethnocentrism, Weber's work offers potential insights about racial group relations and racialized power.

Social science analyses of Weber's work frequently focus upon his studies of the state or his arguments that the state and political realm are as important as class and the economic realm accented by Marxist social scientists. Yet, rarely are Weber's important analyses of ethnic and national loyalties critically examined, nor how his understandings might shape race theory.[31] Moreover, Weber's concept of the highly bureaucratized modern state is often highlighted, while his discussion of the nation-state and ethnicity receives less attention. For Weber, the "specific function of the leading economic and political strata is to be the bearers of the nation's sense of political purpose," and "the worldly organization of the nation's power... is far from being a mere 'superstructure' of the organization of the ruling economic classes."[32]

Weber introduced critical understandings of the social realities of *nationalism* as well as of a dominant ethnic group's power within a nation. For Weber, nationalist and ethnic group loyalties at times trump class and political loyalties. In "The Nation State and Economic Policy," he moves beyond simple descriptions of the modern state and identifies the ethno-national character of the German nation-state. According to Weber, the German nation as a state rests on the German people's and German group's "eternal struggle" to "defend its own culture" and "preserve and raise the quality of [the German] national species."[33] Throughout the essay, Weber contrasts two ethno-nationalist groups: the German nation and the Polish nation, positing Germans as the *superior* national group and the Polish as a culturally less-developed national group. However, two decades later during World War I, Weber developed a more critical analysis of this German nationalism and expressed great concern about the nationalistic expansion of the German state. Additionally, we should note that one of Weber's important contributions to social science analysis was an emphasis on researchers' recognizing their own values and backgrounds—and the need for more critical perspectives in social science.[34]

Significantly, Weber's writings emphasize ethnic and nationalistic issues while not discussing even the racial group issues touched on by Comte, Spencer, and Marx. Like Durkheim, Weber's writings de-emphasize "race," and instead stress ethnic and national identities, groups, and loyalties. While Weber importantly introduced the necessary frameworks of ethnicity and nationality to discuss the European context, he did not present theoretical understandings for critically understanding racial matters and thus wrote little about the major racialized slavery systems and large-scale colonialism existing outside of Europe in his era. He also failed to consider how relations among European nations and how dominant ideologies and material realities within European nations were fundamentally shaped by the global racial dynamics of imperialism, colonialism, slavery systems, and other forms of white dominion over many peoples of color.

We now turn to a critical analysis of the racial theories developed by the most influential and dominant social scientists over the first six decades of the twentieth century.

Notes

1 The socially constructed term "race" has no single meaning; instead the term serves as an umbrella concept or signpost that denotes or implies the multidimensionality of racial matters (racial prejudice, segregation along color lines, whiteness, immigration, racial identity, structural, institutional and systemic racism, colonialism, etc.). While we do not discount the analytic utility of the term "race" as an umbrella concept, and incorporate it in the early parts of our analysis, we prefer using "racial matters" or "racial issues" as a concept that expresses the many layers and features of social reality often associated with the common term or concept "race."
2 See W.E.B. Du Bois, *The World and Africa: An Inquiry into the Part Which Africa has Played in World History* (New York: International Publishers, 1996 [1946]); Paul G. Lauren, *Power and Prejudice: The Politics and Diplomacy of Racial Discrimination* (Boulder, CO: Westview Press, 1996); Charles W. Mills, *The Racial Contract* (Ithaca, NY: Cornell University Press, 1997).
3 Emmanuel C. Eze, *Race and the Enlightenment* (Cambridge, MA: Blackwell, 1997), pp. 33, 118.
4 Ivan Hannaford, *Race: The History of an Idea in the West* (Baltimore: Johns Hopkins University Press, 1996), pp. 205–7.
5 Auguste Comte, *Cours de philosophie positive* (London: Croom Helm, 1974 [1830–42]).
6 See Marvin Harris, *The Rise of Anthropological Theory* (New York: Crowell, 1968).
7 E.E. Evans-Pritchard, *The Sociology of Comte: An Appreciation* (Manchester: Manchester University Press, 1970), p. 14.
8 Harris, *The Rise of Anthropological Theory*, p. 101; Evans-Pritchard, *The Sociology of Comte*, p. 4.
9 Structural functionalism is still operative in a number of areas of contemporary sociology, such as world systems theory, globalization studies, and development studies.
10 Alexis de Tocqueville, *Democracy in America* (New York: Vintage Books, 1945 [1835]), p. 345.
11 Ibid., pp. 344–5. The second quote is on p. 372.
12 See L.L. Bernard, "Henry Hughes, First American Sociologist," *Social Forces*, 15 (1936): 154–74 and Stanford Lyman, "Henry Hughes and the Southern Foundations of American Sociology," in Stanford Lyman (ed.), *Selected Writings of Henry Hughes: Antebellum Southerner, Slavocrat, Sociologist* (Jackson, MS: University of Mississippi Press, 1985), pp. 1–72.

13 George Fitzhugh, *Sociology for the South* (New York: B. Franklin, 1965 [1854]); Henry Hughes, *Treatise on Sociology: Theoretical and Practical* (New York: Negro University Press, 1968 [1854]).
14 See Ronald Takaki, "'Warrenteeism': A Vision of a 'Marx of the Master Class,'" in *Iron Cages: Race and Culture in Nineteenth Century America* (New York: Alfred Knopf, 1979), pp. 128–135; Ronald Takaki, "Pilgrim's Progress of a Southern Fire-Eater," in *A Pro-Slavery Crusade: The Agitation to Reopen the African Slave Trade* (New York: Free Press, 1971), pp. 86.
15 George Fitzhugh, *Sociology for the South*; and *Cannibals All! or Slaves Without Masters*, ed. C.V. Woodward (Cambridge, MA: Belknap, 1960 [1858]).
16 Herbert Spencer, *Social Statics: The Conditions Essential to Happiness Specified and the First of Them Developed* (New York: D. Appleton, 1886 [1851]), p. 46.
17 Herbert Spencer, *The Study of Sociology* (New York: D. Appleton, 1910 [1873]), p. 47.
18 Herbert Spencer, *The Principles of Sociology* (London: Williams and Norgate, 1876), p. 257.
19 Herbert Spencer, "Letter to Mori Arinori," in J.D.Y. Peel (ed.), *On Social Evolution: Selected Writings* (Chicago: The University of Chicago Press, 1972 [1892]), p. 257.
20 See Albion Small and G. Vincent, *An Introduction to the Study of Society* (New York: American Book Co., 1894); L.L. Bernard and J. Bernard, "The Historic Pattern of Sociology in the South," *Social Forces*, 16 (1965): 1–12; see also Mike Hawkins, *Social Darwinism in European and American Thought* (Cambridge: Cambridge University Press, 1997).
21 Richard J. Herrnstein and Charles Murray, *The Bell Curve: Intelligence and Class Structure in American Life* (New York: Free Press, 1994), pp. 295–316.
22 See Sean Elias, *Black and White Sociology: Segregation of the Discipline* (Doctoral Dissertation, Sociology Department, Texas A&M University, 2009), p. 203; R. Peterson, "Marx, Race, and the Political Problem of Identity," A. Valls (ed.), *Race and Racism in Modern Philosophy* (Ithaca, NY: Cornell University Press, 2005), pp. 235–54.
23 Karl Marx, *Capital, Volume I*, trans. Ben Fowkes (New York: Vintage Books, 1977), pp. 915, 926.
24 "Letter from Marx to Pavel Vasilyevich Annenkov," in *Letters of Marx and Engels 1846: Marx-Engels Collected Works* (New York: International Publishers, 1975), Vol. 38, p. 95.
25 Karl Marx, "The Future Results of British Rule in India," *New York Tribune*, June 25, 1853, pp. 76–81; see also Karl Marx and Friedrich Engels, *On Colonialism* (Moscow: Foreign Languages Publishing House, 1959).
26 Émile Durkheim, *The Division of Labor in Society* (New York: Free Press, 1933), p. 384. On justice, see p. 388.
27 See Chad Alan Goldberg, "Introduction to Émile Durkheim's 'Anti-Semitism and Social Crisis,'" *Sociological Theory*, 26 (2008): 299–300; Joe R. Feagin, Hernán Vera and Kimberley Ducey, *Liberation Sociology*, 3rd edn (Boulder, CO: Paradigm, 2015), especially Chapter 2.
28 See Steve Fenton, *Durkheim and Modern Sociology* (Cambridge: Cambridge University Press, 1984).
29 Durkheim's understandings of collective consciousness and social solidarity were challenged by the increasing division of labor between the capitalist class and working class. See Anthony Giddens, *Capitalism and Modern Social Theory: An Analysis of the Writings of Marx, Durkheim and Max Weber* (Cambridge: Cambridge University Press, 1971).

30 J.M. Blaut, *The Colonizer's Model of the World: Geographical Diffusionism and Eurocentric History* (New York: Guilford Press, 1993), pp. 64, 102–3; Edward W. Said, *Orientalism* (New York: Vintage Books, 1979).
31 As Anthony Giddens and David Held observe, "Sentiments of ethnic community or of 'nationalism' for Weber become of major significance in the nation-state. Ethnically based, or nationalist, parties are forms of political mobilization that do not necessarily follow class line." Anthony Giddens and David Held, "Introduction," in Anthony Giddens and David Held (eds.), *Classes, Power, and Conflict: Classical and Contemporary Debates* (Berkeley, CA: University of California Press, 1982), p. 11.
32 Max Weber, "The Nation State and Economic Policy," in *Political Writings* (Cambridge: Cambridge University Press, 1994 [1895]), p. 21.
33 Ibid., p. 16.
34 See Ahmad Sadri, *Max Weber's Sociology of Intellectuals* (New York: Oxford University Press, 1992), pp. 16–18.

CHAPTER 2
RACE THEORY AND THE RISE OF MAINSTREAM SOCIAL SCIENCE

We mark the beginning of the professionalization of social science disciplines in the late nineteenth century and early twentieth century as the advent of *white mainstream* social science. Prior to this point, most white and non-white social scientists were decentralized, non-salaried, and/or worked outside academia. With the professionalization of the social sciences in historically white educational institutions, dramatic changes in social science occurred. Now increasingly numerous white male sociologists, political scientists, anthropologists, and economists possessed new means (salaries, titles) and spaces (academia and think tanks, journals, and presses) with which to generate and implement social scientific knowledge. This mainstream social science development coincided with the great capitalist expansion and increased imperialism of Western societies whose great initial wealth had been substantially generated through major overseas colonialism and the Atlantic slavery system. Since their inception, these mainstream social sciences have been inextricably connected to the power structures of Western societies, more specifically, power relations along racial group lines.

As a result, a white racial framing of society, a worldview often imbedding a deep-seated Eurocentrism, has long permeated much white social scientific thinking. This condition has caused a real segregation of social scientific knowledge and contradicted certain basic principles of the social sciences, which are often said to be rooted in value neutrality, universality, and objectivity. As we demonstrate, however, these are largely unrealized goals of the social sciences in regard to much mainstream racial research. Instead, Eurocentrism, white racial framing, repetition of weak racial theory and methods, biased relationships to racial-power structures, and the marginalization or exclusion of black social scientists and other social scientists of color centrally define the history of the mainstream social sciences. In addition, gender and class marginalization and exclusion have played significant roles in shaping the dominant cultures of the various social sciences, but given the limitations of space we will mostly focus here on how racial matters and, more specifically, a strong white racial framing early shaped mainstream sociology. (See Chapter 9 for a discussion of the role of black sociologists in the founding era of US sociology.)

Robert Ezra Park's White-Framed Sociology of Race

It is important to highlight the influential writings of the major white sociologist Robert Ezra Park, whose professional life as a sociological analyst extended from the early 1900s to the 1940s. Before presenting our critique of Park's role in the development of mainstream social scientific understandings of racial matters, his positive attempts to advance social scientific knowledge about these issues should be mentioned. First, Park did gain firsthand experience of white–black relations in the US South in the early twentieth century while working as a secretary, publicist, researcher, and writer for a leading educator of the day, Booker T. Washington, at Tuskegee Institute, a historically black college in Alabama. Park lived for several years in the Jim Crow south and worked for an employer who was a black American, and lived among black Americans. He came to know personally the difficult social realities of black southerners. This is a commendable feat, because most social scientists researching subordinated social groups do not live extensively among the groups they attempt to research. After Park's employment at Tuskegee, he went on to help develop a major sociology department at the University of Chicago. At Chicago, Park established the study of racial and ethnic matters as a central concern of sociology and helped to integrate a few black students into the budding social science discipline, two very important moves for the early development of a US sociology of "race relations."[1]

While impressive on a number of levels, Park's history and accomplishments in promoting a sociology of racial matters deserve a more critical analysis than they usually receive, especially when considering his problematic views of race and racial relations and his failure to present an analysis of the institutional and systemic dimensions of the white racism he observed up close. Considering that Park lived among many African American students and educators for seven years at Tuskegee and interacted with Booker T. Washington, the most important African American leader of the early twentieth century, was he able to develop critical insights and knowledge about African Americans' social plight and critical views on matters of white racism? Additionally, were Park's efforts to establish studies of racial issues as a central focus of sociology useful if his own racial views were problematic?

One discovers much paradox in Park's life and racial worldview: a desire to learn about race, even firsthand from the perspective of "the other," yet an inability to accurately comprehend numerous fundamental structures and operations of US racism. His motivation to establish racial studies as a central social science concern is offset by his incapacity to develop truly critical social science theories and methods for studying racial matters. Moreover, Park's desire to integrate a few black sociologists into the discipline must be viewed alongside his unwillingness to understand and promote the critical black sociological thought on racial issues of his era and the previous decades.[2] These sets of circumstances are important to acknowledge, because Park's sociology of race established much of the framework for later mainstream analyses of race, up to the present day.

Several key themes problematically shape Park's sociology of race and contemporary mainstream race studies. First, and probably most importantly, Park established the "assimilation" framework as a primary theoretical framework for understanding racial and ethnic adaptations in mainstream social science, one grounded in a white racial framing pervaded by Eurocentrism. Second, Park's conceptualizations of race, ethnicity, nationality, and culture, and their interrelationships are unclear and often conflated, a problem still affecting contemporary racial and ethnic analyses. Third, Park focuses on micro- and meso-level phenomena, such as racial attitudes and small groups, while largely ignoring macro-level racist structures. Fourth, Park's research is highly focused on analyzing people of color and their social pathologies, while completely neglecting analysis of whites' social pathologies and system of racial oppression. Lastly, Park's sociological views about racial matters are linked to his Eurocentrism, his belief that European and European American culture and the behaviors and values of whites should generally be the positive models and norms for all racial-ethnic groups, especially new immigrants. For Park, social "deviance," "pathologies," or "problems" are detected in a group's movement away from these traditional white-framed models and norms.[3]

Park's white Eurocentrism is necessary to consider, because it seeps into his social scientific understandings, and subsequently creates major defects in his theories of racial matters. His Eurocentrism is most noticeable in his views of social groups and of Western "civilization": these are primary subjects in the social sciences. Whites of European descent are "the dominant race" that is physically, intellectually, and socially superior to other racial groups, as well as the sociocultural standard with which to assess these other groups. This is apparent throughout his work, and is explicitly displayed in a 1931 *American Journal of Sociology* article, "Mentality of Racial Hybrids."[4] Presenting a conflicting account of intelligence among racial groups, Park begins by arguing for a social environmentalist understanding of intelligence, and then quickly shifts to biological understandings of racial groups as rooted in "blood" and "heredity." At first he concedes that intelligence "is due to increased education, greater freedom in social contact, greater incentives, higher economic status," a set of social factors, and not "innate and unalterable traits." Yet, in the next sentence Park writes: "there is, nevertheless, no question at all in regard to the actual *superiority* of the mulatto in comparison to the Negro," a view he backs with reference to genetic ancestry.[5]

He goes on to describe mixed-race black Americans (with the derogatory term "mulatto") as "more enterprising," "more intelligent," and more self-aware than "Negroes," and a group that "made a better appearance than the Negro." Speaking of the "defects of the Negro," Park identifies "Negroes" as "docile, tractable, unambitious," and exhibiting "naïveté" and "insouciance."⁶ At several points, Park indicates that "mulatto" superiority over "Negroes" is due to their direct biological and cultural connection to the "dominant white race." He notes that

> If the mulattos display intellectual characteristics and personality traits superior to and different from those of the black man, it is not because of his biological inheritance merely, but rather more… because of his more intimate association with the superior cultural group.⁷

In this influential essay, Park illuminates his Eurocentric understandings of racial group differences. First, he positions whites atop the social hierarchy as the deservedly dominant race and superior cultural group, the racial group that presumably provides "mulattos" with their positive attributes. Yet the latter are never compared with whites, only with blacks. Are they more intelligent than whites? Are they of better appearance, more self-aware and enterprising? Not according to Park, who views "mulattos" as a marginalized group existing between the "superior" cultural attributes and social networks of whites and "inferior" attributes and community of "Negroes."

Not only are European Americans superior to people of color in Park's analysis of mixed-race groups and other subjects, but also European societies are viewed as superior to societies of people of color. He contrasts the "primitive" societies of people of color and the "modern," "civilized," and "complex" societies of Europeans, positioning societies of European civilization as necessarily dominant on the global scene. As he argues, "For four hundred years and more Europe, and particularly Western Europe, has been preeminently the seat and center of greatest intellectual and political activity" while "most of the world outside Europe has been reduced to a position of political and cultural subordination and dependency."⁸

Additionally, Park's primary analytical concept of *assimilation* and his central theoretical perspective on the *racial relations cycle* further reveal his ideas about whites' superiority and people of color's inferiority and helped greatly to imbed them in the then dramatically growing social sciences. The assimilation framework developed by Park has been one of the most influential, long-lasting theoretical frameworks for understanding racial matters in mainstream sociology and other social sciences (see Chapter 7). Reproducing and expanding social science understandings about race that are explicit in the writings of Comte and Spencer, Park's assimilation framework reinvigorates the racial framing and Eurocentrism of his predecessors, but assertively under the guise of social scientific objectivity, value neutrality, and universality. At its base, the concept of assimilation is rooted in a basic proposition: people of European descent (whites) possess the highest level of society and civilization and non-Europeans (people of color) need to assimilate fully to whites' norms and social institutions if they are to become "civilized" and avoid even greater oppression from whites than they currently endure.

Park's understanding of group assimilation is presented in his famous "racial relations cycle"—the four-stage progression of racial relations that begins with (1) contact and competition, followed by (2) group conflict between racial groups, and then a move to (3) accommodation and (4) assimilation by the less powerful racial group to the folkways and structures of the dominant racial group.[9] Park was optimistic about assimilation for the many Southern and Eastern European immigrant groups entering the country in his day, yet pessimistic about full assimilation for black Americans and other people of color into US society.[10] In his racial relations cycle model, Park delineates a conceptual understanding of assimilation that reflects the stages of (white) European immigrant adaptation in the United States, but is unable to develop a scheme of full societal incorporation for African or Asian Americans—that is, Americans of color. Assimilation, moreover, largely represents the processes of group contact and dominance witnessed in US political-economic development. As contemporary sociologist Stephen Steinberg notes, the "logic of imperialism was inscribed on the racial relations model," arguing that the model offered "neo-colonialism in the realm of ideas."[11]

Underlying this still-influential social science theory of both immigrant and other group assimilation are several principal assumptions and logics. First, assimilation theory emphasizes *one-way* assimilation to white norms, ideals, behaviors, standards, social worlds, framing, institutions, and culture. Substantial mutual assimilation or major cross-cultural exchanges are not seriously considered by Park and most other assimilation analysts. Second, this one-way group assimilation is viewed as akin to the "healthy" European processes of modernization, civilizing, and societal advancement that should be models for "Third World" countries and non-Western peoples. That is, this one-way assimilation process is viewed uncritically as a mostly positive and constructive social process for all immigrant groups coming into a Western society. Third, this one-way assimilation is viewed as a *necessary* adaptive process for all immigrant groups that seek white-constructed "citizenship" in the United States and similar Western societies. Lastly, there is a widespread assumption that the study of "normal" one-way assimilation patterns provides the best social science framework for understanding US immigrant adaptation and related racial-ethnic relations. These social scientific notions and logics underlie the concept of assimilation not just in Park's racial relations cycle, for they were to some degree already present in the analyses of Comte, de Tocqueville, Hughes, Fitzhugh, Spencer, and other white sociologists of European descent. Like his predecessors, Park's assimilation framework assumes the "natural" hierarchical organization of racial relations in Western industrialized societies with whites positioned at the top.

Park's racial relations cycle and focus on assimilation continue to inspire many contemporary sociologists working on racial and ethnic issues.[12] Mainstream social scientists still mostly view (one-way) assimilation to a white-controlled culture and society, and the resulting asymmetrical socio-racial relationships, as a desirable process of racial-group socialization and adaptation (see Chapter 7). Most assimilation theorizing assumes increasing adherence to white-established, white-controlled societal norms, institutions, and structures—even when major domains of societal life still imbed much discrimination against people of color.[13] Moreover, assimilation theories often use vague or imprecise language to describe the characteristics and process of assimilation (e.g., the conflicting end goals of one-way "Americanization" or a diverse "melting pot") and avoid directly addressing centuries of white-enforced racial oppression and the consequent and massive unjust impoverishment of people of color. This commonplace concealing language and often uncritical theorizing work to neutralize and objectify assimilation as an unproblematic generic process of "normal" social adaptation.

Gunnar Myrdal's "American Dilemma" Perspective

Gunnar Myrdal was one of the most influential white social scientists of the twentieth century. Researching Jim Crow America, he was responsible for aggressively promoting a Eurocentric assimilation theory. Myrdal and his influential racial relations study, *An American Dilemma* (1944), expanded the assimilation theoretical frame, virtually ensuring its permanence in studies of US racial issues and further naturalizing the assimilationist logic among mainstream scientists.[14] Myrdal, like Park, mostly emphasized the benefits, ideals, and sanctity of one-way assimilation to extant white-normed culture and institutions. Myrdal began his investigation of US racial relations with the commonplace assumption that this social assimilation is the sought-after end goal for all racial and ethnic groups, and certainly for black Americans. According to Myrdal, it is "to the advantage of American Negroes as individuals and as a group to become assimilated into American culture, to acquire the traits held in esteem by the dominant white Americans."[15] He never posed questions about the white-framed ideals and norms ("American" culture) of the societal assimilation process, nor the negative, destructive components of this highly racialized process.

Along with his uncritical perspective on the need for black Americans to assimilate to white-defined and white-controlled institutions, Myrdal did centrally focus on whites' failure to embrace and operate according to their own democratic and egalitarian ideals (termed the "American creed"), most especially in the Jim Crow south where most black Americans then resided. In his view, the US racial problem is not just about black Americans' ability to assimilate to white-framed society, but even more about prejudiced white society's unwillingness to accept them. Thus, Myrdal optimistically viewed the US racial problem as solvable in principle because it was mainly a matter of whites overcoming their failure to fully live up to this American creed. That is, change white prejudices about blacks, and racial relations will significantly improve. As Fred Wacker notes:

> [Myrdal's] optimism with regard to the future of American racial relations was based on his belief that white Americans would not desire to remain inconsistent and ambivalent. White Americans felt a dissonance between their democratic ideals and their treatment of Negroes, a dissonance they would attempt to alleviate because it caused psychic discomfort.[16]

Nonetheless, Myrdal's general conclusions failed to address the structural realities of systemic racism and its legitimizing racial framing that go well beyond some white prejudices. By accenting this white-crafted, white-framed American creed, Myrdal thereby reinforced and elaborated the conventional assimilationist perspective on US society and on visions of its future. As we demonstrate in Chapter 7, acceptance of this one-way assimilationist logic has long had the negative consequence of marginalizing other more critical, competing perspectives on the US system of racial oppression.

One critical perspective on Myrdal's study is that of the brilliant, now often neglected, African American social scientist Oliver C. Cox, who had studied sociology at the University of Chicago, but avoided studying with Robert Park (see Chapter 9). In response to *An American Dilemma*, Cox faulted Myrdal for failing to realize that the problem of white racial oppression cannot be solved in principle because it is not just a problem of white racial ideas and prejudices. Actually, as Cox observes, it is more fundamentally a matter of white economic and political-group interests as these have been generated from different historical conditions and imbedded in all major institutions:

> Seizing the labor of non-Europeans in North America and elsewhere is actually the beginning of modern racial relations. It was

> not an abstract, natural, immemorial feeling of mutual antipathy between groups, but rather a practical exploitative relationship with its socio-attitudinal facilitation... As it developed, and took definite capitalist form, we could follow the white man around the world and see him repeat the process among practically every people of color.[17]

Considering Cox's many important insights concerning racial matters, Stephen Steinberg has asked cogently, "How is it that Myrdal became an exalted figure both inside and outside academia, while Oliver Cox, his brilliant critic, fell into obscurity, relegated to teach at black colleges?" He then rightly asserts that this question has serious implications for the *current* sociology of knowledge, posing the further question: "What does Myrdal's elevation and Cox's marginalization tell us about the formation of sociology's canon? About the racialization of knowledge?"[18] Steinberg is quite accurate in suggesting this is evidence of the contemporary racialization of social science knowledge and marginalization of the critical perspectives of people of color.

Myrdal's failure to investigate the systemic racism context of his optimistically framed notions of black societal assimilation, while focusing on white individuals' and regional groups' racial attitudes and smaller-scale discriminations, is a problem repeated in most contemporary assimilation theory and other mainstream social science research. Additionally, Myrdal fails to interrogate critically his firm belief in the superiority of white-dominated institutions and white-run societies (i.e., "developed nations"),[19] believing that this explicit and implicit whiteness standard is the one to which all people of color should conform. Common to many social scientists of his day and ours, his rather narrow-minded white perspective fails to acknowledge the major contributions of African Americans and other people of color to Western societies and to human civilization generally. This standard constantly emphasizes top-down cultural transmission by the "superior" racial group, whites, not the mutual and extensive cultural exchanges necessary for truly healthy social relations and societies.

Milton Gordon: Refining Assimilation Theory

Following in the tradition of Park and Myrdal, in the mid-1960s, the social scientist Milton Gordon published an influential book, *Assimilation in American Life*, a racial analysis that further elaborated the assimilation model. Yet, unlike Park and Myrdal, Gordon forthrightly acknowledged that the US assimilation processes do involve pressured "Anglo-conformity"—that is, adapting to and embracing the ideas and practices of the dominant Anglo-Protestant whites. Importantly, he recognized there is a US racial hierarchy, as well as substantial religious and national origin differentiation, and he explored alternatives to one-way Anglo-conformity assimilation, including the melting-pot and cultural-pluralism alternatives. Gordon also focused directly on group attitudes concerning assimilation and patterns of racial-ethnic communality, as opposed to just individual racial-ethnic attitudes, to determine how different groups actually embrace or avoid assimilation—and thus the degree to which they accept or reject becoming "Americanized" (white). Nonetheless, despite some improvements over Park and Myrdal's understanding of US racial matters and his introduction of new and useful concepts, such as Anglo-conformity, structural assimilation, and cultural pluralism, Gordon failed to escape numerous pitfalls of his still white-framed assimilationist ideas. Unmistakably and significantly, key elements of his more updated assimilation theoretical framework continue to greatly influence contemporary mainstream racial and ethnic scholarship.[20]

Along with his perpetuation of an uncritical belief in the positive attributes of assimilation to the "core culture" (i.e., white-dominated culture) of the United States, several other missteps in Gordon's theorizing have had a lasting effect in establishment sociologies of race and ethnicity. First, he collapses the socially constructed societal categories of race and ethnicity under the weak umbrella term, "ethnicity." This allows him to largely ignore the centrality of the country's foundational and systemic racism in his social assimilation analyses. Next, Gordon accents generic social scientific terms such as "intergroup relations" and "group life" that generally collapse the very inegalitarian hierarchical divisions of race, class, nationality, and religion into just vague "group divisions." This move to a universalized language of group divisions often de-emphasizes the distinctive societal realities of different US racial, ethnic, and religious groups, all of which have different socio-historical histories, oppressions, and socioeconomic (material) and status positions in this hierarchical society.

Finally, Gordon's understanding of "ethnic" groups fails to adequately address white societal power and dominance. He makes it seem as if British American whites are significantly differentiated from other "ethnic" whites of European descent in many white privileges and advantages. In some contexts, this conclusion is warranted in regard to class differentiation among whites. However, his position overlooks the fact that in societal racial position, the non-British white Americans have long been provided with roughly similar white privileges and advantages in most US institutions. More and more in recent decades, non-British European Americans have even penetrated in significant numbers the upper reaches of US society, such as the US Supreme Court and corporate boardrooms. Today, Gordon's analysis of intergroup relations appears weak and his views of numerous matters of US racism have not withstood the test of time. For one thing, he largely ignores systemic racism, the unjust enrichment for whites and unjust impoverishment for blacks, that was put into place over three centuries of black enslavement and Jim Crow segregation, preferring instead to accent an optimistic view of the ongoing assimilation of (mainly middle-class) black Americans.

Moreover, Gordon's recurring focus on "Negroes, Jews, Catholics, and Protestants" largely ignores the growing and significant group of Latinos (aside from a modest discussion of Puerto Ricans) as well as other historically important groups such as Native and Asian Americans, both of the latter being well established in the United States before many of the Jewish and Catholic immigrants that Gordon does emphasize. Subsequently, Gordon ignores much of the deep history of US racial oppression, including whites' genocidal actions against indigenous Americans, exclusion of Chinese and other Asian immigrants in the late 1800s and early 1900s, and aggressive internment of Japanese

American citizens in World War II concentration camps. One gains a sense of Gordon's skewed understanding of US racial matters, and that of most of his white colleagues in the 1960s, when he writes:

> If... one excludes the special situation of the American Indian, and bars from consideration the remaining Jim Crow laws of the south and the laws forbidding interracial marriage in a number of states..., then it is correct to say that the American political and legal system recognizes no distinction among its citizens on grounds of race, religion, or national origin.[21]

Excluding from consideration Native Americans and much of the experience of African Americans—the two groups, who along with whites, comprised the three primary racial groups in this country's founding era, is an extraordinary and glaring weakness in Gordon's mainstream social science analysis, as is his recurring assumption that US social, political, and economic institutions are mostly colorblind and intrinsically democratic and thus that major government remedial action (e.g., affirmative action) is unnecessary. His white-framed, empirically challenged perspective of a noble US society parallels that of Myrdal, Park, and numerous other early mainstream social scientists.

Nathan Glazer and Daniel P. Moynihan's Problematic White Framing of Racial Groups

Also published in the turbulent 1960s, Nathan Glazer and Daniel Moynihan's major US study, *Beyond the Melting Pot*, has been influential in social science to the present. Yet they repeat numerous problems already observed in the research and theories of Park, Myrdal, and Gordon. Glazer and Moynihan's portrait of racial relations is shaped by a limited and white-framed historical and group focus. For instance, they analyze only certain white ethnic groups (Irish, Italians, Jews), black Americans, and Puerto Ricans. Missing are Native Americans, Asian Americans, many British and other European Americans, and most Latinos—that is, a majority of Americans.[22] Like Gordon, they operate from a remarkably unreflective perspective overemphasizing the significance of "ethnic" differences among white groups, even as these groups were in many ways then downplaying these differences to glean many of the benefits of US whiteness.[23] By the 1960s, the white ethnic groups discussed by Gordon, Glazer, and Moynihan were mostly steeped in the process of substantial de-ethnicization, since numerous benefits of being a successful "American" and living the proverbial American Dream were intertwined with and historically rooted in white racial privileges. Then as now, white identity and its rewards have trumped national-origin loyalties and group ties within much of white America. Like their white predecessors in social science, Glazer and Moynihan also uncritically utilize and further enhance the mainstream assimilationist perspective.

One quickly sees serious fallacies in their theorizing. Early on, they argue that racial-ethnic groups should be viewed foremost as interest groups vying for resources in a fair and even US playing field, where a group's "will to power," its group agency, is what mainly determines success in this societal resource battle. This perspective dehistoricizes different ethnic and racial groups so that all groups are seen as potentially equally successful in demanding their interests, and is oblivious to whites' extensive societal power historically. In their discussion of competing group interests, they reignite the common white racial frame by identifying the interests of whites as mainly work-related and the interests of African Americans and Puerto Ricans, Americans of color, as substantially those of "people on welfare."[24] Remarkably, too, they claim that the commonplace categorization and identification of racial-ethnic groups can be viewed as substantially voluntary, thereby ignoring historical and systemic white oppression, associated racist government policies, and the everyday white-racist framing and discriminatory actions of whites that have greatly shaped major US economic, political, and other social institutions. Ignoring histories of racial group oppression, they write that government remedial actions should not accent group issues but focus only on "individual human qualities."[25] This statement demonstrates Glazer and Moynihan's erasure, among other historical issues, of African Americans' collective history of enslavement and Jim Crow servitude, the latter still in effect when they wrote their book. It posits an individualistic version of the contemporary colorblind philosophy, which repeatedly stresses the central importance of individual qualities of agency and intentionally ignores the foundational and systemic realities of racial oppression.

Another problem with Glazer and Moynihan's understanding of racial matters is their exaggerated focus on certain social problems and assimilation hurdles of "Negroes and Puerto Ricans," without addressing problems of white-imposed systemic racism still targeting these and other Americans of color. Black Americans and Puerto Ricans are highlighted as *problematic* racial-ethnic groups repeatedly, especially as problematic major recipients of public "welfare"—which they say creates white angst and discrimination. In their book's introduction, they demonstrate further flaws in their theorizing by offering a weak explanation of contemporary African American and Jewish American relationships. Their analysis of this complicated subject ignores the white-imposed color line that marginalizes people of color and impedes or prevents their movement up society's socioeconomic ladder. They seem to forget that most Jewish Americans, initially seen as "not white" by Anglo-Saxon Protestant whites in early immigration periods,[26] have been able to successfully battle much overt anti-Semitic discrimination generated by other white Americans and eventually to assimilate substantially to a white identity and to many (but not all) white racial privileges. Avoiding these crucial pieces of the US racism reality, they uncritically discuss supposed ironies of history that "placed Jews disproportionately in positions" of power and influence, with "Negroes, disproportionately, in position of tenants of these landlords, customers of these merchants, patients of these doctors, pupils of these teachers, and clients of these social workers."[27] This supposed irony is explained in large part by the US's long history of extensive anti-black racism and uneven access to racial power, which has a deep foundational and systemic basis.

Conclusion

Social science thinking about racial matters that is rooted in assimilation frameworks pervades many of the major works on racial issues in mainstream sociology today. Park, Myrdal, Gordon, Glazer, and Moynihan, together with many other prominent white male social scientists, did an effective job of firmly establishing this one-way, whitewashed assimilation framework that now informs and is deeply embedded in much social science research. Even with the introduction of concepts such as multiculturalism and cultural pluralism in social science, conventional assimilation understandings generally remain part of the central framework and the standard from which contemporary racial and ethnic groups and their societal development are constantly measured and defined. Assimilation theory continues to frame numerous mainstream social science studies of racial matters, if sometimes in partially revised forms. For instance, contemporary immigration studies and their nationality-based understandings of group dynamics are still often rooted in conventional and often unreflective assimilationist perspectives, as is evident in the next section of this book.

Notes

1 See Benjamin Bowser, "The Contribution of Blacks to Sociological Knowledge: A Problem of Theory and Role to 1950," in Robert Washington and Donald Cunnigen (eds.), *Confronting the American Dilemma of Race: The Second Generation Black American Sociologists* (Lanham, MD: University Press of America, 2002), p. 14; Howard Winant, "One Hundred Years of the Sociology of Race," in Craig Calhoun (ed.), *Sociology in America: A History* (Chicago: University of Chicago Press, 2007), pp. 552–3. For critical views of Park's role, see Aldon Morris, *The Scholar Denied: W.E.B. Du Bois and the Birth of Modern Sociology* (Berkeley, CA: University of California Press, 2015); and Sean Elias, *Black and White Sociology: Segregation of the Discipline* (Doctoral Dissertation, Sociology Department, Texas A&M University, 2009), pp. 238–66.
2 Aldon Morris' pathbreaking research reveals that Park actively attempted to stymie the sociological thought of Du Bois. See Morris, *The Scholar Denied*.
3 See Robert Park, *The City: Suggestions for the Investigation of Human Behavior in the Urban Environment* (Chicago: University of Chicago Press, 1984 [1927]). Park presents a white-framed understanding of the city, equating "evil neighborhoods" with people of color and new immigrant groups who had not yet assimilated to European "civilization."
4 Robert E. Park, "Mentality of Racial Hybrids," in E. Hughes, C. Johnson, J. Masuoka, R. Redfield, and L. Wirth (eds.), *The Collected Papers of Robert Ezra Park, Vol. 1* (New York: Arno Press, 1974 [1929]), pp. 377–92.
5 Ibid., p. 383, emphasis added.
6 Ibid., p. 387.
7 Ibid., p. 389.
8 Robert E. Park, "Race Relations and Certain Frontiers," in E. Hughes, C. Johnson, J. Masuoka, R. Redfield, and L. Wirth (eds.), *The Collected Papers of Robert Ezra Park, Vol. 1* (New York: Arno Press, 1974 [1934]), p. 118.
9 For a detailed description of Park's cycle, see Stanford Lyman, "The Race-Relations Cycle of Robert E. Park," in *The Black American in Sociological Thought* (New York: G.P. Putnam's Sons, 1972), pp. 7–70.

10 Early social scientists such as Auguste Comte, Herbert Spencer, Alexis de Tocqueville, George Fitzhugh, and Henry Hughes believed that assimilation was impossible or unlikely for most people of color. See the debate between Arthur de Gobineau and de Tocqueville in *Correspondence entre Alexis de Tocqueville et Arthur de Gobineau, 1843–1859* (Paris: Plon, 1908); and de Tocqueville's pessimistic view of black assimilation in "The Present and Probable Future Condition of the Three Races that Inhabit the Territory of the United States," in *Democracy in America* (New York: Vintage Books, 1945 [1835]), Vol. 1, pp. 344–5, 372. See also Stanford Lyman, *The Black American in Sociological Thought* (New York: G.P. Putnam's Sons, 1972), pp. 35–44.
11 Stephen Steinberg, *Race Relations: A Critique* (Stanford, CA: Stanford University Press, 2007), p. 61.
12 See Alan Sica, "Editor's Remarks," *Contemporary Sociology: A Journal of Reviews*, 41(4) (2012): 409. See discussion of Richard Alba and Victor Nee in Chapter 7. See also, Joe R. Feagin and José A. Cobas, *Latinos Facing Racism: Discrimination, Resistance, and Endurance* (Boulder, CO: Paradigm, 2013).
13 For example, the US justice system, despite upholding white supremacy in unjustly targeting people of color, is a part of the "legitimate" society that people of color are supposed to respect and assimilate.
14 Gunnar Myrdal, *An American Dilemma: The Negro Problem and Modern Democracy*, Vols. I and II (New York: Harper and Brothers Publishers, 1944).
15 Quoted in Joe R. Feagin and Clairece B. Feagin, *Racial and Ethnic Relations*, 6th edn (Upper Saddle, NJ: Prentice Hall, 1999), pp. 41–2.
16 See Fred Wacker, "An American Dilemma: The Racial Theories of Robert E. Park and Gunnar Myrdal," *Phylon*, 37(2) (1976): 117–25.
17 Oliver C. Cox, *Caste, Class, and Race* (New York: Monthly Review Press, 1948/1959), pp. 332–3.
18 Steinberg, *Race Relations*, p. 3.
19 Myrdal, *An American Dilemma*, Vol. I, p. xlii.
20 Milton M. Gordon, *Assimilation in American Life: The Roles of Race, Religion, and National Origins* (New York: Oxford University Press, 1964); and Feagin and Cobas, *Latinos Facing Racism*.
21 Gordon, *Assimilation in American Life*, p. 4.
22 Nathan Glazer and Daniel P. Moynihan, *Beyond the Melting Pot: The Negroes, Puerto Ricans, Jews, Italians, and Irish of New York City* (Cambridge, MA: MIT Press, 2001 [1963]).
23 See David Roediger, *The Wages of Whiteness: Race and the Making of the American Working Class* (London, Verso, 2007 [1991]); Noel Ignatiev, *How the Irish Became White* (New York, Routledge, 1995); Karen Brodkin, *How the Jews Became White Folks and What That Says About Race in America* (New Brunswick, NJ: Rutgers University Press, 1998).
24 Glazer and Moynihan, *Beyond the Melting Pot*, p. lxxxiv.
25 Ibid., p. lxxxv.
26 See Brodkin, *How the Jews Became White Folks*.
27 Glazer and Moynihan, *Beyond the Melting Pot*, p. lxxxix.

PART II
CONTEMPORARY MAINSTREAM SOCIAL SCIENCE AND RACE THEORY

CHAPTER 3
CHANGES IN THE FIELD OF RACE STUDIES

Our main concern in the next chapters is to investigate key transformations in theories of racial matters that have occurred in the mainstream social sciences during and after this 1960s period of developments in social science theory and research. What elements of white-framed theories and conceptualizations of racial matters of earlier white social scientists were retained, and what elements vanished or were significantly transformed? What are the principal contemporary frameworks that have developed in mainstream sociology and other social sciences, and how do these different frameworks understand matters of "race"?

Few of the social scientific theorists of racial matters reviewed previously would have envisioned the changes in the world's societies and the dramatic cultural shifts and intellectual crises that have occurred in the social sciences and humanities since the 1960s. They likely could not have imagined the election of an African American as US president or the birth of African American studies, Latino studies, Asian American studies, indigenous people studies, and cultural studies programs critically utilizing knowledge from disciplines across the social sciences, humanities, and physical sciences. Nor would they have likely foreseen the deep theoretical divisions among white social scientists in general, and the epistemological divisions among white social scientists who study racial matters in particular.[1] British sociologist Anthony Giddens describes the dissolution of the common ground among mainstream social scientists that occurred during this period:

> The fissures in this common ground opened up remarkably suddenly in the 1960s and 1970s, and they went very deep. There is no doubt that their origins were as much political as intellectual. But whatever their provenance, they had the effect of largely dissolving whatever consensus had existed before about how social theory should be approached.[2]

In both the humanities field of philosophy and its social science cousin, the sociology of knowledge, the ferment of the 1960s and thereafter has brought a significant divide between social thinkers who stress the rationality of human beings and the objectivity of the social world as roots of knowledge and social thinkers who view knowledge more subjectively, relativistically, and contingently, through interpretative understanding (e.g., "hermeneutics"). This latter group has emphasized the irrationality and fallibility of human thought and of the claims of the social and other sciences. Since this period, crises of understanding have developed between the natural and social sciences, between critical theory and hermeneutics, and more specifically between interpretive understanding and scientific explanations, such as in philosophical debates between German sociological theorists Hans-Georg Gadamer and Jürgen Habermas. The battle over the intellectual importance of concepts such as rationality, subjectivity, objectivity, scientific knowledge, and societal progress was significantly developed in epistemological conflicts between Habermas and the radical critics of enlightenment perspectives, such as post-modernists Jacques Derrida and Michel Foucault.[3] Today, this divide still exists, mainly in theoretical disputes between *analytic* and *continental* philosophies and *Enlightenment modernism* and *post-modernity*.

As cultural theorist Patrick Brantlinger observed in the 1980s: "In both the American and European universities since the 1960s, the perception of a crisis in the humanities and social sciences is now common."[4] Similarly, in her discussion of the transitions by some sociologists to a new interest in cultural studies, Elizabeth Long correctly notes that the "fragile postwar unity of American sociology as a discipline... began to fracture during the 1960s."[5] Additionally, part of this sociological fracturing could be seen in the formation of a Black Caucus within the American Sociological Association (ASA) and then partial separation from the ASA by many black sociologists who created the Association of Black Sociologists. Relaying a mainstream response to these associational changes, in 1980 the outgoing ASA president Peter Rossi argued that the "organization's very openness in reflecting so many of the divergent viewpoints in current sociology had produced a condition of intellectual paralysis."[6]

Alvin Gouldner's *The Coming Crises of Western Sociology* (1970), Irving Horowitz's *The Decomposition of Sociology* (1993), Stephen Cole's *What's Wrong with Sociology?* (2001), and, more recently, Alan Sica and Stephen Turner's edited volume, *The Disobedient Generation* (2005), and Craig Calhoun's edited volume, *Sociology in America* (2008), illustrate the important disciplinary debates and intellectual changes occurring in many areas of sociology since the turbulent 1960s.[7] Several of these authors explored the tensions and splintering in social theory and research that have accompanied various social and intellectual "crises." Of significant concern to several of these influential disciplinary analysts, almost all white men, were the changes in US studies of racial-ethnic issues. What exactly were the important changes occurring specifically in the field of racial studies? What were the divergent theoretical frameworks that developed during this period?

Divisions in Racial Theory Since the 1960s

The founding of the Association of Black Sociologists brought the creation or resurrection of theoretical paradigms and concepts into organized space that challenged centuries of white social scientists' misframing of racial matters. Powerful ideas about the "souls of white folk" and "psychological wage of whiteness" observed by W.E.B. Du Bois and the concepts of "institutional racism" and "black power" boldly proclaimed by Stokely Carmichael (Kwame Ture) and Charles Hamilton were increasingly drawn upon and developed theoretically and empirically by numerous critical black sociologists and a few critical white sociologists. This dramatic shift in much social science analysis of US "racial oppression" (now often named as such) shocked the majority of white social scientists and many others. Reinvigorated radical ways of thinking about or theorizing racial matters were often met with hyper-rejection and hostility by white social scientists. Hugely controversial and disruptive analytical works such as Joyce Ladner's *The Death of White Sociology* (1973) and Robert Staples' *Introduction to Black Sociology* (1976) presented what became a more commonplace critical paradigm for understanding racial matters, an aggressively *counter-system* and *counter-mainstream* approach to understanding human relations and society.[8] This new, more revolutionary theory and research was, unsurprisingly, greatly criticized and dismissed by most mainstream social scientists, including some mentioned above. We return to the important strides made in theory and research in this critical black tradition later (see Part III).

As noted previously, our main concern here is investigating some significant transformations in racial theories taking place in the mainstream social sciences after the 1960s period of social science transformation in theory and research. We notice two primary trends in *mainstream* racial theory and research since the 1960s: (1) efforts to dismantle serious social science analyses of racism matters; and (2) efforts to maintain, in new and old forms, certain white-framed social scientific understandings of racial matters. One complex manifestation of these post-1960s theories might be labeled *post-race* or *colorblind-race theory*, a theoretical position that seeks to dismantle analysis of racial matters, while at the same time explicitly or implicitly maintaining the power of a scholarly white racial framing of social reality. Eduardo Bonilla-Silva's analysis of widespread white "colorblind racism," which we cover below, addresses this paradoxical nature of colorblindness in the general white population, which denies current racial realities (e.g., major racial inequalities), while at the same time perpetuating racist ideologies that sustain white racial group power and institutional control. Bonilla-Silva's insightful portrait of ordinary whites' colorblind racism also applies, to varying degrees, to the perspectives of numerous white contemporary social scientists in the United States and elsewhere.[9]

Michael Omi and Howard Winant rightly surmise that in the current century, this colorblindness perspective is pervasive in US society, as the "racial common sense and *desideratum* of our time."[10] Indeed, as we noted previously, this colorblindness has become hegemonic in the United States and other nation-states created by descendants of early European colonists. The colorblind perspective has thus become the racial common sense in much contemporary social science. Because of its force in social thought and race theorizing, we devote the rest of this chapter to examining colorblindness and post-raciality perspectives in contemporary social science, a central aspect of a *white social science framing* of contemporary social realities. After providing this backdrop, we analyze major theoretical frameworks employed by contemporary social scientists to describe and assess racial matters: the deconstruction and reconstruction of the study of racial matters (Chapter 4); class, culture, ethnicity, and nationality paradigms used to replace paradigms of race and racism (Chapter 5); sociobiological understandings of racial matters (Chapter 6); assimilation theory (Chapter 7); and racial formation theory (Chapter 8).

Societal Contexts of Social Science

While our focus is upon colorblindness and post-raciality in contemporary social sciences, we recognize that the social sciences are shaped by their social contexts, a point we suggested in the introduction. To illustrate this important point further, let us first take a brief look at the social environments and contexts, past and present, that have helped shape colorblindness and post-raciality perspectives in US society among ordinary citizens and many social scientists.

Over the past several decades, whites have grudgingly accepted a dismantling of legal segregation, at the same time generating a new orientation of racial power often accenting colorblindness and post-raciality. Today's business and government institutions are subject to federal laws that *officially* establish racial equality, as well as to other policies that supposedly enforce colorblindness among their members.

One powerful institution that officially promotes frames of colorblindness and post-raciality, the criminal justice system, boldly pronounces that "justice is blind," that the US Constitution is indeed "colorblind,"[11] and that racial matters play little or no role in the operation of this "impartial" system. In the first decades of the twenty-first century, the US Supreme Court has aggressively pushed the ideas of colorblindness and post-raciality. Conservative chief justice John Roberts wrote that "The way to stop discrimination on the basis of race, is to stop discriminating on the basis of race."[12] In this and other decisions, he and other court conservatives have clearly signaled that they feel racial discrimination targeting Americans of color is no longer substantial, and that they are much more concerned about government remedial efforts for past racial discrimination that might potentially harm "innocent" whites. A conservative majority of that court pursued a colorblind philosophy that resulted in weakening the 1965 Voting Rights Act and the 1954 *Brown v. Board of Education* school desegregation decision, discounting lawsuits trying to redress discrimination against Americans of color and thwarting affirmative action programs for Americans of color. Yet, the same court went out of its way to bolster "affirmative action" programs for whites, such as in the *Citizens United v. Federal Election Committee* case that legally sanctioned and extended the control of wealthy whites over US politics.[13]

Both major political camps in the United States, Republicans and Democrats, have developed frames of colorblindness and post-raciality. One witnesses the liberal frame of colorblindness espoused by leading Democrats and a conservative frame of colorblindness presented by Republicans, which has so far had much greater resonance in US society. Mainstream media commentators have constantly pressed colorblindness and post-raciality themes into the dominant national discourse. Both conservative and liberal mainstream media deliver such messages. Post-raciality and colorblindness also define much contemporary popular culture. For instance, most commercially successful hip-hop music has been culturally transformed from its roots as socially conscious black music to a form of colorblind "American" music that now largely evades a focus on issues of white racism.

The immense financial success of a number of African American cultural elites—such as the rapper and entrepreneur Jay Z, the talk-show host and entrepreneur Oprah Winfrey, and the athlete and entrepreneur Michael Jordan—are viewed by most whites as examples of how US society has moved beyond substantial racial discrimination and extensive racial disparities. In academia, almost all historically white colleges and universities point to their faculty and students of color to demonstrate their adherence to colorblindness and multiculturalism. Much of academia is so intent to demonstrate its colorblindness that top educational administrators have colluded in the elimination of most substantial affirmative action programs for students of color, albeit often under the pressure of lawsuits from conservative white activists. In a dramatic reversal, today's federal government has moved away from enforcing society's color lines to often enforcing a mythology of colorblindness. These white elite moves to substantially embed colorblind and post-racial beliefs in the US population have succeeded, such that a majority of Americans now claim the country is colorblind in national opinion polls. Indeed, the younger generation of "millennials" is more likely than other Americans to hold such beliefs.[14]

Given this contemporary insistence on a colorblind country, we can now examine briefly its veracity. Paradoxically, visions of a colorblind, post-racial country articulated by white political and media leaders were regularly contradicted by their public reactions to ongoing conflicts between African American communities and the country's criminal justice system. For example, in 2014 an unarmed black man was killed by a white police officer in Ferguson, Missouri. Reacting to the killing and large-scale protests by black Americans and others, some national political leaders publicly discussed the historical legacy of US racism, the history of tensions between the black community and white police officers, and the recurring phenomena of blacks being killed by white police officers. Additionally, public discourse about a post-racial United States was offset by the words of then black attorney general Eric Holder. Holder leveled the scathing counter-colorblind observation: "Though this nation has proudly thought of itself as an ethnic melting pot, in things racial we have always been and I believe continue to be, in too many ways, a nation of cowards."[15] Unsurprisingly, Holder was demonized by many whites for candidly discussing US racial matters. These public race-conscious moments are limited and often punished in US society.

US political and legal systems appear as anything but colorblind and post-racial. The US Senate remains mostly white. The Congressional Black Caucus, Congressional Hispanic Caucus, Congressional Asian-Pacific American Caucus, and Congressional Native American Caucus all still exist. The Republican Party is composed mostly of white voters. For example, in the 2012 presidential election, most voters of color, including 93 percent of African Americans, voted for Obama, the Democratic candidate, while a substantial majority of whites voted for Republican candidate Mitt Romney.[16] Additionally, researchers Jon Hurwitz and Mark Peffley have illuminated the great divide in how whites and blacks view equal treatment in the massive criminal justice system. They found that African Americans are "extraordinarily skeptical that the system can be fair, while whites see the system as essentially colorblind."[17]

African Americans have long demonstrated more skepticism about the US political processes than white Americans. For example, issues surrounding early twenty-first-century efforts by white officials to complicate the voting process for many citizens, particularly moderate-income African Americans and Latinos, represented to them the legacy of past white discriminatory practices (e.g., the Jim Crow south's poll tax) that barred many poor African Americans from voting. Whereas Americans of color often view these unnecessarily strict voter efforts as very discriminatory, those white conservatives pushing for them invoke color-blindness in claims that these are "fair" procedures that all Americans should obediently follow.[18] Moreover, the conflicting intersections of national and international politics stemming from Latin American immigration to the United States are frequently racialized. Images of angry whites blocking buses transporting undocumented Latino immigrants to US detention centers mirror images of angry whites blocking the mostly black civil rights activists marching to protest the policing system's handling of the killings of black men, women, and children. Recurring media images of the brutal racialized realities of social life for Americans of color reveal that institutional racism and racial tensions between whites and people of color are still fundamentally part of US society.

Moreover, in contrast to dominant narratives that argue racism is no longer a relevant concept, much research and other data show that the social constructions of "race" and "color" are still real and significant in social consequences in major US institutions, as well as in other countries. For instance, US businesses generally claim to hire individuals impartially, without regard to a person's race. Yet, ample research suggests that laws such as the 1964 Civil Rights Act banning employment discrimination often remain unenforced, and racial segregation still occurs in workplaces through a variety of supposedly ("colorblind") impersonal employment techniques.[19] Considering the demise of US affirmative action programs, one wonders why potential employees are asked about their race on most job applications if the business world is truly post-race and employers are colorblind. Paradoxically, even with regular sensationalized news coverage of racial matters, most media outlets, conservative and liberal, still incorporate much colorblind, post-racial rhetoric in reporting, even as they simultaneously perpetuate white-framed racial narratives and imagery.

White liberal and conservative media frequently use myths of colorblindness and post-raciality for different purposes. Whereas the liberal language of colorblindness might be described as inflated strategic idealism, conservative colorblind discourse might be referred to as a strategic concealment or erasure of systemic racism and whites' role as the engineers of systemic racism. The former often idealistically seeks colorblindness in a strategic effort to realize the ideal of human equality beyond a racialized social world determined by peoples' skin color. The latter, in contrast, typically accents colorblindness in order to strategically *conceal* whites' contemporary racial power abuses and *erase* whites' past power abuses against people of color. Through its strategic idealism, the liberal version of the white racial frame attempts to promote colorblindness that supposedly benefits all people, while in its strategic concealment the conservative version of the white racial frame promotes colorblindness that seeks to primarily benefit whites and conceal white privilege.[20]

The conservative accent on colorblindness is characterized by a central technique of denying US racial realities while at the same time perpetuating and reifying those realities. Thus, the conservative framing preaches colorblindness and post-raciality, but fails to practice colorblindness and post-raciality. White racism, in forms such as racial segregation and racist beliefs, persists in everyday white practice, but not in the language of most public commentary, including that of the media. Since the 1960s civil rights changes, this white conservative framing has developed to protect white interests in rolling back or containing those changes, and it makes use of relatively new concepts such as "reverse racism" and the "race card." The key paradox of the conservative white framing is that it claims colorblindness and post-raciality despite its color-conscious or race-focused nature in practice. People participating in the conservative framing are those who practice racism without seeing themselves as "racist."[21] They frequently present a frontstage of colorblindness and post-raciality, especially in mixed-race public settings, while attempting to conceal their blatantly racist framing and racist backstage activities. Similarly, those who promote the liberal frame also attempt to conceal their backstage racism and exaggerated views of racial equality. In both examples, colorblindness and post-raciality are *not* achieved social realities, but more recent socially constructed versions of the white racial frame that seek to distance conservative and liberal whites from acknowledging and investigating the harsh realities of contemporary systemic racism.

Moreover, this colorblind and post-racial framing has often been generated by, and greatly influential on, many social scientists across disciplines. Through acceptance of numerous contemporary white racial norms and beliefs, the mainstream social sciences have often incorporated frameworks of colorblindness or embraced post-race and post-racism narratives. Many social scientists have developed or utilized arguments that racism is an outdated or non-viable term of analysis. Many signal in their work that racial relations have improved significantly or have morphed into relatively benign group formations along racial lines.

Colorblindness and Post-Raciality in Past and Present Social Science

Recall that influential social theorists such as Émile Durkheim and Max Weber did little to stimulate necessary racial analyses in the early social sciences. Moving away from racial group analysis that is essential for understanding European and American societies built on colonialism, imperialism, and systemic racism, Weber instead introduced and emphasized concepts of ethnicity and nationality. Although useful concepts for understanding European social relations and nation-state formations, these Eurocentric concepts fall well short of explaining the racialized histories of colonialism, slavery systems, legal racial segregation, and contemporary forms of white oppression targeting people of color. Concepts of nationality and ethnicity fail to describe large-scale, human-constructed divisions in a racial hierarchy, strictly enforced segregation of racial groups, and past and present asymmetric power relations among racial groups. Durkheim's sociology is concerned with how complex modernizing societies achieve social solidarity, integration, and functionality as new ties and networks among people and new social institutions dissolve traditional rural, ethno-racial, and religious ties. For Durkheim, racial-ethnic group identity and relations were disappearing in modern Westernized societies. Focusing on sociological understandings of European societies, Durkheim's analyses mostly ignore the national and international racial oppressions of his time and do not address the expanding white Eurocentric racial frame, the global impacts of colonialism, and racialized slavery and ex-slavery societies operating and structured according to white racial framing and other elements of systemic societal racism.

Even Robert Ezra Park, who was fundamental in establishing studies of racial matters in mainstream sociology and other social sciences, believed that the past and present epochs of racial group divisions and conflict would eventually transform into a modern societal world more shaped by class relations and cultural divisions. According to Park, the

> same forces which brought about the diversity of races will inevitably bring about, in the long, run, a diversity in the people of the modern world corresponding to that which we see in the old. It is

likely, however, that these diversities will be based in the future less on inheritance and race and rather more on culture and occupation. That means that race conflicts in the modern world, which is already or presently will be a single great society, will be more and more in the future confused with, and eventually superseded by, the conflicts of class.[22]

Park envisions a vast transformation from a society shaped by racial oppression and meanings to a modern world where class-based culture and occupations replace "race" and whites' exclusive grip on and inheritance of major societal resources and power. Does he envision that modern class hierarchies and divisions will resemble past hierarchies and divisions among racial groups, with whites and people of color then divided along economic and not racial lines? Will class conflict between whites and people of color replace past racial conflicts? Alternatively, does he mean that a class-based world will emerge that is only divided along these non-racialized cultural and occupational lines—thus a truly non-racist, multicultural social world? If so, one has to wonder what his understanding of culture is, and how closely that concept resembles past understandings of "race." Park lays seeds for a number of problematic moves that did indeed become popular in the contemporary social sciences: conflating "race" and "class," substituting "cultural" divisions as a concept to replace "race" divisions, and, in effect, declaring the end of systemic white racism with its highly unequal and exploitative relationships among racial groups. Park's vision of a de-racialized, class-based, and socioeconomically divided modern world has certainly gained hold in the contemporary social sciences and become linked to a post-racial and colorblind framing among many social scientists.

Increasingly post-racial, colorblind perspectives dominate many areas of social science disciplines at present. A large number of social scientists believe that systemic racism and whites' grip on power have largely faded from society and that "race" no longer remains a central factor or major variable in shaping social worlds. They often argue that new human groupings, boundary formations, and networks have substantially eclipsed relations among racial groups in significance. Many also seem to believe that they themselves are colorblind in their analyses of the social world and that racially framed beliefs and racist social structures, if they exist to some degree, linger mainly outside the supposedly objective terrain of the social sciences.[23]

One manner in which post-racial and colorblind perspectives have gained hold in the mainstream social sciences is seen in the increasing and widespread acceptance among social scientists that racial matters are generally peripheral in the lives of most human beings in contemporary Western societies. While some mainstream social scientists retain a focus on racial matters, many others embrace the post-racial and colorblind narratives popular in "advanced" Western societies and their venerable government, business, media, and academic institutions. Quite clearly, the societal context and dominant worldview of a society greatly affects the ideas and beliefs of most mainstream social scientists.

Contemporary users and proponents of colorblindness in the social sciences have developed a number of approaches for erasing or downplaying analysis of "race" matters. These include social scientists who (1) associate colorblindness with scientific objectivity and value neutrality; (2) discount the social science significance of racist meanings and racist relations; and/or (3) promote colorblindness as a political and analytical tool to fight unjust racial relations and misunderstandings of race.[24] The first approach appears typical of many social scientists, who themselves may or may not view society in post-racial terms, but who view the major contemporary ideas or methods of the social sciences as generally colorblind and not racialized. The second approach generally discounts the social science significance of race and racial groups and the reality of institutional and systemic racism. Some who follow this research approach focus on intellectual arguments in support of colorblindness and post-raciality, while others focus on political arguments. One discovers strategic concealment in this group.

The third colorblind, post-racial approach in the social sciences is quite different from the first two, because it presents a *critical* colorblindness and post-raciality. This strategic approach seeks to dismantle racist systems by eliminating "race" concepts from human language, thought patterns, and practices, including those of social scientists. They do recognize the historical racist realities associated with European colonialism and slavery. Moreover, they understand that the effects of racial discrimination still characterize societies developed through the spoils of historical colonialism and present-day neo-colonialism. However, as an intellectual and political strategy to attack the destructiveness of the public's racist thinking and action, social scientists such as Paul Gilroy seek to discourage reification and analytic usage of old concepts such as "race" and "racism."[25] Summoning strategic idealism, they argue that by eliminating such named concepts from our intellectual and public vocabulary it is possible to *disempower* them and weaken their associated social practices. Pressing modern Western nation-states and power-brokers to live up to their egalitarian ideals of freedom, equality, and justice, these more sophisticated post-racial social scientists seek contemporary language, thought, and social action that strives to be really colorblind and objective. As they see it, a primary method in achieving actual societal and conceptual colorblindness is to eliminate "race" in the ongoing dialectic of thought and praxis, including in the social sciences.

This strategically idealistic, critical colorblindness is very different from the system-defending and overly optimistic colorblindness and post-raciality of social analysts such as David Hollinger, Dinesh D'Souza, and Thomas Sowell.[26] The strategic post-raciality arguments of Gilroy are also quite different from the colorblind post-racial perspectives that condemn race-based preferences and race-based programs to offset damage to people of color caused by systemic racism, such as the views of conservatives Stephan and Abigail Thernstrom and Shelby Steele.[27] While we appreciate the strategic idealism of certain critical theories accenting a need for critical and linguistic colorblindness, such as Gilroy's, we feel that this perspective is ahead of its time and offers only useful social insights, not a substantial framework that can be used to empirically examine actually existing racial oppression in today's societies. Moreover, an eerie similarity exists between this critical colorblindness and the colorblind logic of chief justice John Roberts, noted earlier.

Critical Social Science Responses to Colorblindness and Post-Raciality

A few social scientists have recognized that current claims of colorblind post-racial societies are quite premature and untenable in the face of so much empirical evidence to the contrary. For instance, responding to this colorblind social science, the editors of the critical book *Whitewashing Race* observe that US society is experiencing racial regression, not racial progress, and that social scientists have mistakenly moved away from analyses of white racism. Additionally, they highlight a *false* consciousness of colorblindness and uncritical post-raciality among prominent social analysts such as Hollinger, D'Souza, and the Thernstroms:

> [R]acial justice has ceased to be a priority, and, in some instances, the gains of 1960s and 1970s have been reversed (if they ever took hold at all)... Yet instead of expressing alarm at the persistence of deeply rooted racial inequalities and searching for new ways to reach America's egalitarian ideals, many former advocates of racial equality proclaim the civil rights movement is over and declare victory. Racism has been defeated, they tell us. If racial inequalities persist, they say, it is not because of white racism. Rather, the problem is the behavior of people who fail to take responsibility for their own lives. If the civil rights movement has failed, they insist, it is because of the manipulative, expedient behavior of black nationalists and the civil rights establishment.[28]

Despite an awareness of serious flaws in colorblindness arguments in books like this one, social scientists accenting research on white racism issues are often labeled as old-school thinkers who reify and "essentialize" race and exploit discussions of racial matters for personal ideological reasons. We will see examples of this in some published social scientists' reactions to research and theorizing about racialized social systems (Eduardo Bonilla-Silva) or systemic racism (Joe Feagin), which we address in the next chapter.

Indeed, Bonilla-Silva has been a leader in the charge against the colorblind post-racial approach and significantly advanced our empirical and theoretical knowledge about US racial matters. In his influential research-grounded book *Racism Without Racists*, Bonilla-Silva argues that contemporary US society is shaped by "colorblind racism and the persistence of racial inequality," a reality denying opportunities and resources to Americans of dark complexion. This "colorblind racism" is perpetuated through white-framed ideas and actions. It exists as a racial ideology, that is, the "racially based frameworks used by actors to explain and justify" racial patterns. It also exists as racial structure, that is, the "totality of the social relations and practices that reinforce white privilege." In his view, this now conventional colorblind racism is the new *covert* racism replacing overt Jim-Crow-type racism.[29] This more subtle racism of colorblindness still allows whites a way of maintaining racial domination and upholding racialized structures that benefit them, yet also allows whites to be viewed as no longer racist because they supposedly "don't see color, just people."[30]

In his interview data, Bonilla-Silva examines white interpretive responses to contemporary racial patterns and identifies four important micro-frames of colorblind racism—termed abstract liberalism, naturalization, cultural racism, and racism minimization. Abstract liberalism emphasizes idealistic beliefs in equal opportunity and individual choice, as though racist structures and hierarchies did not exist. Naturalization is the discursive tactic of explaining racial issues as just natural occurrences. The cultural racism view rejects structural-racism explanations and proffers cultural differences to interpret the supposed "inferior" racial status of people of color in society, while the racism minimization framing strongly downplays the reality of racial discrimination and hierarchy in shaping the lives of people of color.[31]

Bonilla-Silva has regularly insisted, too, that much colorblind racist thinking persists in academia. He observes it among numerous students and colleagues who insist that research and teaching on matters of US racism are outdated, unnecessary, and "in and of themselves 'racist.'"[32] Indeed, this type of colorblindness is ubiquitous in academia, and the social sciences are no exception. Bonilla-Silva's work aids understanding the basic micro-frames of colorblindness at work in the everyday social world, and provides critical insights into the ways colorblindness operates in the social sciences. Importantly, Bonilla-Silva identifies colorblindness and post-raciality as micro-frames created by whites. Like Bonilla-Silva, we see this common colorblind perspective primarily as a technique for whites to evade direct discussion of whites' and individual and institutional racism. This evasion is especially problematic when social scientists assigned the task of illuminating racial matters in the social world also dodge serious research on white perpetuation of systemic racism.

In sum, colorblind and post-racial social science perspectives bypass or ignore researching and analyzing these ongoing systemic racism realities and the still-persistent white racial framing that overtly, subtly, and covertly legitimates these realities on a quotidian basis. Indeed, as we show later, even the more obvious, overt, and crude forms of white racial framing remain highly operative today. In this modern racialized world, overt and covert constructions of racist meanings still have great everyday significance, the structuring of asymmetrical and unjust racial relationships persists, and numerous societies long built upon slavery systems, colonialism, and/or contemporary whites' subjugation of people of color mostly remain intact.

Conclusion: White Racial Framing in Social Science

In spite of claims to the contrary, overt, subtle, and covert white racial framing in the social sciences has by no means disappeared, even with the wave of colorblind and post-racial social science frameworks over recent decades. Because we devote most of the rest of this book to explicating different forms of white framing in scholarly research and theorizing, mainly in the social sciences, we provide only a brief overview of this white framing of racial matters here.

Overt, subtle, and covert white racial framing routinely occurs in pages of top journals and books from esteemed university presses; in lecture halls and everyday activities of students, staff, and faculty at colleges and universities; in academic think tanks and research institutes; in meetings of professional social science organizations; and in an array of academic social networks, settings, and activities. To publish research on racial matters in leading mainstream outlets often means succumbing to the constraints and limits of the white racial framing of editors and reviewers and other problematical modes of conventional social science thought. Indeed, this has been the frequent experience of this book's authors and their students and colleagues over several decades now. This social science censorship in turn can require a sacrificing of significant portions of one's scholarship as one is forced by editors and reviewers to adhere to white-legitimated theories and methods of investigation, even if the latter produce limited or misleading social science knowledge on racial matters.

In addition to the constraints of publishing on matters of racism according to these white-generated restrictive customs, social scientists must navigate the white-constructed status hierarchies that exist in the social sciences. These status hierarchies exist in departments, specialized areas of study, and disciplinary fields. Frequently there is a status ranking of schools, departments, journals, presses, and other signposts of distinction that can seriously affect the direction of one's social science scholarship. While these academic hierarchies do not necessarily parallel rankings of knowledge quality, many social scientists operate as if they do. If white-shaped status hierarchies and ranking of social science efforts are defined "as real, they are real in their consequences," as sociologist W.I. Thomas correctly surmised.[33]

Along with these social science status hierarchies are often unspoken but real racial, class, and gender hierarchies in the social sciences. Today, as in the past, most of the social science's elites, those determining much of the research and theory in their disciplines, are white, class-privileged, and/or at elite colleges and universities. There is also variation among social science disciplines. One of the more diverse now is sociology. In recent decades, white female sociologists, sociologists of color, and sociologists from other less privileged backgrounds have been entering the important ranks of the discipline, in some areas to a significant degree. However, at many colleges and universities, old academic hierarchies are still substantially in place despite these advances, with white (often male and elite) sociologists still disproportionately influential. Even though the "liberal" discipline of sociology has increasingly diversified, established hierarchies of "appropriate" methodology, theories, and other aspects of knowledge production are largely intact.[34]

In addition, the "more prestigious" social sciences, such as economics and political science, are diversifying at a much slower pace.

A noticeable divergence has occurred in the continuing white racial framing one finds in the social sciences. On the one hand, there is the elimination or de-emphasis on race in much mainstream social scientific analysis, with its accompanying, often covert or subtle racial framing of colorblindness and post-raciality. On the other, there are the recent movements by some, such as sociobiologists and assimilation theorists, to re-establish an old, more overt white racial framing in the social sciences. For example, some contemporary sociobiologists and socio-geneticists have re-biologized the meaning of "human races" and the old "race" hierarchy, and they often assertively proclaim these biosocial understandings as central to explaining certain contemporary human behavior and social relations (see Chapter 6).

In contrast, an example of a recent technique of covert white framing is that of many social scientists and other academics who use colorblind reasoning to dismiss or marginalize African American, Latino American, Asian American, and Native American studies programs at colleges and universities—and thereby promote white-framed canonical thinking. This move among mostly white academics appears to be colorblind in its dismissing of racial categories, yet a more critical assessment reveals that there is much more involved. While denying the scholarly concerns and racial experiences of Americans of color, many such academics in fact again buttress white-created academic norms discovered in "the Canon" and thereby can prevent the possibility of yet more critical analyses of persisting white racial oppression.

In the following pages, we address in more detail various types of white racial framing found throughout the social sciences. We demonstrate the deficiencies of a more subtle or covert white racial framing in colorblind post-racial perspectives discovered in boundary studies, groupness studies, class-based analyses, cultural studies, and investigations of ethnicity and nationality. Next, we expose defects of more overt white racial framing evident in the contemporary biosocial explanations of race and in the precepts and presuppositions of mainstream assimilationist theoretical explanations of race relations.

Notes

1 See Donald Levine, *Visions of the Sociological Tradition* (Chicago: University of Chicago Press, 1995), pp. 271–2, 280, 285. Levine identifies a number of European/white sociological traditions (using terms such as a "distinctive European sociology") that emerge prior to the "debilitating changes" accompanying the "1960s and 1970s transformations in the social sciences." No non-European theoretical traditions or theorists of color are represented in the 400-year-plus, cross-national analytic portrait of dialogical traditions.
2 Anthony Giddens, *The Constitution of Society* (Berkeley, CA: University of California Press, 1984), p. xv.
3 See, for example, Jürgen Habermas' critique of the post-modernists in *The Philosophical Discourse of Modernity: Twelve Lectures*, trans. Frederick G. Lawrence (Cambridge, MA: MIT Press, 1991).
4 Patrick Brantlinger, *Crusoe's Footsteps: Cultural Studies in Britain and America* (New York: Routledge, 1990), p. 3.
5 Elizabeth Long, "Introduction," in Elizabeth Long (ed.), *From Sociology to Cultural Studies* (Malden, MA: Blackwell Publishers, 1997), p. 11.
6 Levine, *Visions of the Sociological Tradition*, p. 285.
7 Alvin Gouldner, *The Coming Crisis of Western Sociology* (New York: Equinox Publishers, 1970); Irving L. Horowitz, *The Decomposition of Sociology* (New York: Oxford University Press, 1993); Stephen Cole, *What's Wrong With Sociology?* (New York: Transaction Publishers, 2001); Alan Sica and Stephen Turner (eds.), *The Disobedient Generation: Social Theorists in the Sixties* (Chicago: University of Chicago Press, 2005); Craig Calhoun (ed.), *Sociology in America: A History* (Chicago: University of Chicago Press, 2008).
8 Joyce Ladner (ed.), *The Death of White Sociology* (New York: Random House, 1973); Robert Staples, *Introduction to Black Sociology* (New York: McGraw-Hill, 1976).
9 Eduardo Bonilla-Silva, *Racism Without Racists: Colorblind Racism and the Persistence of Racial Inequality in the United States* (Lanham, MD: Roman and Littlefield, 2003).
10 Michael Omi and Howard Winant, *Racial Formation in the United States*, 3rd edn (New York: Routledge, 2015), p. 256.
11 See Andrew Kull, *The Colorblind Constitution* (Cambridge, MA: Harvard University Press, 1998).
12 US Supreme Court chief justice John Roberts, "Opinion in Parents Involved in Community Schools v. Seattle School District No. 1 et al.," *Cornell University Law School*, June 28, 2007, www.law.cornell.edu/supct/html/05-908.ZS.html (accessed August 30, 2015).
13 US Supreme Court decision, "Citizens United v. Federal Election Committee," *Cornell University Law School*, July 21, 2010, www.law.cornell.edu/supct/html/08-205.ZS.html (accessed August 30, 2015).
14 See "2013 NBC News/Wall Street Journal poll," *NBC News/Wall Street Journal*, July 21, 2013, www.nbcnews.com/politics/first-read/poll-57-percent-americans-say-race-relations-u-s-are-n269491 (accessed August 30, 2015).
15 See US attorney general Eric Holder, "Speech at Department of Justice African American History Month Program," February 18, 2009, www.youtube.com/watch?v=2Fy2DnMFwZw (accessed August 30, 2015).
16 See "NBC 2012 Presidential Election Results," *NBS News*, September 2, 2015, http://elections.nbcnews.com/ns/politics/2012/all/president/#.Vee9lSVVh8M (accessed August 30, 2015).

17 See "Interview with Jon Hurwitz and Mark Peffley," *Washington Post*, July 22, 2013, www.washingtonpost.com/news/wonkblog/wp/2013/07/22/white-people-believe-the-justice-system-is-color-blind-black-people-really-dont (accessed August 30, 2015).
18 See, for example, Sarah Childress, "Why Voter ID Laws Aren't Really About Fraud," *Frontline*, October 20, 2009, www.pbs.org/wgbh/pages/frontline/government-elections-politics/why-voter-id-laws-arent-really-about-fraud (accessed August 30, 2015).
19 On white use of social networking for jobs, see Nancy DiTomaso, *The American Non-Dilemma: Racial Inequality without Racism* (New York: Russell Sage, 2013), pp. 64–6.
20 See Joe R. Feagin, *The White Racial Frame: Centuries of Racial Framing and Counter-Framing*, 2nd edn (New York: Routledge, 2013); Michael K. Brown, Martin Carnoy, Elliot Currie, Troy Duster, David B. Oppenheimer, Marjorie M. Shultz, and David Wellman, *White-Washing Race: The Myth of a Colorblind Society* (Berkeley, CA: University of California Press, 2003), pp. vii–viii; Omi and Winant, *Racial Formation in the United States*, 3rd edn, pp. 211–14.
21 See Bonilla-Silva, *Racism Without Racists*.
22 Robert E. Park, "The Nature of Racial Relations," in E. Hughes, C. Johnson, J. Masuoka, R. Redfield, and L. Wirth (eds.), *The Collected Papers of Robert Ezra Park, Vol. 1* (New York: Arno Press, 1974 [1939]), p. 116.
23 This has been the case since social sciences largely dissolved ties with the humanities and moved toward natural science models of understanding, where objectivity, value-neutrality, and data-driven models reign.
24 Like value-neutralists, social scientists who stress "universalism" and "humanism" tend to collapse the idea of distinct racial groups.
25 See, for example, Paul Gilroy, *Against Race: Imaging Political Culture Beyond the Color Line* (Cambridge, MA: Harvard University Press, 2002).
26 For example, David Hollinger, *Post-Ethnic America: Beyond Multiculturalism* (New York: Basic Books, 2006); Dinesh D'Souza, *The End of Racism: Principles for a Multicultural Society* (New York: Free Press, 1995); Thomas Sowell, *Race and Culture: A World View* (New York: Basic Books, 1995).
27 Stephan Thernstrom and Abigail Thernstrom, *Beyond the Color Line: New Perspectives on Race and Ethnicity in America* (New York: Hoover Institute Press, 2001); Stephen Thernstrom and Abigail Thernstrom, *America in Black and White: One Nation, Indivisible – Race in Modern America* (New York: Touchstone, 2009); Shelby Steele, *Content of Our Character: A New Vision of Race in America* (New York: Harper Perennial, 1998).
28 Brown et al., *White-Washing Race*, p. vii.
29 Bonilla-Silva, *Racism Without Racists*, p. 3. For discussion of the overt racism that complements covert racism, see Sean Elias, "Overt Racism" in *The Wiley-Blackwell Encyclopedia of Race, Ethnicity, and Nationalism* (Malden, MA: Blackwell, 2016).
30 Bonilla-Silva, *Racism Without Racists*, p. 1.
31 Ibid., pp. 28–9.
32 Ibid., p. 178.
33 Quoted in W.I. Thomas and D.S. Thomas, *The Child in America: Behavior Problems and Programs* (New York: Knopf, 1928), pp. 571–2.
34 See Joe R. Feagin, Hernán Vera, and Kimberley Ducey, *Liberation Sociology*, 3rd edn (Boulder: Paradigm, 2015).

CHAPTER 4
SUBVERTING RACIAL ANALYSIS
EMPHASIZING PRACTICE, GROUPNESS, BOUNDARIES, AND REFLEXIVITY

Over recent decades, a number of social science and other scholars have promoted conceptual understandings that are challenging and attempting to reshape the subject matter of the field of racial and ethnic studies. Many seek to dismantle and reframe concepts central to race studies, including concepts of race, racial groups, racism, and even race studies. Most question the idea of racial groups labeled as "white" or "black," believing that discussing such groups involves a process of essentialization, reification, or naturalization. They argue that discussion of racial groups is flawed because these groups are merely disingenuous social constructions, not real social entities with significant histories, cultures, and experiences. Like the concept "racial group," the multidimensional conceptual rubric of "race" is discarded and replaced with concepts such as ethnicity, social practices, groupism, and boundary-making. Subsequently, among this group of scholars, discussion of systemic racism, racially oppressive whites, major racial conflicts, and other serious racial matters generally disappears. The following analysis focuses on a few prominent and institutionally well-placed members of this elite scholarly group.[1]

Mara Loveman's Question: "Is 'Race' Essential?"

One increasingly popular contemporary technique for dismantling social scientific discourse of racial matters is to claim that analyses of race and racism are essentialist and reify race. For instance, Mara Loveman's critique of Eduardo Bonilla-Silva's racial understandings, entitled "Is 'Race' Essential?" illustrates well this technique. Loveman argues that Bonilla-Silva's understanding of racialized social systems confounds categories with groups, reifies race, and maintains the unwarranted distinction between "race" and "ethnicity." She states that race (here, used as a reference to racial groups) should not be used as "a category of analysis" and proposes an analytic framework focusing "attention on processes of boundary construction, maintenance and decline—a comparative sociology of group making."[2] Loveman introduces a number of theoretical arguments and concepts mostly stripped from their historical and social contexts—such as "groupness," "group-making," "boundary-making" and "symbolic boundaries"—in a failed attempt to challenge Bonilla-Silva's socio-historically grounded, empirically documented, and theoretically critical explanations of contemporary racism.

For Loveman, race should not be viewed as a category of analysis but rather as a "category of practice." While race can certainly be viewed as practice, it should not be discarded as a category for analysis. Like Bonilla-Silva, we view race as an analytic category that describes concrete racialized practices and systems, as well as social structures and forces that reinforce analytic categories of race. One cannot successfully describe racial practices or phenomena without reference to the historically and *socially constructed* categories of race. Loveman criticizes Bonilla-Silva for reifying race, accusing him of categorizing races as "real groups and collective actors." She argues against the view that races "exist as bounded, socially determined groups" and thus views race as a "category of practice" and "flexible and subject to context."[3]

Like many of her contemporaries in mainstream social science, Loveman turns to a classical European social theorist who never studied racial matters for conceptual understandings of race and racism. In probing racial boundary-making, thus, she relies on Max Weber's concept of "social closure."[4] This tendency, turning to white European theorists as authorities on racial matters and as those best equipped with supposedly legitimate intellectual tools for understanding them, is repeated by numerous contemporary social scientists who attempt to describe or discount contemporary racial matters. This inclination will be seen in several other examples in the following pages.

Along with Bonilla-Silva, we view social "race" as a social category that resulted from the historically racialized practices of people of European descent. The human social practices associated with the category of race are impossible to analyze deeply without critical concepts and theories that dissect the specific "race" categorizing processes. One also cannot analyze these oppressive white practices well without historical and other *empirical* data specifically collected on how whites have thought and acted in terms of their white-framed concept of "race." According to Loveman, racial categories and racial groups are confused in Bonilla-Silva's analysis and should be kept analytically distinct in order to not foreclose on "potentially rewarding avenues of research and theorization."[5] However, there are no races or racial groups without the white racial categorizing processes implemented in various societies over the centuries. The continued realities of group segregation and power imbalances among racial groups exist only because of the centuries-long, white-controlled process of racial categorization and hierarchical ranking. The latter were well institutionalized to create and sustain great wealth and power for whites. Today, contemporary versions of the centuries-old white racial frame cut across time and place, constantly generating new systemically racist arrangements that greatly resemble the racially oppressive social worlds of past colonialism and slavery.[6]

Rogers Brubaker's Race Without Races

According to sociologist Rogers Brubaker, the "reality of race… does not depend on the existence of 'races.'"[7] In his published articles, such as "Ethnicity Without Groups," and his book *Grounds for Difference* (2105), he argues that ethnicity, race, and nation should not be conceptualized as substantial social entities. For instance, instead of viewing "race" as a concept denoting groups of people, Brubaker proposes a dramatic shift in social science understandings of racial and other human groupings, one that considers race, together with ethnicity and nation, *solely* as "practical categories, cultural idioms, cognitive schemas, discursive frames... and contingent events."[8] Brubaker criticizes what he terms *groupism*—that is, treating ethnic groups and races as entities with human interests and agency. Thinking of ethnicities, races, and nations as groups is a bad habit and the product of "folk" sociologies that inappropriately reify and naturalize groups of people.[9]

Brubaker evokes post-modernist understandings of identity—specifically, the supposed disappearance of group identity—to explain why social scientists should eliminate thinking about race, ethnicity, and nations in group terms. Human relations are viewed as ephemeral, and human interactions are seen as losing clear boundaries. Thus, there are no stable groups. Race is thus relational and eventful, not concrete or bounded.[10] He urges social scientists instead to focus on group-making instead of the group (e.g., racial group), to distinguish between groups (fixed and given) and groupness (variable and contingent), and between groups and categories of analysis such as group-formation.

With these abstractions, Brubaker is emphasizing action instead of representation, the verb over the noun. Race is not an entity or group to be defined or substantiated but an ongoing action and dynamic of human interaction always in flux. This view of racial groups is echoed in the analysis of Loveman. Racial groups are not meaningful when viewed as distinct groups, but become meaningful entities when understood as actions and performances of assorted actors.

Despite some important insights about group-making in this analysis, overall, Brubaker's attempt to discard social scientific analyses of racial *groups* is theoretically and empirically weak on a number of levels. To begin, racial groups as entities unquestionably exist as demonstrable empirical realities, and therefore the concept of racial group is necessary for substantial analysis of the contours and operations of centuries-old systemic racism. Additionally, racial groups cannot be accurately lumped together, as Brubaker does, with ethnic and religious groups.[11] Distinctive histories and common social experiences of oppression—as well as shared home and resistance cultures, languages, and societal positions—are some key factors uniting certain racial groups that are divided from yet other groups according to physical markers. In our racial group analysis, we recognize that these groups are social constructions that fluctuate to different degrees and are contingent on historical time, geographical place, and dominant racial framing. It is analytically useful to understand how racial groups operate as *groups*, even while realizing that multiracial *individuals* often challenge their categorization into one racial group or another.

Although some individuals might challenge their racial group categorization, this does not mean that this everyday racial categorization does not regularly intrude on and shape their lives and those of most others in a racially structured society. In contrast to Loveman, Brubaker, and other mainstream theorists' emphasis on the fragmentation and ephemeral character of racial groups, the empirical literature on certain major racial groups shows that their morphing or disassembling, while occurring to some degree, is less common than their *persistence* over long periods of time as substantially racially defined and oppressed groups. Most oppressed racial groups remain defined by the dominant group as such, as well as by their strategic cohesion and a largely shared worldview and response to racialized oppression. In most cases, the white racial group works to stagnate subordinated groups' lower positionality in a racially constructed hierarchy.

Problematically, scholars such as Brubaker dismiss or downplay the major racial conflicts and the racial hierarchy generated by whites and thus bypass central features of US modernity—white-created colonial, imperialistic, enslavement, and Jim Crow systems of racialized oppression.[12] Indeed, terms and concepts such as racial exploitation, racial oppression, institutional racism, and systemic racism do not appear in Brubaker's *Grounds for Difference*, nor are there references to W.E.B. Du Bois and other key social science figures in the centuries-old race-critical tradition.[13] Nowhere is there discussion of the role of white agents and actors in creating contemporary racial phenomena. Yet, race-critical concepts and theories are necessary for understanding the empirical reality of racialized social groups and the sharp division between those who sustain racial oppression in its various forms and those against whom that oppression is directed. Without serious acknowledgment of these empirically demonstrable group differences in power and position in a historically and socially constructed racial hierarchy, the concepts of race and racism have little meaning. As we will see in later chapters, systemic racism, a fundamental and material feature of past and present US society, is sustained by whites' extensive racist framing and action directed at people of color—without question, groups are an essential part of any racial analysis.

More radically, Brubaker even suggests a future dismantling of the social scientific domain of racial studies. That is, "by raising questions about the *unit* of analysis—the ethnic [or racial] group—we end up questioning the *domain* of analysis: ethnicity [or race] itself."[14] While he raises important questions about the complexity of analyzing racial and ethnic groups, he does not come close to presenting a successful argument for their removal from social scientific analysis of the historical and contemporary empirical realities of systemic racism.

Andreas Wimmer on Ethnic Boundary-Making

Andreas Wimmer has advanced a nuanced understanding of ethnicity that offers some helpful insights about the framework of ethnic boundary-making. For instance, he examines the range of weak-to-strong ethnic boundaries and usefully investigates possible explanations for the range and flexibility, formation and dissolution, and embrace or rejection of ethnic boundaries. Wimmer aims to develop a "comparative analytic of ethnic boundary-making," one that embraces key features of the constructivist tradition, but goes farther by asking questions, such as "how and why ethnicity matters" to different degrees depending on social contexts. He also raises questions about why ethnicity, race, and nationality differences are sometimes associated with group oppression and inequality, yet in other cases "do not structure the allocation of resources, invite little political passion and represent only secondary aspects of individual identity."[15] Unlike other constructivists who view race and ethnicity as ephemeral, unstable, or porous, Wimmer suggests that some ethnic and racial boundaries are indeed lasting, stable, and less permeable. Overall, he attempts to explain how such boundaries arise and how they are often altered over time—that is, "how and why they might be redrawn to include new groups of people or hitherto accepted ones, how they might become blurred, fuzzy, and porous and perhaps eventually dissolve altogether, or, to the contrary, remain stable and persist over time."[16]

Pointing out that ethnic and racial boundaries are not necessarily ephemeral and unstable, Wimmer appears to challenge the attempts at dismantling ethnicity and race increasingly popular among numerous contemporary social scientists. However, his understanding of ethnic and racial boundary-making has some problematical features. To take a major example, he subsumes race and nationality groups, like many scholars mentioned already, under an all-encompassing rubric of ethnicity. Race and racial groups are thus only a "subtype of ethnicity."[17] This old analytical move to integrate race, ethnicity, and nationhood under the concept of ethnicity, and thus to view them in similar terms and as part of one conceptual family, seems to again be gaining currency in the social sciences, as we see in the works of Rogers Brubaker and others.[18]

While the conceptual frameworks of race, ethnicity, and nationhood certainly can and do overlap and intersect, they relate to distinctive social histories and realities and do not necessarily intermix or coincide. Comparative field research on different societies shows that all three have conceptual utility and relate to distinctive social realities in human societies. For the most part, in these societies ethnicity is different from race and nationhood, race is different from ethnicity and nationhood, and nationhood is different from race or ethnicity. Their placement into one conceptual category or their development as a hybrid understanding distorts a multifaceted, complex social reality. For Wimmer and numerous other social scientists, ethnicity is posited as the central concept around which the others are defined or understood, but in this process racial groups and nationality groups tend to be downgraded, absorbed, or peripheralized.[19] This disregard of race and nationhood as distinctive societal entities and the failure to see that these frameworks exist *beyond ethnicity* is problematic.

Additionally, a conceptual framework that seeks to understand "strategic struggles" over group boundaries is important, but only one piece of the theoretical puzzle of understanding issues of race, ethnicity, and nationality. Social boundary-making or the dissolving of social formations (i.e., groups) only tell social scientists so much about social reality. They do not provide a comprehensive theoretical means of viewing and studying the broad range of social relations, including those of racial oppression arising from histories of Western colonialism and imperialism. Wimmer's main contribution to race and ethnic discourse appears to be his analyses of "strong" and "stable" ethnic and racial boundaries, yet under a closer reading he seems to be shaky on this point, for he chides the contemporary scholars who "dare to argue for the givenness, trans-situational stability, and deep-rooted character of ethnic cultures and identities." Finally, we disagree with his claim, a common one among some (white) social analysts today, that there is a major danger in seeing "race, ethnicity and nationhood wherever one looks."[20] While it is obvious that not every social interaction and human construction can be directly linked to race, ethnicity, or nationhood, nevertheless there are still fundamental patterns of racialized social organization in the modern era that are deeply embedded in societies across the globe.

Mustafa Emirbayer and Matthew Desmond: Race and Reflexivity

In a well-received article, "Race and Reflexivity," in *Ethnic and Racial Studies*, Mustafa Emirbayer and Matthew Desmond address a range of significant issues in contemporary racial studies.[21] One issue they focus on involves the degree of reflexivity or reflectivity of social science researchers dealing with racial issues. They call for thoughtful consideration by social scientists of their own positions in the racial order and the social structure of social science, as well as their relationships to the broader intellectual world. Yet, despite this call, they largely ignore the insights and intense reflexivity of decades of African American sociology, a well-established tradition that competently frames reflective thought about race. They overlook, for example, John Stanfield's work *Black Reflective Sociology* (2011) and numerous other works that demonstrate the decades-old scholarly reflectivity of black sociologists.[22] Moreover, their article embarks on a highly abstract exploration of scholarly reflexivity with little consideration of the ubiquitous and influential macro-social structures of the established racial order.

Evoking the work of W.E.B. Du Bois, Emirbayer and Desmond point out a fundamental concern about scholarly reflexivity in racial studies, the hidden assumptions of most white scholars that include using white understandings as the standard for evaluating social science research questions. In our view, they correctly argue that whiteness is now the implicit or explicit reference category in much social science and for the importance of bringing critical-race and intersectional theories into contemporary racial studies.[23]

Another of their important points is the call for "rigorous institutional analyses of the social and historical structures that condition one's thinking" and for social science analyses of "institutional settings in which race scholars are formed, the structures and processes whereby their hidden assumptions about the world are forged." However, we disagree with their follow-up statement that indicates that analyses of these institutions should seek out "advanced and sophisticated instruments of scientific objectification."[24] Unfortunately, the advanced and sophisticated scientific instruments they seem to have in mind have long been used to avoid critical institutional analyses and have actually perpetuated white-framed understandings of societal matters. Moreover, Emirbayer and Desmond's recognition of the importance of institutional analysis at the very end of the article appears to be tangential to their main focus on the reflective thought of individual social scientists. They do not offer any race-critical analysis of the social institutions that maintain this racial order, but rather explore how a scholar should become more critical in her or his analyses of social institutions and aware of the role the latter play in shaping their thinking.[25]

Several observations in Emirbayer and Desmond's important article contradict themselves and are analytically problematic. In a critique of the article, Mary Pattillo focuses on the tension in their prescription to embrace the knowledge of ordinary people at one moment (implementing sociologist Pierre Bourdieu's idea) and to reject the knowledge of ordinary folk the next moment (implementing Émile Durkheim's idea). They oscillate between demanding a reflexivity that avoids abstract theory and one that actually seeks abstract theoretical development.[26]

Additionally, we find their analysis overly optimistic about social scientists' ability to address issues of power, and thus to be truly reflexive. For instance, they use the phrase "analysts of racial domination" to describe those who study racial matters, yet few race analysts fall into this the category; most such analysts shy away from questions regarding highly racialized power structures. They include themselves in this group of analysts of racial domination and, despite the potentialities in their analysis of whiteness, nowhere in their article do they critically analyze white racial agents, structural racism, systemic racism, or institutional racism—all key features of racial domination.[27]

Their race and reflexivity analysis references mostly *white* social scientists and social thinkers (John Dewey, Karl Manheim, Karl Marx, Émile Durkheim, Antonio Gramsci), many of whom never seriously studied racial matters. The article's primary concept used to discuss race, "reflexivity," is derived from the contemporary white sociologist Pierre Bourdieu, who wrote little about racial matters, as they themselves note. Bourdieu is not a scholar who spent time seriously analyzing racial matters, nor did he develop theoretical understandings about Western racial oppression. His intellectual popularity in the largely white-framed, Eurocentric social sciences may have to do with his European background and respect in largely white academic worlds in the West. Problematically, there is a disturbing trend in much Western social science to seek a certain type of Eurocentric sanctioning of knowledge, and thus a regular resorting to a white framing of social reality.

Emirbayer and Desmond's discussion of the insider doctrine in social science research makes several claims. They dispute the idea that "an insider's vantage point in and of itself leads to scientific discoveries unavailable to the outsider." This point seems reasonable, but it is important to critically assess their next statement: "The notion that white scholars, strictly because of their whiteness, are blind to certain dimensions of racial domination, while nonwhite scholars, strictly because of their nonwhiteness, are keen to these dimensions, is too simplistic a proposition."[28] While not all white scholars are blind to deep understandings of racial domination, a great many are; conversely, while not all scholars of color are conscious of that racial domination, a great many are.

Moreover, considering mainstream white scholars' centuries-long mis-theorizations and misconceptions of race documented in several scholarly books,[29] one might think that Emirbayer and Desmond would consider and assess how white social analysts have historically failed to develop significant theoretical insights about patterns of racial domination. If they were to fully address the work of social scientists of color, aside from W.E.B. Du Bois, and, in fact, understand his work more deeply and thoroughly (see below), they would realize that these scholars of color have for centuries provided many of the keenest insights about racial oppression. Black social thinkers in the late 1700s and early 1800s were already developing sounder theoretical sociological arguments and concepts of racial matters than are found in the contemporary racial scholarship of many white social scientists.

Another troubling argument involves their take on the debate over how to define racial groups. They cite and agree with Rogers Brubaker and others in regard to the "fallacy of analytic groupism," which they view as the "tendency to take discrete, sharply differentiated, internally homogenous, and externally bounded groups as basic constituents of social life, chief protagonists of social conflicts, and fundamental units of analysis."[30] As we indicated previously, we find the argument against identifying and analyzing empirically society's racial groups as one of the intellectually puzzling and inept arguments made by some prominent scholars dealing with racial matters, as it discards societal history and present-day societal realities in grand fashion. The argument against the analytic utility of substantially bounded racial groups does not hold up in the empirical research world and has no strength as realistic social science theory.

As we have observed previously, to do away with studying the empirical reality of subordinated and racialized groups is to ignore the systemic racism of colonialism, slavery and apartheid systems, and modern-day exploitation of people of color (for example, US prison systems) that were created by the elite white architects of these racialized systems. It is also to discount the actions of people of color who have generated different and resisting worldviews, histories, values, and social practices than the whites who have oppressed them. Racialized social systems and racial groups have been socially created and powerfully maintained by whites, despite the desire of individuals of color or groups of color to challenge and eradicate these oppressive structures and their white-imposed human groupings. To acknowledge, discuss, and research the social construction and current reality of racial groups is not the same thing as legitimizing or reifying this horrific racial oppression.

In addition, Emirbayer and Desmond criticize what they view as an unproductive trend in race studies, that stigmatized minorities are either overly celebrated through epistemic privilege and racial romanticism or overly demonized through condescension and being labeled as inferior. They put Afrocentric manifestos in the first group. However, as the critical race scholar Wendy Moore notes, they are creating a straw man. The second trend has "become embedded in mainstream academic scholarship about people of colour, the other has not."[31] The social sciences have a history of pathologizing people of color and valorizing whites. Not only do Emirbayer and Desmond fail to address this fact, they uncritically link Du Bois to what they consider to be "cult-like celebration" of racial groups without recognizing his balanced view that addresses groups' virtues and problems. It appears that their reading of Du Bois, who left many volumes of racial analyses, needs greater attention.[32]

The most serious error is their failure to incorporate the substantial knowledge and insights about reflexivity found in the work of critical social scientists of color, particularly critical African American sociologists. The latter have developed some of the most useful tools in racial analysis and some of the most important steps toward scholarly reflexivity. In a number of places, their analysis would have benefited greatly by addressing the insights and realities of this African American sociological tradition. For example, when describing scholars as "a class having leisure" who are "protected against the more serious perils which afflict the mass of humanity," they might have been describing the life-world of a majority of white scholars, but as the history and narratives of African American social scientists regularly reveal, they are mostly *not* in the leisure class and have often faced serious life perils (see Chapter 9). Given this reality, one must seriously consider how reflexivity is both contextualized and racialized. In many cases, the social reflexivity of most white scholars might be different than that of most black scholars for a whole host of social, economic, cultural, and historical reasons linked in many ways to the context of systemic racism.[33]

In their discussion of scholars who are aware of their statuses in overlapping societal hierarchies, Emirbayer and Desmond could have used numerous black social scientists' writings as prime examples of this reflexive awareness. Moreover, they could have critically noted how and why few white social scientists engage in similar reflexivity about their hierarchical positioning. Critical black social scientists are often forced to reflect on discrimination and their position in a racial hierarchy, while white social scientists, because of their privileged hierarchical position, mostly have the luxury to avoid this type of reflexive inquiry.

Reference to black sociological works would also have complicated their deconstruction of racial groups. Many black sociologists stress the epistemological importance and strategic necessity of recognizing and critically analyzing racial groups as long as the dominant white racial frame is maintained and white oppressors continue to sustain systemic racism and socially stratify and categorize people into racial groups (see Chapter 9). Emirbayer and Desmond argue that racial groups differentiate and reify themselves, mostly ignoring the larger societal structures—the legal system, segregated social spaces, dominant racial framing—created by whites that have long established very concrete mechanisms of racial group differentiation and oppression.

By paying greater attention to black social science writings in particular and black literature in general, Emirbayer and Desmond might also not have been dismissive of the relationship between biography and racial understandings. For example, critical autobiography was a major vehicle for Du Bois discussing his own racial experiences and viewpoints, and thus for brilliantly researching and theorizing the dimensions of racial oppression. His own biography and issues of racial oppression are in conversation in his key writings, such as *The Souls of Black Folk* (1903) and *Darkwater* (1920). One of his most sociologically informative and scholarly works, *Dusk of Dawn: An Essay Toward an Autobiography of a Race Concept* (1940), demonstrates by its title and in its text that Du Bois discerns a strong social interrelatedness of race concepts and his racialized biography and thus aims to demonstrate their related analytical importance.[34]

In his essay, "W.E.B. Du Bois: The Autobiographer as Sociological Theorist," the contemporary African American scholar Rutledge Dennis has described how Du Bois used autobiographical writings to dissect and foreground issues of ongoing racial prejudice and discrimination. Du Bois uses his autobiographical narrative to reveal the racist "paradoxes, conflicts, and ambiguities of American society."[35] As an insightful researcher and a white-racialized subject, he thereby critically explained the larger worlds of racial oppression. Indeed, Du Bois and numerous other black scholars and writers—for example, Henry Louis Gates and Maya Angelou—have used such autobiographical theorizing to analyze in great detail the painful realities of white racial oppression. In our view, contemporary racial theorists such as Emirbayer and Desmond should pay much greater attention to this type of black self-reflection on individual positioning in the racial structure, especially when that positioning shares numerous similarities with many other people of color. Autobiographies of people of color often provide well-informed observations of the sociologically significant experiences of individuals who have been aggressively racialized and have thus experienced extensive material racism, including racial stratification and stigmatization.

Social Science Attempts to Bypass or Dismantle Research on Systemic Racism

Important scholars such as Loveman, Brubaker, Wimmer, Emirbayer, and Desmond have sought to deconstruct, dismantle, and/or reframe contemporary research and theorizing about race and ethnicity. They have resurrected old ideas about these racial-ethnic matters and also introduced a range of new concepts and theoretical claims. They and others have often tried to erase or marginalize the concept of "racial groups," a move that ultimately eliminates or downplays sociologically significant, cogent discussions of systemic racism, the racialized character of colonialism and imperialism in the past and present, racial group resistance against this racial oppression, and government policies such as immigration control measures that target people solely because of their racial group profiles. Many other important topics about contemporary white racism are also downplayed or erased by this approach.

In their dismissing or deconstructing of racial-group issues, such scholars stress individual agency over structure and the flexibility of social relations instead of the stubborn stability and persistence of racialized social systems, societies, built on whites' past and present subjugation and exploitation of people of color. Restricted and restricting in their use of racial-group concepts, they thus downplay or evade entirely discussion of long-lasting structural, institutional, and systemic racism—key concepts for understanding the history and current landscape of the United States and other societies. In this process they ignore what is one of the most important forms of social explanation and power in the modern period, *white supremacy*, a term and historically rooted social reality that never forcefully arises in their writings.

Another member of this cadre, Pierre Bourdieu's student, Loïc Wacquant, has described the study of racial domination as an area of current social science research "where political posturing and moral ranting too often take precedence over analytic rigor and the quality of empirical materials" and warns of the "slippery and loaded notion of 'racism.'"[36] Oddly uninformed about much contemporary empirical research on systemic racism as it operates in everyday life, he too proclaims that racial division is not "a thing but an activity." Like those discussed above, he overemphasizes a dissipating activity in ethno-racial divisions, rather naively denouncing the largely stable, static social realities of racial and ethnic relations that have been shown by extensive social science research in the field to exist in many US and other societal contexts well into the twenty-first century.[37] Like the others, he discourages social science research that separates race and ethnicity, echoing Loveman's weak criticisms of Bonilla-Silva's supposed pitfall of "distinguishing analytically between 'race' and 'ethnicity.'"[38] While we could address other problematical issues raised by these scholars, we believe it is important to conclude with a discussion of the differences between "race" and "ethnicity," an analytic distinction often exorcized by those who seek to reduce or dismantle deep theoretical and empirical probing of the persistent systemic racism of Western societies.

Distinguishing "Race" and "Ethnicity"

Many social scientists whose work we addressed previously are opposed to viewing race and ethnicity as distinctive societal realities requiring different conceptual frameworks to fully understand. Some would do away with the study of racial-group matters altogether in favor of "ethnicity" studies. Others would still address racial matters as such, but only as a less important subset of issues related to the umbrella concept of ethnicity. Approaches that marginalize racial-group issues or confuse them with other social-group realities and conceptual categories are, as we have previously noted, quite out of touch with the extensive historical and contemporary empirical research on many societies' often brutal and extensive racial realities.

Rather than understanding the racial group as a subtype of ethnicity, we find much more analytic clarity in viewing "ethnic groups" as largely separate social formations and "racial group" formations as involving more powerful and encompassing social structural realities in many societies and globally. The English word "ethnic" (from Greek ethnos for "nation") comes into English with the early explorations and conquests of Europeans outside Europe, first appearing in the 1400s as a word to describe culturally different "heathen" (not Christian) countries.[39] Not until the 1930s and 1940s, however, does the regular use of "ethnicity" and "ethnic group" to denote national-origin groups appear in social science, then being applied to the large immigrant groups that had come to the US from Southern and Eastern Europe. W. Lloyd Warner and his colleagues seem to have been the first social scientists to make extensive use of the terms "ethnicity" and "ethnic groups," with the latter viewed as social groups primarily marked off by their cultural or nationality differences. Racial groups, in contrast, were socially marked by the dominant racial group primarily by selected physical differences.[40] Notice that these understandings emphasize the social and societal construction of both racial groups and ethnic groups and reject the biological determinism that views such groups as self-evident with unchanging physical or cultural characteristics. Human beings, outside and inside racial and ethnic groups, determine when certain physical or cultural characteristics are important enough to mark off a group for social purposes, for good or for ill.

Those contemporary scholars discussed previously overestimate the power of an umbrella ethnicity conceptualization to explain racial phenomena. Moreover, one major problem that we often see among such social scientists is that they also argue that assimilation and related societal experiences of "non-white" groups are generally similar to those of white groups. This usually ensures less scholarly and public policy attention to the extensive white racial oppression long faced by racialized groups. Thus, this public and scholarly use of the umbrella term "ethnic group" frequently has overtones of racial bias. As the scholar Philomena Essed has noted, the "substitution of 'ethnicity' for 'race' as a basis of categorization is accompanied by increasing unwillingness among the dominant group to accept responsibility for the problems of racism."[41]

Historically and empirically, racial groups and ethnic groups are mostly distinct social realities, best analyzed by different conceptual approaches to understanding groups, social relations, societies, and global relations. Indeed, fully examining historical and contemporary racial matters is a vast empirical and theoretical undertaking and thus examining differences between race and ethnicity approaches is only one step to understanding these racial matters, yet it is an essential one.

Our understanding of the difference between "racial group" and "ethnic group" is clear-cut with regard to how and why these human groupings were created, principally by white Europeans and their descendants in past centuries. Racial groups ("races") are socially and historically constructed *crude* categories of people based mainly on physical features such as skin color. They typically were constructed during histories of highly exploitative relationships between peoples from different geographical regions of the globe. While socially and historically constructed and human-made, crudely defined racial groups have, as a result, come to represent very real social realities for those who identify or are identified within one racial category or another. This is due to the very *material* construction and maintenance of a racial hierarchy by dominant white groups in modern societies, wherein different groups are labeled, ordered, and rewarded or penalized according to a racial classification system developed and substantially maintained by whites.

Over the past centuries, whites have devised a simplistic but socially powerful color-coded racial classification system that conceptually and materially divides people of the globe into major racial groups based on certain physical characteristics. As we noted in Chapter 1, since the eighteenth and nineteenth centuries, a typical racist categorization system runs something like this: "whites" (Europeans); "reds" (Native Americans); "yellows" (East Asians); "browns" (Latin Americans, Middle Easterners); and "blacks" (Africans). Whites are at the top of this hierarchy, with the darkest-skinned groups (for example, blacks) at the bottom. Throughout the modern period, European and European American science, religion, laws, and other cultural structures have propped up and enforced this aggressively white-framed racial hierarchy (see Chapter 1). Hierarchical divisions are directly linked to the unequal life-worlds and opportunities of racially constructed groups. Through European and US colonialism, slavery systems, and continued systematic subjugation of people of color, whites have regularly created and maintained a highly racialized social world and empirically well-defined "color line" between whites in general and people of color in general. They have generated and racialized this materially oppressive world so that they can profit economically and in numerous other ways.[42]

In contrast to systemic racism's physically-coded breakdown of racial groups, ethnic groups are socially constructed groups primarily distinguished by cultural or geographical characteristics such as religion and national origin. For example, in the socially constructed white racial group, one finds different national origin (ethnic) groups such as Irish and Italian Americans. These groups broadly share a socially distinguished "white" phenotype as well as historical connections to European nations or their colonies outside of Europe. Yet, they are ethnically diverse, especially in earlier generations, often displaying differences in religion, language, and national loyalties. Similarly, among socially defined "black" people one finds numerous ethnic groups with distinctive identities and cultural backgrounds. Multigenerational African Americans with distant links to ethnic groups in Africa during the slavery era have been joined, more recently, by national-origin groups such Ethiopian, Haitian, and Nigerian Americans.[43]

Ethnicity shapes the social world in many societies where racialization (race) plays little or no role, such as those where the population is racially homogenous. For example, ongoing ethnic conflicts within Eastern Europe long after the demise of the old Soviet Union point to nationalistic tensions without apparent connections to racial issues. Theories that address national origins are useful for assessing societies that are predominately marked by ethnic group organization. Ethnicity in this sense is conceptually important, and for this reason should be viewed as a social group category substantially distinct from racial group, with its own set of historical and contemporary understandings and examples. Interestingly, perception of a common ancestry, real or mythical, has been part of ethnic groups' self-definitions. Max Weber described ethnic groups as "groups that entertain a subjective belief in their common descent."[44] Thus, we do not discard ethnicity in favor of race, as ethnicity is as socially real as racial grouping in many societies.

Certainly, many societies are not racially *homogenous*, particularly societies that were European colonial outposts and/or had European-generated slavery systems. A number of contemporary societies, such as the European "settler" countries the United States, Australia, Canada, New Zealand, and South Africa, are thus multiracial. They have largely been defined by social relations among racial groups in which the white racial group has maintained great socioeconomic power over the others. Even societies once defined by their mostly homogeneous racial character are becoming increasingly racially diverse as they become even more globally connected through changes stemming from increased immigration and international relations. A steady racialization of numerous European countries has accompanied the migration of people of color to them, migrations that often have their roots in past European colonialism and slavery systems. Many of the people of color who immigrate and try to gain citizenship in these European nations were once the subjects of racialized colonialism in their home societies.

For example, Great Britain's growing "brown" and "black" racial groups are predominately from Pakistan, India and the Caribbean islands, once key outposts of the British colonialism and slavery systems.

With the twentieth-century racialization of Europe defined by the migration of formerly colonized people of color has come social unrest among white Europeans who feel "their" countries are being invaded and corrupted by growing numbers of brown and black immigrants and their descendants. One finds numerous nativistic books in Europe, such as Ed West's *The Diversity Illusion: What We Got Wrong About Immigration & How to Set It Right*.[45] Early examples of this sentiment, which especially targeted the United States, can be found in the nativistic screeds such as Madison Grant's *The Passing of the Great Race or The Racial Basis of European History* (1917) and Lothrop Stoddard's *The Rising Tide of Color Against White World-Supremacy* (1920). More recently, this same type of racialized nativism can be found in Samuel Huntington's books, *The Clash of Civilizations and Remaking of the World Order* (1996) and *Who Are We? The Challenges to America's National Identity* (2004).[46]

Racial group conflicts have increasingly developed in European nations such as Great Britain as black and brown residents, especially immigrants, are viewed through a white framing as major sources of national economic and social maladies.[47] These racial conflicts are distinct from ethnic conflicts, as they have different social histories and disparate social contexts. They exhibit different social group formations and hierarchies because they usually emerge from the racial constructions of highly exploitative and oppressive European colonialism and slavery systems, and they involve the continued maintenance of white-framed social structures, including white-run economic, political, justice, and educational systems. Moreover, in most cases, racial conflicts over a range of issues favor whites and perpetuate imbalanced power relations between them and people of color. The social construction and perpetuation of the dominant white frame, at work for several centuries, continue to generate racialized social worlds that divide and stratify groups of people into different racial groups. In turn, the societal ordering of racial groups, based on a racial hierarchy created long ago by whites of European descent and largely persisting into the present, continues to reinforce socially constructed beliefs about the racial superiority of whites and racial inferiority of people of color.

We recognize and emphasize that the social constructions of racial and ethnic groups are historically contextualized, and can shift over time and agree with the theorists critically analyzed in this chapter that racial-ethnic categorizing and hierarchical placements do sometimes shift in certain ways over the course of history and through social contexts. For example, researchers such as St. Clair Drake and Frank Snowden have demonstrated that in the first centuries of European contacts with African peoples, including the Greek and Roman periods, European outsiders mostly attached greater significance to Africans' culture and nationality than to their physical characteristics. While in this era some Europeans did express negative views of Africans' physical characteristics, there was no systematic racialized enslavement of Africans by Europeans, and these European views did not develop full color consciousness and other racially framed views of Africans that would come with later large-scale exploitation. Virulent white-racist framing emerged only in the modern world, during the imperial expansion into Africa, Asia, the Island nations, and the Americas by European countries seeking wealth through means of colonization and enslavement of peoples of color between the 1400s and the 1800s.[48] These historical and contemporary processes of highly exploitative oppression have regularly shaped whether and how skin color and other physical characteristics become group markers principally established by the oppressor group.

Conclusion

Racial matters are firmly and deeply rooted in the modern social world, regularly shaping and affecting many contemporary societies. Thus, it is very puzzling that all the contemporary theorists discussed in this chapter seem to ignore or have a limited awareness of the now extensive empirical research literature that demonstrates this fact about contemporary white racism.[49] We will return to this critical empirical reality and the research on it, a requisite consideration for accurate and honest race theory, in Chapters 9 and 10.

Additionally, class, culture, ethnicity, and nationality are also products of modernity that significantly shape contemporary societies. In the next chapter, we demonstrate how today's social scientists too often conflate the concepts of class, culture, nationality, and ethnicity with race. Instead of eliminating, dismantling, or disempowering the framework of race, we propose viewing the intersectionality and interrelationships between race and class, race and culture, race and ethnicity, and race and nationality.

Notes

1. Interestingly, all are at elite US universities.
2. Mara Loveman, "Is 'Race' Essential?" *American Sociological Review*, 64(6) (1999): 891.
3. Ibid., pp. 891–5.
4. Ibid., pp. 896–7.
5. Ibid., p. 892.
6. See Joe R. Feagin, *Racist America: Roots, Current Realities, and Future Reparations*, 3rd edn (New York: Routledge, 2014).
7. Rogers Brubaker, "Ethnicity Without Groups," *Archives Européenes de Sociologie XLIII*, 2 (2002): 163–89.
8. Ibid., p. 167. See also Rogers Brubaker, *Grounds for Difference* (Cambridge, MA: Harvard University Press, 2015), Kindle loc. 110–11.
9. Brubaker, "Ethnicity Without Groups," p. 166.
10. Ibid., p 164–7.
11. Brubaker, *Grounds for Difference*, Kindle loc. 110–11.
12. Brubaker, "Ethnicity Without Groups," p. 166.
13. Brubaker, *Grounds for Difference*. See Kindle loc. 948 for his abstract way of describing racial violence.
14. Brubaker, "Ethnicity Without Groups," p. 186.
15. Andreas Wimmer, *Ethnic Boundary Making: Institutions, Power, Networks* (New York: Oxford University Press, 2013), p. 2.
16. Ibid., p. 4.
17. Ibid., p. 7.
18. See Andreas Wimmer, "Ethnic Boundary Making as Strategic Action: Reply to Critics," *Ethnic and Racial Studies* 37(5) (2014): 834–42.
19. Wimmer's problematic views about race, including his erasure of the racial group and white actors as racial oppressors, persists in "Race-centrism: A Critique and a Research Agenda," *Ethnic and Racial Studies*, 38(13) (2015): 2186–205. One also notices the eclipse of race by "ethnicity" in numerous areas, including the headings of the *Contemporary Sociology* review journal.
20. Wimmer, *Ethnic Boundary Making*, pp. 2, 5.
21. Mustafa Emirbayer and Matthew Desmond, "Race and Reflexivity," *Ethnic and Racial Studies* 35(4) (2012): 574–99. Many of their key arguments are repeated or amplified in their book: Mustafa Emirbayer and Matthew Desmond, *The Racial Order* (Chicago: University of Chicago Press, 2015). *The Racial Order* is similarly steeped in Eurocentric intellectualism that attempts to build racial knowledge on the ideas of white European social scientists and intellectuals, most of whom never studied racial matters

seriously. While noting social scientists of color in passing, they spend little time analyzing their ideas.
22 See Joyce A. Ladner (ed.), *The Death of White Sociology* (New York: Random House, 1973); James E. Blackwell and Morris Janowitz (eds.), *Black Sociologists: Historical and Contemporary Perspectives* (Chicago: University of Chicago Press, 1974); Robert E. Washington and Donald Cunnigen (eds.), *Confronting the American Dilemma of Race: The Second Generation Black American Sociologists* (Lanham, MD: University Press of America, 2002); John Stanfield II, *Black Reflective Sociology: Epistemology, Theory, and Methodology* (Walnut Creek, CA: Left Coast Press, 2011).
23 Emirbayer and Desmond, "Race and Reflexivity," pp. 575, 579, 580, 587. See also Emirbayer and Desmond, *The Racial Order*.
24 Emirbayer and Desmond, "Race and Reflexivity," pp. 591–2.
25 Ibid., p. 592.
26 Mary Pattillo, "The Tension between Abstraction and Specificity in Enacting Reflexivity in Race Scholarship," *Ethnic and Racial Studies*, 35(4) (2012): 620.
27 On p. 579, Emirbayer and Desmond quote Roediger (reference below): "Few Americans have ever considered the idea that African Americans are extremely knowledgeable about whites and whiteness." Yet, they do not follow up on this point and suggest the need for incorporating African American social scientific perspectives. See also David Roediger, *Black On White: Black Writers on What It Means to Be White* (New York: Schocken, 1998).
28 Emirbayer and Desmond, "Race and Reflexivity," p. 582.
29 See Joyce Ladner (ed.), *The Death of White Sociology* (New York: Random House, 1973); Stanford James McKee, *Sociology and the Race Problem: The Failure of a Perspective* (Urbana, IL: University of Illinois Press, 1999); Robert Staples, *Introduction to Black Sociology* (New York: McGraw-Hill, 1976); Stephen Steinberg, *Race Relations: A Critique* (Stanford CA: Stanford University Press, 2007).
30 Ibid., p. 585.
31 Wendy Moore, "Reflexivity, Power, and Systemic Racism," *Ethnic and Racial Studies*, 35(4) (2012): 618.
32 In *The Philadelphia Negro: A Social Study* (1899) and *The Souls of Black Folks* (1903), two of his most noted works, Du Bois seriously discusses pathologies in the black community. See W.E.B. Du Bois, *The Philadelphia Negro: A Social Study* (Philadelphia: University of Pennsylvania Press, 1996 [1889]) and *The Souls of Black Folks* (New York: Penguin, 1995 [1903]).
33 This tension is not absolute. Some black scholars share positions of reflexivity similar to their white colleagues; conversely, some white scholars share many of the qualities of the reflexivity of black scholars. Additionally, other people of color, in many cases, demonstrate unique types of reflexivity rooted in social context and group experience.
34 See W.E.B. Du Bois' works: *The Souls of Black Folks* (New York: Penguin, 1995 [1903]); *Darwater: Voices From Within the Veil* (Mineoloa, NY: Dover Publications, 1999 [1920]); *Dusk of Dawn: An Essay Toward an Autobiography of a Race Concept*, in N. Huggins (ed.), *W.E.B. Du Bois Writings* (New York: Penguin, 1986 [1940]).
35 Rutledge Dennis, "W.E.B. Du Bois: The Autobiographer as Sociological Theorist," *Perspectives*, 29(1) (2006): 3.
36 Loïc Wacquant, "Marginality, Ethnicity and Penality in the Neoliberal City: An Analytic Cartography," *Ethnic and Racial Studies*, 37(10) (2013): 1695.
37 See references in note 48 below.
38 See Pierre Bourdieu and Loïc Wacquant, "On the Cunning of Imperialist Reason," *Theory, Culture, and Society*, 16(1) (1999): 41–58; Loveman, "Is 'Race' Essential?" pp. 894–5.

39 William M. Newman, *American Pluralism* (New York: Harper & Row, 1973), p. 19.
40 W. Lloyd Warner and Leo Srole, *The Social Systems of American Ethnic Groups* (New Haven, CT: Yale University Press, 1945), pp. 284–6.
41 Philomena Essed, *Understanding Everyday Racism* (Newbury Park CA: Sage, 1991), p. 28.
42 See Joe R. Feagin, *Systemic Racism: A Theory of Oppression* (New York: Routledge, 2006); Sean Elias, "The Colour Line," in *Wiley-Blackwell Encyclopedia of Race, Ethnicity, and Nationalism* (Malden, MA: Blackwell, 2016).
43 See Joe R. Feagin and Clairece B. Feagin, *Racial and Ethnic Relations*, 9th edn (New York: Pearson, 2011), Chapters 1–2.
44 Max Weber, "Ethnic Groups," Talcott Parsons et al. (eds.), *Theories of Society* (Glencoe, IL: The Free Press, 1961), Vol. 1, p. 306.
45 Ed West, *The Diversity Illusion: What We Got Wrong About Immigration & How to Set It Right* (London: Gibson Square, 2013).
46 Madison Grant, *The Passing of the Great Race or The Racial Basis of European History* (London: Wermod and Wermod, 2012 [1917]); Lothrop Stoddard, *The Rising Tide of Color Against White World-Supremacy* (Honolulu: University Press of Hawaii, 2003 [1920]); Samuel Huntington, *The Clash of Civilizations and Remaking of the World Order* (New York: Simon and Schuster, 1996); Samuel Huntington, *Who Are We? The Challenges to America's National Identity* (New York: Simon and Schuster, 2004).
47 Paul Gilroy, *"There Ain't No Black in the Union Jack": The Politics of Race and Nation* (Chicago: University of Chicago Press, 1991).
48 St. Clair Drake, *Black Folk Here and There* (Los Angeles: UCLA Center for Afro American Studies, 1987), Vol. 1, p. xxiii; Frank Snowden, *Color Prejudice* (Cambridge, MA: Harvard University Press, 1983), pp. 3–4, 107–8.
49 See, for example, Elizabeth Higginbotham, *Too Much to Ask: Black Women in the Era of Integration* (Chapel Hill, NC: University of North Carolina Press, 2001); Louwanda Evans, *Cabin Pressure: African American Pilots, Flight Attendants, and Emotional Labor* (Lanham, MD: Rowman & Littlefield, 2013); Joe Feagin and José Cobas, *Latinos Facing Racism: Discrimination, Resistance and Endurance* (New York: Paradigm/Routledge, 2014); Brittany Slatton, *Mythologizing Black Women: Unveiling White Men's Racist and Sexist Deep Frame* (New York: Paradigm/Routledge, 2014).

CHAPTER 5
CLASS, CULTURE, ETHNICITY, AND NATIONALITY— ANYTHING BUT "RACE"

The deconstruction and downplaying of racial analysis have spread across contemporary social sciences, appearing in various forms, a number of which we addressed in the last chapters. Social scientists have devised a variety of arguments that discount racial oppression in favor of some other explanatory principles, in many cases further promoting notions of post-raciality and colorblindness. *Class*, *culture*, *ethnicity*, and *nationality* studies are presented as alternative analytic frameworks to racial analysis and have gained considerable currency in the social sciences. Each offers an alternative perspective for understanding the social world. Because class-based analyses of race have had such a powerful impact in dismantling racial analysis, particularly in the United States and Britain, we devote a good portion of this chapter to critically examining the US class-based theories of William J. Wilson and the British neo-Marxist understandings of race as laid out by John Solomos. To conclude, we briefly illustrate ways that culture, ethnicity, and nationality paradigms, like class-based understandings of race, subsume or discount racial matters.

Class-Based Analyses of Race and Racism

Demonstrating the close, inseparable relationship between race and social class is an important task for social scientists. However, attempts by contemporary social scientists to elude or downplay racial analysis in favor of class analysis present questionable social knowledge about societal issues of race and class. In the US, sociologist William J. Wilson's argument that social class has overtaken race as the key variable affecting the lives of African Americans has been greeted with both controversy and wide acclaim.[1] Across the Atlantic, class-based understandings of racial matters in Britain rooted in Marxist analysis, such as that of John Solomos, have also often worked to diminish the social significance of race as such.

William J. Wilson: The Declining Significance of Race
William J. Wilson's *The Declining Significance of Race* (1978) was a pivotal book in discouraging or dismantling racism analysis in the social sciences, even if that was not exactly the author's intent. Wilson's argument goes like this: In the present post-industrial age, matters of social class and economics are more significant factors affecting the life chances of most black Americans and the relevant structures of institutions and social relationships than are the traditional racial factors, including institutional and systemic racism. Wilson stresses problems associated with the changing economic realities of the present-day high-tech, post-industrial global economy. These include the lack of technical job skills, adequate job training and education, and job availability in "underclass" communities, as well as greater job competition because of the globalizing economy and US corporations seeking cheaper labor in "less-developed" countries across the globe. For Wilson, these global economic structures are the primary impediments to advancing the life chances of the large working-class majority in US black communities. Jim-Crow-like structural organization of US racial relations and other institutionalized racism are no longer the key factors in black socioeconomic troubles as in previous eras. Subsequent books have reinforced his class-based analysis of the growing divide between this black underclass and the black middle class, and his emphasis has remained on the large-scale socioeconomic transformations of US inner cities that negatively and greatly affect underserved black communities.[2]

Wilson has argued for decades that US society is no longer one in which major institutions are substantially governed by decisions made out of a white-racist ideology; it is now a society in which the class position of most individuals of color is not greatly shaped by traditional racial discrimination. The primary evidence provided for this shift to a society where class trumps race is the developing divide between the "underclass" and middle-class black Americans. While recognizing that income divisions between middle-class whites and blacks are a reality, nonetheless he argues that divisions *among* blacks, not between blacks and whites, are now more pronounced and have greater implications for the black community's economic problems in the United States.[3]

In his 1980s book, *The Truly Disadvantaged*, Wilson continues with his central argument that class issues are generally more significant than racial issues for black communities. He addresses criticism of his earlier focus on socioeconomic improvements for the black middle class and relative neglect of the plight of lower-income black Americans. In contrast to older concepts such as the working class or lower class, Wilson's notion of the "underclass" describes a significant class segment of black Americans facing long-term poverty and dependence on government programs. In his view, and that of many popular authors, this underclass is overwhelmingly steeped in negative "ghetto" values and behavior, and is thus often out of the national mainstream of healthy families.[4] Wilson candidly focuses on the particular economic problems of black inner-city residents, again making a solid case for class-specific government policies. Exploring why these problems have grown over recent decades, he offers explanations emphasizing social dislocations especially affecting residents of inner-city neighborhoods. He also examines conflicting social science analyses of black community problems that have emerged as major public topics since the 1965 publication of the government monograph called the "Moynihan Report" and presents a critique of liberal and conservative perspectives on black poverty and "pathologies."[5]

Wilson's critique of liberal perspectives on contemporary racial realities is important for understanding his shift to a class perspective and for detailing his pointed criticisms of researchers arguing for the reality of contemporary racism. As he sees it, some liberal approaches evade addressing the significant pathologies of black low-income communities. This liberal approach is manifested in an over-valorization of black culture, in an increased focusing on the positive attributes of black communities, and in underestimating the reality of black poverty. Wilson critiques the liberal approach to studying problems in black inner-city neighborhoods that emphasizes "racism," which he largely defines in individualistic terms as a psychological state of prejudiced white minds.[6] According to Wilson, these serious community problems, as well as the growing class divide between the black poor and the black middle class, cannot be explained with a white-racism thesis.

For Wilson, the liberal accent on the continuing importance of contemporary racism fails to distinguish between the severe past racism and the current racial inequalities that must now be understood substantially in terms of non-racial causation, especially by "economic-class position and modern economic trends."[7] Government social policies based on race-based understandings of issues in black communities will not have the same satisfactory effects as government policies that address non-racial class factors. He accuses liberals of disingenuously employing the racism argument, stating that even they know racism is "too easy an explanation."[8] Because the liberal perspective has failed to adequately address extensive changes in inner-city communities, an array of conservative perspectives on the black underclass has taken hold in public and policy discussions. Conservative perspectives on changes in black communities routinely evoke culture-of-poverty arguments with little attention to economic contexts and trends. Wilson pursues the tensions between liberal and conservative perspectives on contemporary racial matters facing African Americans in his later books, including *When Work Disappears: The World of the New Urban Poor* (1996) and *More Than Just Race: Being Black and Poor in the Inner City* (2009).[9]

In *When Work Disappears*, Wilson does identify race as a social structural variable reflecting an individual's racial position and networks. However, in his view the liberal explanations of social inequality emphasize racial causation while ignoring what he views as non-racial economic issues and black cultural issues, whereas conservative explanations downplay all structural variables and stress black cultural values and lifestyles to explain racial group differences. Wilson thus argues for an approach to inner-city communities utilizing economic-structural, cultural, and psychological variables.[10] He argues against focusing on racial tensions and inequalities in society, and instead for focusing on a positive perspective that "promotes values of racial and intergroup harmony and unity and rejects the commonly held view that race is so divisive that whites, blacks, Latinos, and other ethnic groups cannot work together in a common cause."[11] Moreover, *In More than Just Race*, Wilson continues to employ a combined economic structure and cultural analysis to better understand why the inner-city "ghetto" persists, as well as in making sense of the troubled situations of black males and the chronic breakup of black families in such areas. He also continues to describe conservatives as accenting black cultural causation and liberals as mostly accenting the structural factors associated with white racism.[12]

Insights and Blind Spots in Wilson's Class-based Understandings

Wilson's work is clearly important on a number of fronts. He has developed a conceptual framework that informs social scientists and the general public about key issues and tensions in contemporary racial relations, specifically debates about the interconnections of race and class. Significantly, his sociological analyses have sought to explain the socioeconomic plight of blacks in the contemporary period and provide real policy solutions for that reality. His analyses have positively addressed the economic concerns of African Americans and importantly alerted social scientists about significant changes in the black community that have accompanied the dramatic US socioeconomic restructuring during recent decades of heightened deindustrialization and corporate globalization. Despite its controversial title, his concept of a black "underclass" presents a tragically accurate assessment of a large segment of the black population facing large-scale economic change. Additionally, Wilson's assessments of some gains by the slowly growing black middle class have advanced social scientific analysis by highlighting empirical realities of black success that offset anti-black stereotypes created by whites for centuries. In his writings over the decades, he has notably addressed heterogeneity in the black community, the effects of globalization on black communities, and the related shortcomings in numerous social scientific analyses of US racial matters.

While acknowledging these very important contributions, we still observe a number of blind spots, miscalculations, and tensions in Wilson's class-based understandings of racial matters. We are unconvinced that racial oppression has been replaced by economic class restructuring and subordination. Indeed, this economic class subordination has been and continues to be a part of a larger systemically racist social structuring. A focus on racial group conflict does not obscure the relations between racial oppression and class oppression but sharpens understandings of this often very close relationship. While understanding economic problems is fundamental to understanding society, we do not view them as more fundamental than problems associated with racial hierarchy and oppression. In fact, considerable empirical data demonstrate that historical and contemporary economic problems and racial problems have often been closely and foundationally entwined. Indeed, the global capitalistic economic shifts Wilson regularly references are directly linked to *past* European and US colonialist and slavery systems. These shifts are substantially part of the continuing acquisition by (mostly white) corporate executives and their corporations of the resources and labor of (mostly) peoples of color across the globe.

Mounds of empirical data that we have previously cited demonstrate that US society is still foundationally and systemically racist, despite the unconvincing contemporary arguments of "racial progress" and improved racial relations (see Chapters 8 and 10). Wilson's argument that the rise of the black middle class signifies that classism is now more significant than racism is not backed up by major studies of the extensive white discrimination faced by the black middle and working classes.[13] Another argument can be made that, with shifts to colorblind racism and claims of post-raciality, whites with great societal power and resources are now pressured to be at least partially diversity-oriented and to promote significant career success for some people of color. However, in many cases, powerful whites foster the careers only of blacks and other people of color who largely conform to white norms and/or acquiesce quietly to persisting white power and control.

Wilson's claims that white-constructed racial barriers and overt oppression facing people of color are crumbling are at best half-truths.

Yes, numerous official segregation barriers have come down since the Jim Crow era, but others not so immediately noticeable have persisted or been newly erected. While deliberate and overt racial oppression might not always be displayed publicly as much as in the past, it still often appears in numerous societal environments, including workplaces and schools.[14] Additionally, less overt discrimination and covert discrimination has become routinized and a popular strategic form of establishing or reestablishing white oppression of people of color in many societal arenas. Wilson argues that focusing on white racism ignores complex socioeconomic issues that are hard to explain. This might be true for analyses focusing on individual white bigotry that fail to account for complex racism issues, but a race-specific, systemic racism perspective can address these complex socioeconomic issues by analyzing, for example, the social reproduction of unjust enrichment for whites and unjust impoverishment for blacks over 20 US generations. Considering the divide between the "haves" and "have-nots" in the black community, Wilson argues that white racism cannot account for these major class divisions. Again, whites' covert and overt maintenance of systemic racism regularly operates to maintain white socioeconomic resources, privileges, and power even if that means occasionally taking down or weakening old racial barriers in response to organized pressures from people of color. The fact that the black middle class has had to fight twice as hard for every inch of their socioeconomic gains should indicate the great and persisting reluctance among most whites to cede significant resources and power.

Wilson's distinction between historic and current white racism is also problematic. To say that slavery does not represent the same social realities as Jim Crow segregation is true, as is the view that contemporary racism is different from Jim Crow. Yet, much white racial framing, many discriminatory tactics, and other characteristics of the white oppression of the slavery and Jim Crow eras did not suddenly disappear. Even though the face of white racism has morphed to some degree, especially on the surface level, many deep structural and institutional elements of earlier systemic racism remain intact, as we demonstrate throughout this book. In addition, the unjust enrichments that the majority of white families gained in that past racist era have persisted as major resource and capital inheritances across many generations to the present day.

While Wilson's class-trumps-race theory has received legitimate criticisms, largely and most pointedly from other African American sociologists,[15] a majority of the largely white social science establishment and the broader white community embraced, praised, and promoted his stated idea of the "declining significance of race." As sociologist Aldon Morris has explained, "For whites generally the message was embraceable, for it suggested that America had finally overcome its racist past."[16] Morris' deft review of *The Declining Significance of Race* underscored potential problems in the book addressed by numerous other black sociologists, reviews that were mostly drowned out by the generally positive reception of the book by the mainstream white press and academia.

While many mainstream sociologists uncritically embraced the declining-significance thesis, critical sociologists of various backgrounds have continued to highlight numerous flaws in Wilson's main theses. Many have countered them by pointing to abundant empirical evidence of the persistence of major racial divisions and of the racially discriminatory realities that continue to unjustly shape life-worlds and life chances of racial groups such as black Americans. Like many contemporary social scientists who study racial matters, Wilson's research focuses primarily on white racial attitudes, and not on the persisting structures of white institutions, organizations, and networks—the systemic racism that constantly defines and maintains the societally significant life-worlds of whites and "others." Wilson's critics have also pointed out that modern capitalism would not exist without the extreme white exploitation of people of color and their lands and resources in earlier centuries.[17] Modern capitalism, like nation-states and other major features of the modern world, developed to a substantial degree out of racial exploitation of people of color, and not the other way around. "Modernity" is indeed a product of the white racial framing and other forms of systemic racism constructed over centuries of European and European American colonialism and slavery systems. The riches and "progress" of the white world—the developments of capitalism—did not come without the great and exploited labor of people of color, which produced much of the basis for the excessive wealth and leisure of people of European descent to the present day.

John Solomos: A Neo-Marxist Deconstruction of Race
The British sociologist John Solomos is currently a central figure in ethnic and racial studies, specifically as a neo-Marxist analyst of racialization and racial categorization who problematizes "racial relations" research and the use of "race" as an explanatory concept. In his work, Solomos presents an illuminating analysis of Marxist social scientists' attempts to address racial matters, demonstrating theoretical divisions among Marxists with regard to the meaning of race and its place in social science analysis.[18] His essays provide important insights into various angles of Marxist analyses of racial matters, demonstrate the close relationship between racial matters and class, and reveal numerous Marxist contributions to understanding of racial matters in Western societies. Yet, on a number of levels, they also expose the limitations of historical and contemporary Marxism in regard to analyzing many racial matters.

Solomos argues that older mainstream Marxism mostly evaded discussion of racism and racial group relations and subsumed race under class. More recently, this has given way to a heterogeneity of Marxist approaches that address social divisions and conflict other than class, including issues of racism, sexism, and non-class political organization. He discounts the view that Marxism is incapable of addressing racial matters, must subsume race under class, and is inextricably rooted in economic determinism.[19] Responding to one such critique, Solomos notes the increased interest among Marxist theorists in analyzing racial and other non-class social divisions that are part of late capitalist societies. It is a mistake to view contemporary "Marxism as a monolithic set of assertions or to assimilate it wholesale into some notion of economic determinism or class reduction… it is best viewed today as consisting of a spectrum of competing schools of thought."[20]

He discusses three neo-Marxist approaches to racial issues: the relative autonomy model, the autonomy model, and the migrant labor model. In brief, the relative autonomy model is associated with the work of the Birmingham Centre for Contemporary Cultural Studies

(CCCS), whose common concern centers on a serious analysis of racism that recognizes "its relative autonomy from class-based social relations."[21] Solomos recounts the importance of the center's director, Stuart Hall, in directing analysis toward British racism, citing important books produced under his directorship, especially *Policing the Crises* (1978) and *The Empire Strikes Back: Race and Racism in 70s Britain* (1982).[22] These works introduced substantial racism analyses into contemporary Marxist dialogues. Solomos addresses Hall's attempt to develop a multidimensional analysis of racism that emphasizes that racism is not a general feature of all societies, but rather what exists are historically specific "racisms." Hall argues that racism cannot be reduced to other oppressions, that it has some autonomy, and he argues against a social science theory that posits a dichotomy of race and class.[23]

Some contemporary Marxist theorists are not satisfied with the view that racism is relatively autonomous from classism, but also wish to abandon the class-reductionism common to much Marxist theorizing. Solomos addresses the work of scholars John Gabriel and Gideon Ben-Tovim, who take this viewpoint and highlight how racism has been generated by historical struggles that created distinctive and irreducible racist phenomena. They view "race" as socially constructed. According to Solomos, their autonomous model prioritizes ideology over social practice, viewing racist ideologies as driving economic and political actions in those nation-states where such racism exists. Embedded in this autonomous model is the view that the modern nation-state is not monolithic or permanent, but instead a sociopolitical site of constant racist and anti-racist *struggles*.[24]

Another neo-Marxist model for understanding race issues is the migrant labor model developed by Robert Miles and Annie Phizacklea. Miles and Phizacklea reject the concept of "race in itself" and focus on *racism* as an ideology created and shaped by particular ideological and political-economic contexts such as labor migration. Additionally, Miles and Phizacklea argue that studies of the race–class interrelationship are misdirected and that class is the more significant analytical category. As Miles sees it, racism is only "one of the means which transform the positions occupied by class fractions in capitalist societies."[25]

In an effort to incorporate the insights and eliminate the problematic ideas of these neo-Marxist approaches, Solomos presents his own analytic framework exploring the dialectical relationships of race, class, and nation-state. In his view, the problems of racial relations are closely interwoven with the particular economic, political, and ideological characteristics of capitalist societies. A general Marxist theory of racism is inadequate because every historical situation should be "analyzed in its own specificity." He also accepts the claim of certain contemporary neo-Marxist theorists that racial-ethnic divisions of societies are not "completely determined by the structural contradictions" in various capitalist societies.[26] However, Solomos concludes his essay by observing that, while Marxist "race" theories are diverse, they are united in the belief that there is "no racial relations problem as such" and that "there is no problem of racism which can be thought of as separate from the structural features of capitalist society."[27]

A decade later, Solomos teamed up with social theorist Les Back to further explore developments in contemporary neo-Marxist understandings of racism issues. In their view, recent neo-Marxist approaches have focused more exclusively on political institutions, on the "role of the state as a site for the reproduction of racially structured situations."[28] They revisit theoretical developments among neo-Marxists of the 1970s and 1980s—specifically Robert Miles and CCCS theorist Paul Gilroy, one of Stuart Hall's students. They examine early neo-Marxist criticisms of race relations research by Miles, who rejected a named "sociology of race" and argued for a focus on an analyses of *racism* viewed within the context of capitalist arrangements. For Miles, "race" is only a conventional human construct, not an analytically useful concept.[29] Solomos and Back also turn to CCCS contributions to contemporary Marxist theoretical understandings of race. They discuss the center's view of race as a contested social construction, not one simply imposed by the state. Specifically, they note, Gilroy envisions collective racial identities as a "means to coordinate action and create solidarity." Racial identity thus coexists with other political identities and is "relatively autonomous" from relationships based on class.[30] The CCCS analysts also incorporate feminist perspectives on race and class and introduce gender analysis into their neo-Marxism. Moreover, the center's collaborative work, especially the book *The Empire Strikes Back*, served as a catalyst for important political debates surrounding racial relations research, especially a critique of Eurocentrism in the sociology of racial and ethnic studies.

Toward the close of their essay, Solomos and Back delineate a shift in certain neo-Marxist approaches to racial matters, with some theorists prioritizing racial over class identity and others promoting the move to a post-modernist understanding of race largely incompatible with many concerns of classical Marxists and neo-Marxists. At the heart of this theoretical shift is the question of the role of culture in racial matters and a focus on cultural forms of racial discourse in literature and media.

Neo-Marxists identified with this cultural turn avoid a monolithic definition of racism. An example is David Theo Goldberg, who notes that a view of Western racism as monolithic is being replaced with a concern with its "multifarious historical formations."[31] They additionally observe a new "cultural racism" resulting from societal conflicts associated with the rise of the political right, especially in Britain. Significantly, some academic writings on this "new racism" examine "how contemporary manifestations of race are coded in language that aims to circumvent accusations of racism. In the case of new racism, race is coded as culture."[32]

Solomos and Back strongly assert their central message—that knowledge concerning race and racism is highly politicized and its societal contexts must be well understood. Critical theorists must get beyond just the tools for racial analysis to examine comparatively the various Marxist paradigms, including the contextual debates over what should be analyzed. Conceptualizing race and racism issues involves much more than academic analysis, for there is a much larger political context that actually or potentially shapes such analysis. Because of this political nature of theorizing racism, they suggest viewing "race" solely as a political *construct* that can appear in many forms, such as in the view of race and culture in cultural Marxism perspectives. Contemporary racism is also viewed as evolving in relation to changing social and historical circumstances. The meanings of race and racism need to be understood as situated in "particular fields of discourse" and within specific and larger socio-historical settings. In this regard, Solomos and Back also underscore a popular trend in contemporary social science: the proclamation of the death of racism and "race" and the evident resurgence of emphasis on "ethnicism and cultural differentiation."[33] Moreover, somewhat surprisingly, since most neo-Marxist analysts neglect a focus on whites as such, Solomos and Back suggest the need for neo-Marxist analyses of race to address the "politics of Whiteness," including the ways in which this whiteness is "equated with normality."[34] They do not pursue this insight in any detail, but it is significant that they at least raised this major issue of whiteness.

A Critique of Neo-Marxist Understandings

As a rare critical theory of societies, Marxist analysis offers numerous conceptual tools that benefit racial analysis, and it has positively influenced the field of racial and ethnic studies in certain ways. Neo-Marxism's effect in theoretical analyses of racial matters has been most pronounced in Europe, especially in Britain. Because of a long McCarthyist tradition, Marxist theorizing of race has been less common or overt in the United States. Exceptions to this can especially be seen in the work of forward-thinking African American social scientists such as Oliver Cox and W.E.B. Du Bois, whose Marxist analyses of racism are sometimes recognized, but often misinterpreted, by many European Marxists. In contrast to the *theoretical* focus on racial matters in the analyses of many British Marxists, most US Marxist scholars who address racial matters—for example, Philip Foner, Eugene Genovese, Edna Bonacich, and Robert Blauner—are generally much more empirically oriented and less theoretically abstract in their sophisticated analyses. This is the major reason for our focus on contemporary British neo-Marxist theorists who attempt to *theoretically* explain racial matters, not just empirically describe them.[35]

Analyses of racial issues raised by European neo-Marxists present theoretical perspectives that deserve serious consideration and sometimes integration into critical theoretical discourses of matters of racism. One significant contribution of neo-Marxist analyses is actually directing serious analysis to matters of societal "racism," explicitly named as such. Yet, while they highlight the study of racism, none in our view provides a theoretically sound and detailed definition, and most present misleading or problematical understandings of societal racism. First, they tend to focus on localized forms of societal racism (e.g., Stuart Hall's "historically specific racisms") and thus fail to assess thoroughly the commonalities in white-framed, systemically racist social systems seen in several major Western societies over long time periods. They tend to avoid a probing analysis of the dominant (white European) racial group, including its role as the main oppressor group perpetuating systemic racism in these societies. In short, most European neo-Marxists attempt to explain societal racism without a full-featured historical and contemporary analysis of racial group dynamics and of the broad racist framing and extensive institutionalized practices created by the dominant white group in modern societies.

Colonialism, slavery systems, and new structures of white oppression against people of color are historically specific phenomena and realities that frequently traverse *very* long historical periods and great social space. They thus deserve central analytical attention. Oddly, given their concerns with the capitalist class, in the past and the present Marxists generally ignore elite whites in their analyses. One wonders how contemporary neo-Marxists can attempt to produce adequate analyses of societal racism without analyzing those powerful whites who historically created, and now recreate and maintain, systemically racist social systems. While historically specific white racisms are indeed created across the globe, they are mostly linked and fueled by a central dynamic: the white racial framing of the social world and the systemically racist social systems that perpetuate and uphold this globalized framing. This avoidance of examining elite and ordinary white domination across long periods of time and much space—issues discussed by early black class-conscious thinkers such as Cox and Du Bois—is most likely the result of the inherently Eurocentric nature of most neo-Marxist racial analysis.[36]

One way of incorporating some Marxist insights into contemporary racial analysis more fruitfully would be to compare the similarities found in Karl Marx's understanding of the class conflict between capitalists and workers and the real-world racial conflicts between whites and people of color. Just as Marxism recognizes capitalism as a historical process with solid structural features that cut across time and place, contemporary Marxist analysts of racial matters should realize that white racism is a historical process with structural features that cut across time and place as well. Questions contemporary Marxists analysts of racial matters might ask include: What are the commonalities between Marx's understanding of class consciousness and ideas about racial consciousness? How does the false consciousness of the working class resemble the false consciousness of racially oppressed groups? Additionally, does modern capitalism emerge out of the systemically racist social systems of colonized and slavery societies? Are class relations a subset, distillation, or other face of racial relations? How do racial matters shape matters usually seen as just related to class—that is, states, economies, and class hierarchies? These are critical questions about systemic racism and classism that contemporary Marxists and other social scientists might ask to improve our critical knowledge of societal worlds.

While the field of conceptual Marxism has diversified, expanding its range of analysis, we do not agree with analysts such as Solomos that the formation of neo-Marxist explanations of the social world have migrated far from certain key Marxist understandings. Solomos argues that contemporary neo-Marxism—with its concerns with other major forms of social divisions—does not subsume race under class or reduce racial matters to class analysis. Yet, Solomos and many other neo-Marxists do continue to frame racial matters greatly in the context of class analysis and of the political economy, and some do in effect reduce race structures to class structures. For example, Solomos begins by arguing that racism has to be understood in the context of a capitalist society, as a social reality that emerges from the operations of capitalism. Moreover, while the CCCS relative autonomy model views racial matters as distinct yet intertwined with matters of class, racial matters are still perceived as offshoots of capitalist development. Hall frames racial matters in the context of capitalism. Most neo-Marxists do discard the economic determinism of conventional Marxist theory, yet retain a very heavy focus on the political-economic capitalistic context that purportedly greatly shapes white racism.

As we make clear in later chapters, we are influenced by some of the neo-Marxist insights about modern capitalism, but we propose instead a different starting point for analyzing racial matters. Rather than begin by asking how (often vaguely defined) racism develops within a capitalistic society, we ask how does capitalism develop in white-racist societies. In other words, we find the conceptualization of a *racist society* (and *systemic racism*) to be a more precise starting point for social analysis of modern social formations than the conceptualization of a separate *capitalist* society. Instead of just focusing upon the structural features of a capitalist society, we are concerned with examining the structures, political-economic contexts, and broad framing that define a racist society. We investigate the ways that economic systems, political systems, and other social relations (e.g., gender and class) are shaped by, and constantly co-reproductive with, systemic racism and its legitimating white racial frame. Certainly, one major reason for this co-reproduction of the major systems of oppression in Western societies is that mostly the same group of elite white men are in the top positions in the racial, class, and gender hierarchies.

Additionally, the focus on "ideologies" and "political contexts" of numerous neo-Marxists ignores the fundamental historical realities shaped by *white-racialized social structures*. Neo-Marxists mostly neglect investigating the socio-racial practices of whites who benefit from systemically racist social systems, and they largely neglect the significant impacts of the countering praxis of people of color who have long faced systemic racist oppression. Analyses of ideologies and political contexts are too often mired in ambiguity and misunderstandings without the necessary historical context and analysis of *patterns* of racialized social practices over time. For example, Hall's analysis of historically specific racisms fails to foreground and assess the broad white racial framing and other aspects of systemic racism that cut across most specific white-imposed racisms, crisscrossing historical periods and different societies and social worlds within those societies. Moreover, in contrast to neo-Marxists who deny the analytic utility of the term "race," we argue for its continued analytical usage as an umbrella concept that denotes the multidimensionality of socially and societally constructed racial matters. As noted earlier, "race" ("racial matters") does not refer to any one specific Western social reality, but rather stands as an umbrella term under which a number of white-racialized social realities (e.g., European colonialism, Jim Crow segregation in the United States, indigenous genocides, "model minority" mythology) can be linked together, critically discussed, and better understood. Unsurprisingly in the past and present these racial matters have cut across the social realities of structure and agency, class and gender, and national and international boundaries. They have penetrated dominant cultures and counter-cultures, and they have shaped and intertwined with a large array of economic (i.e., capitalistic), political, and other social structures.

Wilson, Solomos, and the neo-Marxists who deconstruct "race" and "racism" are part of a larger movement in contemporary social sciences stepping away from a critical in-depth analysis of well-institutionalized and systemic racism perpetuated by whites in all social classes. Moreover, along with these class-oriented analysts who shy away from critically addressing systemic racism, specifically whites' racial power,[37] other influential theoretical camps that study the political economy—for example, state-centered theorists, world-system theorists, and neo-liberalism theorists—are also usually guilty of evading serious analyses of systemic racism. Contemporary class relations and capitalism have not somehow eclipsed or eradicated systemic white racism, but rather class relations and capitalism are manifestations of, and co-reproductive with, unequalized racial relations and systemic white racial oppression.

The Cultural Eclipse of Racial Matters

Culture has long been a central social science concept used to discuss various social phenomena. To simplify discussion, we follow Raymond Williams' understanding of culture as "a particular way of life, whether of a people, a period or a group."[38] The field of cultural studies developed during the 1970s in Britain as an assorted collection of ideas and methods from an array of social science and humanities perspectives. A cultural studies' mantra often invokes the intersecting frameworks of race, class, and gender as essential subject matter for the social sciences and humanities. In many cases, however, collapsing race, class, and gender under the rubric of cultural studies has weakened or disempowered these particular critical perspectives and understandings of social structures by locating these realities more broadly in culture itself and in the field of cultural studies.

Our concern here is with the complex relationship between culture and race and the problematic ways that culture has frequently become a substitute framework for understanding race. As discussed previously, Robert Park was one of the first influential social scientists to substitute "culture" for "race" when explaining human behavior of different groups, thereby raising the question of whether cultural analysis supplants the need for analysis of racial matters. In one of the contemporary cultural criticisms of racial analysis, Anthony Appiah answers in the affirmative. Thus, Appiah's important critique of W.E.B. Du Bois' explanations of racial matters argues that such discussions of "race" are problematical. According to Appiah, where "race works—in places where 'gross differences' of morphology are correlated with 'subtle differences' of temperament, belief, and intention—it works as an attempt at a metonym for culture; and it does so only at the price of biologizing what is culture, or ideology."[39] We observe several problems with this and other views in Appiah's critique. Seeking to discredit biological understandings of race, in particular Du Bois' early attempts to address such understandings, Appiah overlooks race's larger political, economic, cultural, and psychological dimensions. Indeed, Du Bois identifies and examines these latter institutional and systemic dimensions of race and racism thoroughly throughout his many writings.

By viewing "race" just in biological (physical) terms, Appiah allows no room for discussing racial matters in a broader societal context and ignores Du Bois' sophisticated multidimensional understanding of matters of societal racism.[40] Moreover, a physical-characteristic element to matters of societal racism is inescapable at present so long as human beings intellectually differentiate and socially divide people according to differences in physical morphology. Certainly, contemporary color/racial divides in human populations across the globe are social-structural, psychological, *and* cultural in their everyday operations. Yet, singled-out physical differences among human beings, especially skin color, have been at the root of the social construction of discriminatory racial lines for centuries. To acknowledge a physical element in the way racial groups have become socially defined in the modern period does not lead to biological essentialism, as Appiah implies. Moreover, Du Bois argued that the biological aspect of race had no meaning, socially or sociologically, other than that of Europeans seeking to oppress groups of people by utilizing a color-coded hierarchy and framing. To dismiss the biological coding aspects of the *social construction* of racial groups in the past or present is flawed, despite Appiah's and other cultural analysts' intention of erasing biological understandings of race. We view culture as one feature of racial matters, and not as a concept to be used in opposition to race.

Ethnicity's Sublimation of Racial Matters: Contemporary Theorizing
As we have previously noted, in much social science, ethnic groups (ethnicity) and national groups (nations/nationality) have often become synonymous with racial groups (race), continually replacing a racial/racism theoretical perspective. Numerous contemporary social scientists prioritize the conceptual usage of ethnicity over race and/or perceive race as a subtype of ethnicity. For example, Richard Jenkins argues that racial differentiation and racism "should perhaps best be viewed as historically-specific forms of the general—perhaps even universal—social phenomenon of ethnicity."[41] Donald Horowitz similarly argues for an umbrella view of ethnicity embracing "differences identified by color, language, religion, or some other attribute of common origin." For him color-group relations are not necessarily different from other ethnic-group relations, because "non-visible" characteristics of groups are equally as important as the "visible" sign of color.[42] Similarly, Sandra Wallman proposes that phenotype is just one more "element in the repertoire of ethnic boundary-making."[43] She and other scholars, such as the aforementioned Mara Loveman (see Chapter 4),

claim there is no substantive difference between ethnicity and race. Ethnicity is also central to understandings of nationalism in the writings of numerous scholars who view nations and nationalism as a product of ethnicity outside the realm of racism matters.

Whereas nationality primarily remains a focus of European theorists, ethnicity theory is popular among US and European social scientists, as it has been for some decades now. US analysts such as Milton Gordon and others (Chapter 2) have long focused on a model of European immigrant (ethnic) group assimilation, while in many cases ignoring the dynamics of racial-group exploitation and incorporation—including forced immigration—that has been foundational and systemic for the United States. Immigration studies are often framed in terms of ethnic groups and ethnicity, although much US immigration has long been a racialized reality. Today, for example, most whites identify Latino immigrants as a racial group different from the majority white racial group; they are thus usually treated differently from European immigrants of varying nationalities. Like some British colleagues, numerous US analysts of immigration have often disempowered the study of racial (white-racism) meanings in favor of the study of the meanings of ethnicity and ethnic group formation, from Milton Gordon and Stanley Lieberson to Nancy Foner and Herbert Gans.[44] Such social scientists retain a focus on the ethnic-immigrant assimilation process and often neglect the highly racialized structures and operations that shape this societal process for immigrants of color and their descendants, a process that is much different from that of white immigrants. They have frequently provided inaccurate or partial portraits of human social relations in US society, portraits that reinforce a white racial framing of immigration by such strategies as focusing on the proverbial "melting pot" for white ethnic groups or downplaying the white-imposed oppressive realities facing immigrants of color.

As we discussed previously, by lumping ethnic groups and racial groups together, many ethnicity theorists in the social sciences confuse two quite different societal realities. The assimilation of white (ethnic) immigrant groups cannot be understood in isolation from the racial exclusion and societal discrimination that face racial groups such as black Americans, Native Americans, Asian Americans, and other Americans of color. In the US context, ethnicity studies do help explain the experiences of many white immigrants, yet they provide little explanation of the experiences of immigrants and other people of color who are negatively viewed in the white-framed assimilation and other societal integration processes. The assimilationist theorists often hold that European immigrants partially or substantially dissolve their home cultures into a predominantly Anglo-Saxon core culture—and thus become fully "white American." They can also retain some sense of ethnic (nationality) group affiliation in addition to their new and predominant white American identity. Yet, understanding white immigrant integration into societal institutions of systemically racist societies provides little understanding of the larger, racially structured, hierarchical group relations of the society.[45]

Conventional concepts such as the melting pot, ethnic pluralism, and immigrant assimilation have generally been reserved for social science analysis of white immigrants, in the past and present. These concepts are mostly ineffectual for analyzing the adaptive social experiences, socialization, and societal positioning of immigrants and other people of color. For example, sociologist Mary Waters discusses "ethnic options," the choosing of ethnic identities, in which ethnicity is thus "a subjective identity, invoked at will by the individual." As she notes, whites are generally free to choose an ethnic group identity, yet "those defined in 'racial' terms as non-whites much less."[46] Acknowledging that those in the black community have no real option but to identify as black, she nonetheless proceeds to develop a general theory of the "new ethnicity" in the United States and the idea of "flux and choice" in this new ethnicity. This is a conceptual framework of ethnicity that is effectively limited to people with substantial European ancestry. If Waters and other scholars are positing that white national-origin groups should generally be viewed as ethnic-option groups, and that people of color fall well outside this domain of options (i.e., as racial groups), we can accept this argument. However, it appears that she and others have developed an understanding of ethnicity that does not carefully account for the continuing racialization of immigrants and other people of color. Without the ability to account for this often aggressive white racialization of people of color, we again strongly question the utility of a general ethnicity paradigm, aside from its usefulness in understanding European immigrant developments. We will return in more detail to these and other problems in assimilation theorizing in Chapter 7.

Nationality and Nationalism Theory: Insights and Problems

Studies of nations, national identity, nationalism, and ethno-nationalism have directed the social sciences to important sets of sociological issues in the development of modern societies. "Modern nations" and the nationalism that sustains them have arisen powerfully with the transformation of numerous societies across Europe over the past several centuries. There have also been major societal and national identity changes on continents that have been colonized by Europeans. Major social shifts in European, American, and other "settler" societies have taken place with new in-migrations and new group formations of formerly enslaved or colonized peoples who challenge the older meanings of nationality within increasingly diverse countries.

Two social scientists at the forefront of theoretically addressing matters of nationality and nationalism are Anthony Smith and Walker Connor. Both have alerted social scientists and policy analysts to the importance of nationalism in the social construction of modern Europe's nation-states and in the formation of similar societal groups within other countries. Both provide nuanced understandings of ethnicity, nationality, and nationalism that can aid in the understanding of some racial matters.[47] Thus, Smith usefully describes a nation as a "named human population sharing an historic territory, common myths and historical memories, a mass, public culture, a common economy and common legal rights and duties for all members."[48] Moreover, both Smith and Connor usefully distinguish between the meanings of "state" and "nation." According to Connor a *state* is best defined "in quantitative terms" that depict the size of population, GDP, and territorial boundaries. But conceptualizing *nation* is "much more difficult because the essence of a nation is intangible." He also presents a solid argument that many social scientists concerned with nation-building have long neglected issues of ethnic diversity, which signals social scientists' evasion of the major ethnic roots of much contemporary nationalism.[49]

Working in the same vein, Anthony Smith rightfully argues for understanding "national as opposed to other kinds of collective cultural identification" and aims to demonstrate the role of divergent "ethnic bases" in the growth and development of early and contemporary nations, thereby untangling misunderstandings surrounding nationality.[50] Modern nations emerge most notably from earlier ethnic group formations or communities termed "ethnies." Smith introduces the concept of core ethnies to demonstrate how European nations have formed. There are similarities between ethnies and nations, yet nationality involves a *conscious* awareness of a group's communality and involves significant political organization around that sense of group belonging. Most of these contemporary European nations are polyethnic; after they were formed around a core ethnic, they often "annexed or attracted other ethnies or ethnic fragments into the state." Subsequently, the "presumed boundaries of the nation are largely determined by the myths and memories of the dominant ethnie."[51]

Although Smith's and Connor's analyses do help us better understand issues of European nationality and nationalism, we question whether their version of these concepts is of much use outside of European contexts. Key questions come to mind: how does analysis of the development of ethnies into nations in Europe help explain often highly exploitative social relations between white Europeans and peoples of color across the globe? Is nationalism here just a Eurocentric concept with little validity in analyzing the social relations of peoples outside Europe? Despite our reservations about European ethnicity-based nationalism as presented by Connor and Smith, we do think that one can analyze *racial nationalism* in conjunction with ethno-nationalism, the former being a concept appropriate to discuss both European colonizers' nationalisms and the colonizing-resistance nationalisms such as black nationalism in the US case. If a more general concept of nationalism is to be of use to social scientists, we argue that multiracial states must also be carefully examined, and not just multiethnic nations. Should the concept of nationalism retain its analytic significance, the racialized nation and state with its core racial group is equally as important for analysis as the ethnicized nation and state and its ethnic core group, for not all modern nation-states have emerged centrally from a type of *ethno*genesis.

Additionally, their concept of "ethno-nationals," while applicable to social relations between white ethnic groups within Europe, has less utility in analyzing the highly racialized contexts of colonialism, slavery, and contemporary forms of white exploitation of people of color. The European ethnic groups, despite different loyalties, mostly share the physical characteristics and privileges of "whiteness." Sociopolitical divisions and conflicts such as those between English and Irish Europeans may be pronounced, but are of a different character from the divisions and conflict between, for example, US whites and blacks. The latter division is based on long-lasting *social constructions* of certain physical characteristics with major collective and societal impacts, including the rationalization of systemic racial exploitation, not just beliefs and practices rooted in certain cultural differences. Connor and Smith importantly point to the more malleable ethnic basis of certain forms of nationality, primarily within the European context, but fail to recognize the more structured and long-enduring *racialized* basis of yet other social groupings and therefore of major *multiracial* nation-state formations. (Indeed, Smith also problematizes the idea of "race" groups.)[52] Not only are modern nation-states multiethnic, but several modern nation-states are multiracial and largely controlled by a dominant racial group whose "myths and memories" also shape those nations' character and greatly influence their economic, political, and other social structures and operations. The latter include the oppressive realities of systemic racism imposed by whites.

We might add that this critique can be extended to various state-centered social theorists who overlook the critical multiracial dimensions of modern state formations and often ignore issues of racial conflict. Most modern states are now composed of a multitude of ethnic and/or racial groups, with one dominant racial or ethnic group that promotes its own sense of nationalism, including its own sociopolitical ideology and sense of ethnic or racial loyalty. Still, Connor's and Smith's analyses seem to offer many fertile understandings of ethnicity/nationality that, at least by analogy, can advance and complement understandings of racial matters. Commonalities, including a shared sense of history, that unite ethnic groups within nations often unite racial groups within nations in somewhat similar ways. In sum, studying the ideologies and worldviews of racial groups in multiracial nations is just as important as studying the ideologies and worldviews of ethnic groups in multiethnic nations.

Conclusion

As we have attempted to illustrate, the various class, culture, ethnicity, and nationality perspectives present important understandings of the social world. Contemporary class theorists point to the importance of certain class-linked racism studies, cultural theorists point to new coded types of racism, and ethnicity and nationality theorists expose tensions and adaptation processes facing white immigrants and their descendants. Nevertheless, these theoretical perspectives do not stand in isolation from major patterns of systemic racism in Western societies or as primary theoretical frameworks that explain systemic racism. Rather, class, culture, ethnicity, and nationality approaches ought to be viewed as investigations into the societal formations that have accompanied and/or are interlaced with the racialized developments and structures of the modern world. Social scientists discussed above mostly focus on ways that class, culture, ethnicity, and nationality shape or replace racial matters. In contrast, we argue that social scientists need to recognize the ways that the realities of systemic racism can shape or co-reproduce, without overshadowing, the realities of class, culture, ethnicity, and nationality. This starting point of societal analysis generates substantially different knowledge about societal worlds and their constituent human beings than the starting points of the theorists considered in this chapter, as we will further demonstrate in Part III.

Notes

1 Approval of Wilson's arguments has been most pronounced among mainstream social scientists, whereas he has received far less support among less visible sociologists, such as a significant number of members in the Association of Black Sociologists.
2 See William J. Wilson's works: *The Declining Significance of Race: Blacks and Changing American Institutions* (Chicago: University of Chicago Press, 1978); *The Truly Disadvantaged: The Inner City, the Underclass, and Public Policy* (Chicago: University of Chicago Press, 1987); *When Work Disappears: The World of the New Urban Poor* (New York: Vintage, 1996); and *More Than Just Race: Being Black and Poor in the Inner City* (New York: W.W. Norton, 2009).
3 Wilson, *The Declining Significance of Race*, pp. x–xi.
4 Wilson, *The Truly Disadvantaged*, p. 7.
5 Ibid., p. 6.
6 Ibid., pp. 10–11. Wilson defines contemporary racism rather narrowly as "conscious refusal of whites to accept blacks as equal human beings and their willful, systematic effort to deny blacks equal opportunity."
7 Ibid., p. 11.
8 Ibid., p. 11. Here Wilson offers a limited view of racism as a "psychological state of mind."
9 See Wilson, *When Work Disappears*.
10 Ibid., pp. xiv, ix, xix.
11 Ibid., p. xxi.
12 Wilson, *More Than Just Race*, pp. 23–4.
13 See, among previously cited sources, Louwanda Evans, *Cabin Pressure: African American Pilots, Flight Attendants, and Emotional Labor* (Lanham, MD: Roman and Littlefield, 2013) and Joe R. Feagin, *Racist America: Roots, Current Realities, and Future Reparations*, 3rd edn (New York: Routledge, 2014).
14 See Evans, *Cabin Pressure*.
15 For example, see Aldon Morris, "What's Race Got to Do With It?" review of *The Declining Significance of Race* in *Contemporary Sociology: A Journal of Reviews*, 25(3) (1996): 309–13; Charles V. Willie, *Caste and Class Controversy* (New York: General Hall Publishing, 1979), which contains the "Statement of the Association of Black Sociologists" condemning Wilson's book; Charles Willie (ed.), *Class and Caste Controversy on Race and Class: Round Two of the Willie/Wilson Debate* (Lanham, MD: Roman and Littlefield, 1989); Melvin Oliver, "The Enduring Significance of Race," *Journal of Ethnic Studies* 7(4) (1980): 79–91.
16 Morris, "What's Race Got to Do With It?" p. 311.
17 See W.E.B. Du Bois, *Color and Democracy: Colonies and Peace* (Millwood, NY: Kraus-Thomson, 1975 [1945]) and *World and Africa: An Inquiry Into the Part Which Africa Has Played in World History* (New York: International Publishers, 1996 [1946]).
18 See John Solomos, "Varieties of Marxist Conceptions of 'Race,' Class and the State: A Critical Analysis," in John Rex and David Mason (eds.), *Theories of Race and Ethnic Relations* (Cambridge: Cambridge University Press, 1986), pp. 84–109; John Solomos and Les Back, "Marxism, Racism, and Ethnicity," *American Behavioral Scientist*, 38(3) (1995): 407–21.
19 See Frank Parkin's critique of Marxism, *Marxism and Class Theory: A Bourgeois Critique* (London: Tavistock, 1979).
20 Solomos, "Varieties of Marxist Conceptions," p. 84.
21 Ibid., p. 89.

22 Stuart Hall, Charles Critcher, Tony Jefferson, John Clarke, and Brian Roberts, *Policing the Crises* (London: Macmillan, 1978); The Centre for Contemporary Cultural Studies, *The Empire Strikes Back: Race and Racism in 70s Britain* (London: Hutchison, 1982).
23 Solomos, "Varieties of Marxist Conceptions," p. 92.
24 Ibid., p. 92, 95.
25 Ibid., p. 104.
26 Ibid., p. 104.
27 Ibid., p. 107.
28 Solomos and Back, "Marxism, Racism, and Ethnicity," p. 408.
29 Ibid., p. 409.
30 Ibid., p. 412.
31 Ibid., p. 414; also see David T. Goldberg, *Anatomy of Racism* (Minneapolis: University of Minnesota Press, 1990).
32 Solomos and Back, "Marxism, Racism, and Ethnicity," p. 414.
33 Ibid., p. 418.
34 Ibid., pp. 415–16. We are surprised that Solomos and Back mention "whiteness," considering their analysis and that virtually all neo-Marxists' analyses avoid discussion of whites. While they in fact do not analyze whites, they do point to Marxism-influenced scholars whose work addresses this indispensable subject matter.
35 British neo-Marxists provide certain rich analytic tools for racial analysis, but poor explanations of the empirical realities of racial matters. US social scientists tend to offer meaningful extrapolation of empirical realities but little theoretical development.
36 See Cedric Robinson, *Black Marxism: The Making of a Black Radical Tradition* (Chapel Hill, NC: University of North Carolina Press, 1990).
37 See, for example, Jonathon Feldman, "Ferguson, Racial Tropes, and the Politics of Scarcity," *Counter Punch*, December 1, 2014, www.counterpunch.org/2014/12/01/ferguson-racial-tropes-and-the-politics-of-scarcity (accessed August 30, 2015). Feldman presents a flawed neo-Marxist analysis of the 2014 events in Ferguson, Missouri, after the shooting death of a black teenager by a white officer. He argues "race" is overvalued in analyses of this situation.
38 Raymond Williams, *Keywords* (London: Fontana, 1983), p. 90.
39 Anthony Appiah, "The Uncompleted Argument: Du Bois and Illusion of Race," in Henry Louis Gates Jr. (ed.), *"Race," Writing, and Difference* (Chicago: University of Chicago Press, 1986), pp. 35–6.
40 See Lucius T. Outlaw Jr., "'Conserve' Races?': In Defense of W.E.B. Du Bois," in Bernard W. Bell, Emily R. Grosholz, and James B. Stewart (eds.), *W.E.B. Du Bois: On Race and Culture* (New York: Routledge, 1996), pp. 15–38; Robert Gooding-Williams, "Outlaw, Appiah, and Du Bois's 'The Conservation of the Race,'" in Bell et al. (eds.), *W.E.B. Du Bois: On Race and Culture*, pp. 39–56. Also, see Lucius T. Outlaw Jr., *On Race and Philosophy* (New York: Routledge, 1996).
41 Richard Jenkins, "Rethinking Ethnicity: Identity, Categorization, and Power," in John Stone and Rutledge Dennis (eds.), *Race and Ethnicity: Comparative and Theoretical Approaches*, (Malden, MA: Blackwell, 2003), p. 67.
42 Donald Horowitz, *Ethnic Groups in Conflict* (Berkeley, CA: University of California Press, 1985), pp. 41–51.
43 Sandra Wallman, "Ethnicity and Boundary Process in Context," John Rex and David Mason (eds.), *Theories of Race and Ethnic Relations* (Cambridge: Cambridge University Press, 1986), p. 229.
44 Milton Gordon, *Assimilation in American Life: The Role of Race, Religion, and National Origins* (New York: Oxford University Press, 1964); Stanley Lieberson, *A Piece of the*

Pie: Blacks and White Immigrants Since 1980 (Berkeley, CA: University of California Press, 1980); Nancy Foner, *In A New Land: A Comparative View of Immigration* (New York: New York University Press, 2005); Herbert Gans, "Symbolic Ethnicity: The Future of Ethnic Groups and Cultures in America," *Ethnic and Racial Studies* 2(1) (1979): 1–20.

45 See Joe R. Feagin and Clairece B. Feagin, *Racial and Ethnic Relations*, 9th edn (Upper Saddle River, NJ: Prentice Hall, 2011).

46 Mary C. Waters, *Ethnic Options: Choosing Identities in America* (Berkeley, CA: University of California Press, 1990), pp. 7, 18.

47 See Walker Connor, *Ethnonationalism: The Quest for Understanding* (Princeton, NJ: Princeton University Press, 1994); Anthony D. Smith, *National Identity* (Reno NV: University of Nevada Press, 1991).

48 Smith, *National Identity*, p. 14.

49 Connor, *Ethnonationalism*, pp. 41–2.

50 Smith, *National Identity*, p. viii.

51 Ibid., pp. 39–41.

52 Ibid., p. 21; for Smith, an "ethnie" must be "sharply differentiated from a race in the sense of a social group that is held to possess unique hereditary biological traits that allegedly determine mental attributes of the group." By mistakenly viewing race mainly in biological and not socially constructed terms, he provides only a partial and inadequate portrait of social group formation in modern nations.

CHAPTER 6
RACE AND THE GENOME
BIOSOCIAL THEORIES OF RACE

Unlike the theorists discussed in the last two chapters, contemporary biosocial theorists of race do not attempt to eliminate or de-emphasize analyses of racial matters. Thus, on one level, the social sciences are experiencing a resurgence of white-framed biosocial explanations of race and debates surrounding that resurgence. In recent years social science journals have published symposia and essays that address the rise of biosocial explanations of racial matters. The major journal *Sociological Theory* presented a symposium on "The Genomic Challenge to the Social Construction of Race."[1] *Contemporary Sociology*, a major social science book review journal, published an essay by Dalton Conley and others on "The Emergence of Socio-Genomics."[2] Additionally, in *Contexts*, the popular social science journal, a number of social thinkers have addressed the question, "What's biology got to do with it?"[3] These articles and debates reveal that biosocial explanations of racial matters are still employed and expressed in forms old and new in the contemporary social sciences, and that numerous social scientists have developed arguments that support or reject this resurgence of race viewed in biosocial terms.

The renewal of interests in biological understandings of racial matters is not confined to academia, as mainstream media have also contributed to the discussion and debate. A recent *Time* magazine article by Nicholas Wade, a former *New York Times* science editor, sparked an international controversy with his claims that analysis of "genomes from around the world establishes that there is a biological basis for race." In the article, Wade asks, "why is it apparently so hard for tribal societies like Iraq or Afghanistan to change their culture and operate like modern states?" His answer is that this tribal behavior has "a genetic basis." Wade's book, *A Troublesome Inheritance: Genes, Race, and Human History* (2014), although popularized and often well received in the mainstream media, was met with great criticism by many population geneticists and other bio-specialists who argued that Wade had cherry-picked their research and misappropriated their findings.[4] Nevertheless, *Time* chose to feature Wade's biosocial arguments about race and numerous media outlets gave prominent voice to his white racist framing of various racial and ethnic issues across the globe.

Despite broad pushback among many biologists and social scientists, theories of the biosocial basis of contemporary racial matters have retained some sense of scientific legitimacy, particularly in areas of pharmaceuticals and medical research and practice. Additionally, social scientists, if only a growing minority now, show a commitment to the renewed genomic understandings of social behavior and racial groups.

Pierre van den Berghe: Biosociality and Race

Before exploring contemporary debates, let us first analyze perhaps the most prominent contemporary social science exponent of biosocial understandings of racial matters, Pierre L. van den Berghe. He has long articulated biosocial ("sociobiological") understandings, even during the 1970s and 1980s when this theoretical approach was more marginalized in social science. For decades he has written extensively on the principal ideas of sociobiology that are re-emerging in new genomic debates.[5]

In the 1970s, E.O. Wilson's book *Sociobiology* reawakened social science debates over the degree to which human behavior is influenced by genetics and evolutionary factors.[6] Supporting Wilson's claims, van den Berghe argued that understanding specific human behavior requires understanding that it is genetically based and shaped. Van den Berghe claims he is not a biological determinist, for he views culture as a variable in regular interaction with human biological developments. Culture is involved "in adaptive co-evolution with reproducing biological organisms." Yet, biological reproductive success is also central to human groups. In his view "nepotism based on proportion of shared genes" is the "basic mechanism of ethnic (or racial) solidarity." This commonality of genetic interests is significantly different from other human interests, including those of class. According to van den Berghe, many of the sciences support his emphasis on the genetic basis for human behavior.[7]

Van den Berghe posits that human culture has evolved in part genetically because the human brain's capability for developing culture is "genetically channeled." He links the development of ethnic groups, which are based on patterns of human descent, as bounded by both the cultural and the genetic boundaries of an in-breeding population. Cultural and genetic evolution are thus constantly interactive and intertwined. Yet, he recognizes that human cultural evolution has had emergent properties and partial autonomy from genetic evolution. From his viewpoint, the goal of the social sciences should be to research and discover the "multiple and complex mechanisms of gene-culture co-evolution, mediated through the human brain."[8]

Moreover, in an important 1978 article, van den Berghe specifically addresses "race." He argues that the social reality of both ethnicity and race are extensions of the human reality of biological descent and kinship groups; "race sentiments are to be understood as extended and attenuated form of kin selection."[9]

Problematizing van den Berghe's Sociobiologistic Understanding of "Race"

Disentangling van den Berghe's understanding of "race" is no easy task, considering that, at times, he presents seemingly contradictory arguments. While we find a number of questionable claims, in some cases his arguments make empirical or theoretical sense. His explanation of modern racism is mostly accurate. In his view, European colonialism brought a great expansion of Eurocentric racism, in part because skin color could be used in making an "accurate kin selection judgment from a distance of several hundred meters," thereby making the killing of kin unlikely.[10] This perception is obvious and has been discussed by numerous other scholars.[11] What is not obvious is van den Berghe's claim that this European colonial expansion was the "overwhelmingly important genetic event of our species." In contrast, we argue that this rise of European colonialism and imperialism is historically and socially rooted in economic exploitation. It had impacts on global genetic mixing, but was not genetically based.

As we previously noted, physical differences among human beings do play a central and recurring role in the social construction of race. However, van den Berghe's claim that understanding human group behavior requires understanding its link to a major genetic foundation is problematic. Whereas van den Berghe views biology as an essential starting point and component for understanding the emergence of ethnic and racial groups, we can point to historical and contemporary data that shows this supposed biological inevitability actually involves major human *social constructions* designed, in the case of racial groups, to socially divide human beings according to perceived physical differences, and often for the purpose of socioeconomic exploitation and subordination. Commonplace biological understandings of race are, in fact, social constructions imposed by dominant groups that shape much human behavior. The latter are not inherent or intrinsic biological realities that inevitably shape individual or group behavior. These socially constructed biological (physical) interpretations do not necessarily represent real biological "nature," but only powerful human beings' interpretation of that nature. While van den Berghe speaks of the co-evolution of biological organisms and cultures, he often prioritizes genetics or the biological organism as somehow more important than culture.[12] Yet many social scientists have demonstrated that human understandings of this nature are culturally rooted, that culture regularly shapes biological organisms, and that genetic understandings themselves have evolved from human cultural meanings and analyses.

Another problem in van den Berghe's sociobiology is his confusing account of race and ethnicity. In some of his work he distinguishes between race and ethnicity, but in other work he subsumes racial matters under the umbrella of ethnicity, virtually eliminating an explicit discussion of race and racism. He does acknowledge that his focus is on ethnicity and not on race. Moreover, he also says that he is opposed to viewing a race as a biological sub-species and instead understands it as a social race involving human categorization based on "biologically trivial phenotypes." Thus, race has "no intrinsic biological significance, as indicated by the fact that only a few of the world's societies use primarily morphological phenotypes to define themselves, and to differentiate outsiders." Acknowledging that this view seems to invalidate his larger sociobiological argument, he proposes that sometimes phenotype characteristics such as skin color are used to define racial groups, but that the "cultural criteria of membership are far more salient than physical ones" and that societies stressing "physical phenotypes more than cultural traits are exceptional."[13]

Van den Berghe's stated view that few of the world's societies primarily use physical characteristics (phenotypes) to define themselves is empirically erroneous. The whole history of European colonialism, slavery societies, and modern-day white oppression of people of color has seen the successful social division of human beings into "race" groups based on some aspect of phenotype differences. After centuries of whites' racial framing and oppression of people of color, a great many societies have used phenotypes as markers to define themselves and to differentiate yet others, a primary activity of modernity that van den Berghe does not address. His theorizing ignores large parts of the globe where physical markers continue to play a great role in determining individuals' and groups' life chances and status in society. Overall, van den Berghe's sociobiological explanations of race and ethnicity fall short of providing much useful social scientific knowledge about human beings and social groups, particularly racial groups. His understandings of human cultures appear to be backward. Culture is not primarily the product of genetics, but rather genetic understandings are to a substantial degree culturally constructed.

A Genomic Challenge to the Social Construction of Race

In 2012, Jiannbin Lee Shiao, Thomas Bode, Amber Beyer, and Daniel Selvig's article "The Genomic Challenge to the Social Construction of Race" was published in *Sociological Theory*. The authors state that contemporary research "on the human genome challenges the basic assumption that human races have no biological basis." The article's goal is to thus offer a theoretical synthesis that accepts research on genetic clusters as being congruent with existing racial classifications but "without diminishing the social character of their context."[14]

These researchers argue that social construction analyses of race have evaded addressing the biological basis of human group variations and that the mainstream social sciences are inclined to a pro-nurture bias overlooking recent advancements in genomic understandings from computerized analysis of genetic data. They use the term "clinal classes" as the parallel biological term to socially constructed racial and ethnic group terms. In their view, contemporary research shows that human genetic variation is "composed of not only clines but also clusters that are homologous to racial and ethnic categories."[15] They present research showing "ubiquitous partial heritability supports the existence of nondeterministic genetic effects, whereas the practice of controlling for population stratification suggests that those genetic effects include group differences in the frequency of alleles associated with the heritability of morphological, personality, and cognitive characteristics." They further propose that their "bounded-nature reformulation" of races is able "to distinguish the levels of social process that are more or less directly affected by genetic effects."[16]

Several social and natural scientists published a response to the Shiao et al.'s challenge in a *Sociological Theory* symposium that addressed these genomic arguments. Ann Morning, Daniel HoSang, and the team of Joan Fujimura, Deborah Bolnick, Ramya Rajagopalan, Jay Kaufman, Richard Lewontin, Troy Duster, Pilar Ossario, and Jonathan Marks uniformly discredit the article's major arguments.[17] For instance, Ann Morning counters their assertion that there is a disconnect between social constructionist views of race and human biology, for genetics-based claims about the biological basis of "race" are themselves social constructions. Research on human genetic variation is greatly influenced by the researchers' own human assumptions and decisions, including their choices about "whose DNA to sample and which types of genetic data to analyze." Researchers' portrayals of human genetic structures are "themselves so culturally conditioned that it would be a mistake to conclude that they represent objective biological measurement."[18]

Human decision-makers, not abstracted genetics, are the creators of racial categories. Additionally, even statistically aggregated genetic clusters have a historical and social basis that social constructivists regularly accent in looking at racial matters. Morning makes it clear that some socially constructed groups "come to be roughly distinguished by biological differentials," but that does not mean that *pre-existing* biological differences actually equate to racial group categories created by powerful human beings.[19] In her view, which we share on the basis of extensive data review, these renewed attempts to argue that socially defined "races" closely map on statistically defined genetic clusters are yet more attempts to assert a biological basis for socially constructed racial groups, a key effort in the history of white racist framing.[20]

The arguments of Joan Fujimura and her colleagues provide a similar critique of Shiao et al.'s article. They also note that much "sociocultural and historical evidence has demonstrated that human race and ethnic categories are socio-historically constructed, changing over time and differing by locale." Pointing to research studies that demonstrate the flexibility of racial classifications across time and place, they observe that the "consensus of social and historical scholarship is that racial and ethnic categories are formed through—and should be studied as—political, social, cultural, and psychological processes." In their critique, they observe that sociocultural and political-economic processes, larger contexts, shape the biological researchers' decisions "about which samples to compare together, and their interpretations of results" and thus that "previously determined information about individuals' nationality, ethnicity, or linguistic group may be used to decide which groups to compare."[21] Fujimura and her colleagues further note that the statistical genetic clusters sometimes do not correlate with racial-ethnic categories and that the concept of "clinal classes" is substantially the same as the older concept of discrete biological "races." Social typologies are again imposed on the biology of the human species, exposing circularity in this biosocial analysis. More specifically, Shiao et al. predefine "groups and identifying specific genetic markers with frequency differences that differentiate those groups," and then "use those markers to recreate the same clusters of individuals."[22] In opposition to Shiao et al.'s claims about the biological basis of human behavior, Fujimura and her colleagues argue that "existing genetic research suggests that it will be exceedingly difficult to identify any specific genetic factors that have a large effect on behavioral traits."[23]

Daniel HoSang's critique of Shiao and colleagues observes that certain social scientists they reference have produced little new understanding about the structure of ancestry relationships and migration patterns and also that their findings using sophisticated software potentially misrepresent understandings of genetic clusters. One of the disconcerting claims they make is that genetics or biosocial causation might explain "unequal distribution of personality, cognitive, and other characteristics between racialized groups," such as individual and group ethnocentrism. As HoSang notes, there is no heritable basis for ethnocentrism in any of the genetics research that they actually reference.[24] Next, HoSang discusses the racialized agendas of two theorists used in the analysis of Shiao et al., those of Stephen Hsu and Neven Sesardic. Hsu runs a privately funded research program that explores the "heritable basis of intelligence" and promotes eugenics-based government intervention. Sesardic argues that there are inherited psychological and intellectual differences that separate racial groups. His research agenda, substantially supported by the eugenics-oriented Pioneer Fund, is to demonstrate whites' genetically based racial superiority.[25]

As HoSang and other critics suggest, this new genomic challenge to the social construction of race is fraught with serious misperceptions, a shaky literature review, and highly questionable methodology. Reading the article, it becomes clear that Shiao and colleagues almost worship the science of genetics for purportedly providing a form of scientific legitimacy that can ground the variability in socially constructed knowledge of racial groups in biological understandings. One witnesses an overvaluing of quantitative analysis and explanations produced by lab sciences that are completely divorced from social reality. Lab-based quantitative analysis only makes sense when supported by substantial qualitative (e.g., interpretive) analysis based in critical empirical research existing outside the lab in the real social world. In our view, quantitative analysis should be viewed as an ancillary approach to producing such broad social knowledge, not the starting point or primary data-gathering procedure. Here genomic claims are made with little or no evidential backing, and geneticists' research is misrepresented, interpreted improperly, or omitted when it weakens their argument. We concur with much in these aforementioned criticisms of the genomic challenge to the social construction of race. The critics' main argument against the genomic alternative is that knowledge produced in genetics research and biological understandings are themselves social constructions, not objective realities discovered by scientists. In short, Shiao and colleagues confuse what biological beings do (social constructs) with what biological beings are viewed to possess (human traits).

The Emergence of Socio-Genomics: A Systemic Racism Critique

An article on "socio-genomics" by Dalton Conley, Jason Fletcher, and Christopher Dawes in the major social science book review journal *Contemporary Sociology* raises many of the same theoretical concerns we find in the Shiao et al. article. Conley and his colleagues also present unsubstantiated claims about the usefulness of contemporary genetics in understanding human behavior and groups. For example, at the beginning they strongly argue that all "human outcomes and traits are increasingly explained by discoveries in genetics." Like other researchers examined above, Conley et al. are enamored with statistical techniques used by geneticists, arguing that the latter are making great strides in understanding the degree of heritability involved in particular human traits. Like others before them, they rely on problematical twin and sibling studies to insist that the "total of all nucleotide differences… provide a measure of genetic stock… predictive of important social outcomes." Genetic factors and environmental factors interact "in a complex and dynamic feedback loop that begins to explain further several aspects of behavior of humans and societies."[26] Resorting to a discussion of "risky" and "safe" genes, they present old arguments about the genetics-based success of some individuals and groups in certain environments and the genetics-rooted failure of others, claiming evidence exists for gene–environment interactions that favor or disfavor some genes in some social environments at certain times.

Possibly the most problematic assumption in Conley and his colleagues' essay involves their belief that genetic understandings of human behavior can play a positive role in deciding *public policy* matters. In an ambitious yet contorted attempt to demonstrate how a smoking tax policy had little effect on the current generation of smokers, they propose that 1960s smokers as a group were genetically different from contemporary smokers as a group. They then argue for personalized policy for current smokers, claiming that "[e]vidence has shown that some educational interventions have greater or lesser effects depending on… genotypes."[27] Moving beyond explanations of the genetic basis of smoking, they further argue that modern genetic analyses provide information that helps us develop better macro-historical analyses. To demonstrate this, they address the large macroeconomics question about why certain countries thrive and others stagnate. In addition to the rather obvious environmental, institutional, and geographic factors, they argue for serious consideration of the population genetics factors.[28]

A central theme in their work, as with other sociobiologists, is that sociology and the social sciences will become irrelevant in research and analysis of human behavior unless they embrace the growing amount of new genetic data and analysis. Like other sociobiologists, they present numerous unfounded claims, such as "genes matter for both IQ and social class," that scientists are now able to "generate an unbiased estimate of the genetic contribution of a given trait," and that "new discoveries in genetics can tell us about… racial identity." Nowhere in their article do they present cogent detailed evidence that backs up these old and discredited claims. Instead, one discovers rather improbable genetic explanations. Their "tax on smoking" analysis, for example, presents undocumented claims that one generation of smokers is genetically distinct from another and that certain people are more prone to smoking because of a "nicotinic receptor gene."[29] In several cases, they incorrectly substitute the biological "gene" for the social "person."

Instead of ascribing common human behaviors to "genes," we suggest an alternative explanation for behavior with more empirical backing: an individual who makes socially shaped choices (and behaviors), not some biologically programmed subject acting on hidden genetic impulses. Stated differently, the social scientists' job is to explain people's behavior not the behavior of genes.

Conley et al. and other sociobiologists assume that sophisticated statistical analyses of genetic data can greatly aid in understanding human behavior and societies. Yet, they do not provide the substantial and detailed evidence that would back up such claims. Moreover, attempted genetic explanations of human behavior have a long history of getting such assumptions and predictions wrong, thus generating dangerous government policies to the detriment of certain human populations (for example, sterilizing or killing people judged genetically inferior).[30] Addressing the value of socio-genomic research today should at a minimum include a serious analysis of the past misunderstandings and policy horrors associated with attempted genetic explanations of human behavior. Thus, Conley et al.'s claim that current genetic research can be wisely applied to current public policy is not supported by their weak claims about genetically different generations of smokers and national populations. If this is the evidence they present in support of contemporary genetic research's input into public policy, one can envision the development of a series of problematical genetic explanations used to dictate public policies that risk causing great harm to human populations.

What's Biology Got to Do With It?

In 2014 the popular social science journal, *Contexts*, brought together several social scientists to discuss the "biological turn" in social science research. In the symposium titled "What's Biology Got To Do With It?" social scientists Karl Bryant, Kristen Springer, Alondra Nelson, Roger Lancaster, and Dalton Conley provided various viewpoints on issues surrounding the possibility of a new biosocial zeitgeist in the social sciences. One motivation for the symposium was that biologically minded sociologists have formed a section in the American Sociological

Association titled "Evolution, Biology, and Society." The section's perspective includes the view that a supposed biophobia in social science is retarding understandings of human behavior that can be explained by major biosocial theories.[31]

Demonstrating biology's increasing interest in social science, all but one in the *Contexts* debate perceive a significant role for biological understandings of human beings in the social sciences. In his article, Dalton Conley supports integrating genomic concepts into research on social mobility. As in earlier racist social science interpretations of human beings, Conley speaks of genetic endowment as a "lurking" variable or human fact that social scientists must heed. Individual genotypes "may be the prism by which we come to understand why some individuals react so differently to the same stimuli… perhaps innate disposition can provide a rational accounting of them."[32] Conley's use of language is revealing, for at one point he asserts genetics as a fact in human behavior, yet also uses words such as "may," "perhaps," and other uncertain terminology.

In contrast, Roger Lancaster develops a critique of attempts at genetic reductionism in researching human behavior and institutions. Dissecting research on political attitudes among poor, working-class, and middle-class whites, his essay demonstrates how easily studies that attribute genetic explanations to human behavior are disproved. He notes how genetic reductionism has found a home in areas of psychology, a discipline that often ignores or downplays full sociological understandings.[33] In the US, biology and genetics are frequently placed on a scientific pedestal and given great legitimacy, since their analyses often "*sound* scientific because they've got *genes* and *numbers* and even sometimes *correlations*." Yet the reduction of social facts to genetic and other biological factors requires a social and historical neglect of or amnesia about human "migrations, class struggles, ethnic resentments, and institutional changes—that is to say, almost everything that might make social facts intelligible.[34]

In her insightful essay, Alondra Nelson delivers a complex understanding of the ways that genetics research may potentially assist social scientific understandings. She explains how genetics research can yield significant information about certain ethnic African and other characteristics of African Americans, such as those whose bones were discovered at a New York burial site. She argues that genetics research can reveal much about these exhumed bodies, often including population origins, physical quality of life, and "biological and cultural transition from African to African-American identities."[35] This type of genetic analysis usefully demonstrates that in the past African Americans were very complex human beings, with more diverse African and American histories and ancestries than have often been historically recorded. It certainly makes scientific sense to utilize genetics (DNA) research to amplify this historical record and its complex effects on contemporary African Americans, yet we suggest that such use of genetics research should be careful to constantly link it to the relevant social constructions and contexts that greatly shape and channel these racial realities.

Additionally, in this discussion of the biosocial turn, Kristen Springer and Karl Bryant also argue that biological research is relevant to developing a social science that has a "more grounded" explanation of human behavior. Springer's essay argues that biological research aids in sociological understandings of patterned inequalities. She cites biological research that has demonstrated great biological similarities between men and women, offsetting past dominant narratives stressing biological differences. She notes that research shows how "sociocultural practices shape bodies," and her own research explores physiological responses to gendered threats that challenge male individuals' masculinity.[36] While these are interesting findings, none of the interesting conclusions about society's gendered realities necessarily require genetic/biological explanations. That bodies are biological tells us nothing about their social function and positioning; actual social relations and social constructions, past and present, best explain actual gender role differences in any society.

Positing that the nature–nurture debate presents a false dichotomy, Karl Bryant also argues there are important examples of the "interplay of bio-physiological factors and social factors in shaping human bodies and experiences."[37] However, like some others mentioned, Bryant offers no proof to support this claim other than reference to his own research on a "Gender Identity Disorder of Childhood," a socially constructed psychiatric diagnosis. This impressive-sounding, scientifically defined "disorder" is supposedly biologically rooted at some level. How it is actually rooted is not explained. Bryant claims social scientists should embrace a sociologically informed approach to biological issues in order to understand human bodies and their physical experiences. Like Springer, he views human bodies as somehow standing opposed to or outside sociocultural practices and the social world. Biological research understandings do offer useful information related to the physiology of human *bodies*, but provide no direct information about human *beings'* actions and interactions in the social world. From cradle to grave, human beings are far more than biological bodies. Indeed, speaking of bodies in place of human beings presents a narrow picture of individuals and, in our view, social scientists ought to consider the limitations, misuse, and problems associated with that uncritical use of the term.

These *Contexts* articles in the debate over the use of biology and genetics research in social sciences fail to present convincing arguments for integrating biological understandings of human beings' social behavior into the *heart* of the contemporary social sciences. Most analysts offer numerous unsupported claims and/or present an overly optimistic view about genetic and other biological research's contributions to contemporary social science. If a biosocial revolution is in fact taking effect, they do not cite the numerous new knowledge-producing studies that demonstrate the importance and reliability of biosocial causation and the links between biology and social sciences. At present, there are mostly citations of a few weak and controversial biosocial studies that have produced no shattering understandings of human behavior and societies. One gets a sense that many of these social scientists are resorting to socio-genomic and other biological explanations in an attempt to make their work, or social science more generally, appear more "scientifically" legitimate and up-to-date. Unfortunately, this pursuit often has the opposite effect, as it can resuscitate the pseudo-scientific fallacies of past attempts to biologize social realities in the interest of dominant groups.

Nonetheless, we do think it is important for those who study how social environments shape the health and bodies of human beings to stay in regular dialogue with biological and health researchers who do pay serious attention to social environments and their impacts on human biology and health. The emerging field of behavioral *epigenetics* has shown how some human genetic material, often ignored or unknown in past genetics research, plays a key role in triggering or blocking expression of inherited genes. Epigenetic "switches" of current individuals can be greatly shaped by social environments—social nurturing, diet, toxin exposure, discrimination exposure—that they or their recent ancestors have endured.[38] Keeping the focus clearly on the effects of these social environments, including difficult and destructive socio-racial contexts, should be the main task of social scientists working in this area of study of the relationships of biology, health, and systemic racism.

Current Biosocial and Socio-Genomic Explanations of Racial Matters

Ironically, many social scientists who seek scientific legitimacy by turning to biosocial causal explanations of human beings and society, including racial matters, are in fact demonstrating a retreat from most of the pertinent ideas and research methods that make for sound social and physical sciences. In several ways, many of today's socio-genomists are not much different than the nineteenth-century phrenologists,[39] aside from the fact that latter group attempted to explain human behavior and social reality through measuring visible features and the outer body of human beings, while the former now attempt to explain humans and social realities by measuring the inner biological workings of human beings.

Reading through the literature of socio-genomics, behavioral ecology, behavioral genetics, evolutionary psychology, and other perspectives that produce or elevate most recent biosocial explanations, one discovers why many social scientists' obsession with seeking such scientific legitimacy is harmful in the production of accurate social knowledge. Most social scientists involved in this type of interpretive work ignore the necessary research analysis of the real social worlds outside the biological laboratory and often attempt to describe the biologically unknowable or unobservable. Most dodge the relevant, often deep historical and societal analysis necessary, thereby highly limiting their focus to certain types of human behavior. Considering all that is empirically observable in social worlds and human beings' actions and interactions—and indeed often unresearched—it makes little sense that certain social scientists retreat to analyses of biological phenomena that are generally imperceptible without reference to contrived statistical tools and associated statistical models. In our view, this type of hyper-scientism among some social scientists needs to be checked, and the often undeserved authority and the numerous fallacies of their supposedly scientific findings need to be critically exposed.

Along with the socio-genomists analyzed above, another group of social scientists are in our view moving down the wrong track to sociological knowledge. These "evolutionists" include social scientists such as Gerhard Lenski, Stephen Sanderson, Jonathan Turner, Heinz-Jürgen Niedenzu, and Alexandra Maryanski. They frequently view human beings as primarily biologic animals programmed according to their evolutionary heritage and/or biological development. While an evolutionary model of human beings and of society has produced useful information—for example, how human beings have historically adapted to different physical environments—this type of evolutionary theory, in and of itself, offers a weak *general* model to explain human behavior and society. This model certainly should not serve as a grand social theory, as many such social scientists claim. The reason is that humans are a unique social animal whose behaviors develop and manifest contextually and socially well beyond the confines of conventional evolutionary principles and models.

It is puzzling how certain social scientists who toy with socio-genomics and advance theories of biosocial human behavior usually *ignore* scientific leaders in the field of genetics and human biology who warn against, or discount applying, genetic and biosocial understandings to present human behavior. Even certain applications of genetics to medical understandings of human beings—specifically in using "race" groups for medical purposes—are fraught with serious problems, as experienced social scientists such as Troy Duster, major epidemiologists such as Jay Kaufman, and distinguished biologists such as Ruth Hubbard have shown. Hubbard, for example, has pointed out the major problems in the medical use of "racial" gene clusters to try to predict or prevent human diseases:

> For one thing, the manifestations of inherited conditions can vary considerably and unpredictably from one person to another and, indeed, in the same person at different times. This is so because many factors, both within and outside ourselves, affect the ways we develop and function. This is true of our biological characteristics as well as our psychological and social ones. Even conditions such as cystic fibrosis or sickle cell anemia, which follow predictable patterns of inheritance, can exhibit a wide range of symptoms that differ in their severity in different people or, indeed, in the same person at different times. When it comes to the more common and prevalent health conditions or diseases, such as the various cancers or the vascular conditions that can lead to heart attacks or strokes, genes do not predict the fact or time of their occurrence or their severity with any degree of accuracy. For these sorts of conditions, a *person's life circumstances*, beginning at birth (or indeed during gestation) are better predictors than their genes are.[40]

There is also the matter of the search for corporate profits. Corporate capitalists are directly driving some of this socio-genomic revolution in regard to medicine and health care. Pharmaceutical companies vie for knowledge of human genetic makeup (DNA mapping) that might give them an edge in producing the latest profitable drug. The $50 million investment in the genetic database firm 23andMe and the $415 million buyout of the deCODE genetics firm by the large biotech firm Amgen demonstrate the large-scale corporate commitment to such genetic research.[41] Numerous university genetics departments are also scrambling for the expanding private and government funding thereby generated.

In addition to the problems associated with the relationship between socio-genomic research and big corporations is the question about the ways that new genetics research, intentionally and unintentionally, is used by sociobiologists to reproduce or increase society's racial inequalities and thus systemic racism. No longer are just visible physical attributes of human beings used to distinguish, separate, and oppress racial groups. Rather, now, the inner DNA make-up and invisible genetic operations of human beings are being used by some to distinguish, separate, and oppress. Anthony Hatch emphasizes how this social science turn to such socio-genomic understandings of racial groups is not a random occurrence, for, on certain levels, it coincides exactly with whites' "colorblind" racist framing of US society. This white "colorblind" framing is actually a cover-up of persisting and systemic white racism, and one of its examples is a new form of colorblind scientific racism that tries to explain away the still harsh and extensive "realities of extreme racially coded inequality."[42]

Conclusion

The socio-genomics of race and biosocial explanations of race noted in this chapter generally present far more problems than solutions to understanding racial inequality and other racial patterns in societies. That these types of explanations only focus on human bodies (individuals associated with racial groups), and often do a poor job at that, demonstrates their limited and flawed approach to achieving broader understanding of racial matters, such as institutional and systemic racism, the history of Western colonialism, and the everyday racialized interactions among people of different racial groups. Social scientists working to provide useful information about racial matters are best served by avoiding the detours and traps of socio-genomic and biosocial explanations of race, which mostly provide murky understandings or complete misunderstandings of a very limited set of racial matters.

One of the intriguing beauties of human beings and their social worlds is that not everything is immediately knowable—that is, present to current scientific knowledge. "Being" conceals itself as well as reveals itself. Thus, biological scientists can study the neural pathways of the physical brain, but their studies tell us little about the incorporeal human "mind" and "consciousness," and thus nothing directly about the social patterns of behavior created by human consciousness.

Notes

1 See Jiannbin Lee Shiao, Thomas Bode, Amber Beyer, and Daniel Selvig, "The Genomic Challenge to the Social Construction of Race," *Sociological Theory*, 30(2) (2012): 67–88. In the issue of *Sociological Theory*, 32(2) (2014): 189–258, see these articles: Ann Morning, "Does Genomics Challenge the Social Construction of Race?"; Joan H. Fujimura, Deborah A. Bolnick, Ramya Rajagopalan, Jay S. Kaufman, Richard C. Lewontin, Troy Duster, Pilar Ossorio, and Jonathan Marks, "Clines Without Classes: How to Make Sense of Human Variation"; Daniel Martinez HoSang, "On Racial Speculation and Racial Science: A Response to Shiao et al."; and Jiannbin Lee Shiao, "Response to HoSang; Fujimura, Bolnick, Rajagopalan, Kaufman, Lewontin, Duster, Ossorio, and Marks; and Morning."
2 See Dalton Conley, Jason Fletcher, and Christopher Dawes, "The Emergence of Socio-Genomics," *Contemporary Sociology: A Journal of Review*, 43(4) (2014): 458–67.
3 In *Contexts: Understanding People in Their Social Worlds*, 13(4) (2014): 15–23, see Jodi O'Brien and Arlene Stein, "Editors' Introduction to "What's Biology Got to Do With It?"; Dalton Conley, "How I Became a Socio-Genomicist"; Roger N. Lancaster, "Cultural Institutions Do Not Reduce to Genes"; Alondra Nelson, "Genetic Ancestry Testing as an Ethnic Option"; Kristen Springer, "How Biology Supports Gender as Social Construction"; and Karl Bryant, "Teaching the Nature-Nurture Debate."
4 Nicholas Wade, "What Science Says About Race and Genetics," *Time*, May 9, 2014, http://time.com/author/nicholas-wade (accessed September 1, 2015); Nicholas Wade, *A Troublesome Inheritance: Genes, Race, and Human History* (New York, Penguin, 2014). More than 140 respected scientists who study genomics signed a letter criticizing Wade's misuse of their work and sent it to *The New York Times Book Review*, August 8, 2014, www.nytimes.com/2014/08/10/books/review/letters-a-troublesome-inheritance.html?_r=0 (accessed September 1, 2015).
5 See Pierre L. van den Berghe's works: *Race and Ethnicity* (New York: Basic Books, 1970); *Race and Racism* (New York: Wiley, 1978); "Race and Ethnicity: A Sociobiological Perspective," *Ethnic and Racial Studies*, 1(4) (1978): 401–11; "Ethnicity and Sociobiological Debate," in John Rex and David Mason (eds.), *Theories of Race and Ethnic Relations* (Cambridge: Cambridge University Press, 1986); and, *South Africa: A Study in Conflict* (New York: Praeger, 1980), pp. 246–63.
6 See E.O. Wilson, *Sociobiology* (Cambridge, MA: Belknap, 1975); Marshall Sahlins, *The Use and Abuse of Biology* (London: Tavistock, 1977); Mary Midgley, *Beast and Man: The Roots of Human Nature* (New York: Meridian, 1978); Stephen J. Gould, *The Mismeasure of Man* (New York: W.W. Norton, 1996); Richard Lewontin, Steven Kamin, and Leon Rose, *Not In Our Genes: Biology, Ideology, and Human Nature* (New York: Pantheon, 1984); Ruth Hubbard and Elijah Wald, *Exploding the Gene Myth: How Genetic Information is Produced and Manipulated by Scientists, Physicians, Employers, Insurance Companies, Educators, and Law Enforcement* (Boston: Beacon Press, 1993).
7 Van den Berghe, "Race and Ethnicity: A Sociobiological Perspective"; van den Berghe, "Ethnicity and Sociobiological Debate," pp. 247–54. Also see critiques of sociobiology by Joe R. Feagin, "Review of *The Ethnic Phenomenon*," *Contemporary Sociology*, 10 (1981): 835–6; William M. Newman, "Review of *The Ethnic Phenomenon*," *Social Forces*, 61 (1982): 291–3.
8 Van den Berghe, "Ethnicity and Sociobiological Debate," p. 258.
9 Van den Berghe, "Race and Ethnicity: A Sociobiological Perspective," p. 403.
10 Ibid., p. 407.

11 See George Frederickson, *Racism: A Short History* (Princeton, NJ: Princeton University Press, 2002); Winthrop Jordan, *The White Man's Burden: Historical Origins of Racism in the United States* (New York: Oxford University Press, 1974).
12 Van den Berghe, "Ethnicity and Sociobiological Debate," p. 247.
13 Van den Berghe, "Race and Ethnicity: A Sociobiological Perspective," p. 406.
14 Shiao et al., "The Genomic Challenge to the Social Construction of Race," p. 67.
15 Ibid., pp. 68–72.
16 Ibid., pp. 79–84.
17 See footnote 1 above.
18 Morning, "Does Genomics Challenge the Social Construction of Race?" p. 190.
19 Ibid., pp. 190–1.
20 Ibid., p. 204.
21 Fujimura et al., "Clines Without Classes," p. 211.
22 Ibid., pp. 209–14.
23 Ibid., p. 220.
24 HoSang, "On Racial Speculation and Racial Science," pp. 235–8.
25 Ibid., p. 237.
26 Conley et al., "The Emergence of Socio-Genomics," pp. 459–60.
27 Ibid., p. 462.
28 Ibid., p. 463.
29 Ibid., pp. 462–3.
30 See Edwin Black, *War Against the Weak: Eugenics and America's Campaign to Create a Master Race* (New York: Dialogue Press, 2012).
31 O'Brien and Stein, "Editors' Introduction to "What's Biology Got to Do With It?" p. 15.
32 Conley et al., "The Emergence of Socio-Genomics," p. 16.
33 Lancaster, "Cultural Institutions Do Not Reduce to Genes," pp. 17–18. In contrast, for an example of the legitimization of integrating of genetics and social sciences, see Jeremy Freese, "Integrating Genomic Data and Social Science: Challenges and Opportunities," *Politics and the Life Sciences* 30(2) (2011): 88–92; see Jeremy Freese, "Genetics and the Social Scientific Explanation of Individual Outcomes," *American Journal of Sociology*, 114 (2008): 1–35.
34 Lancaster, "Cultural Institutions Do Not Reduce to Genes," p. 18, emphasis in original.
35 Nelson, "Genetic Ancestry Testing as an Ethnic Option," p. 19.
36 Springer, "How Biology Supports Gender as Social Construction," pp. 20–2.
37 Bryant, "Teaching the Nature–Nurture Debate," p. 23.
38 Tabitha M. Powledge, "Behavioral Epigenetics: How Nurture Shapes Nature," *BioScience*, 61 (2011): 588–92, http://bioscience.oxfordjournals.org/content/61/8/588.full (accessed July 28, 2015).
39 See Troy Duster, "Race and Reification," *Science*, 307 (2005): 1050–1.
40 See Troy Duster, "Lessons from History: Why Race and Ethnicity Have Played a Major Role in Biomedical Research," *Journal of Law, Medicine, and Ethnics* (2006); also see Jay Kaufman, "The Anatomy of Medical Myth" (2006) and Ruth Hubbard, "Race and Genes" (2006) on the "Is Race Real?" web-forum established by the Social Sciences Research Council: http://raceandgenomics.ssrc.org (accessed September 1, 2015). Emphasis added.
41 Adrianne Jeffries, "Genes, Patents, and Big Business," *The Verge*, December 12, 2012, www.theverge.com/2012/12/12/3759198/23andme-genetics-testing-50-million-data-mining (accessed September 1, 2015).
42 Anthony Hatch, "Transformations of Race in Bioscience: Scientific Racism and the Logic of Colorblindness," *Issues in Race and Society: An Interdisciplinary Journal*, 2(1) (2014): 30.

CHAPTER 7
ASSIMILATION THEORY'S DOMINION IN SOCIAL SCIENCE

A national narrative that valorizes the quest for societal assimilation and highlights the virtues of Americanism exists in US social sciences and, more broadly, in US society. In popular culture, this narrative of the unquestionable significance of assimilation and becoming "American" cuts across the news media, political discourse, the business world, and most institutions, especially educational institutions. To question the assimilation process or what exactly it means to be American is viewed as being "un-aspirational" or "un-American" and going against the grain—the norms, beliefs, and value system—of US society. The assimilation-to-become-American narrative is based on several assumptions. First, this narrative presents an unquestioned belief that societal assimilation is generally positive and a necessary part of the US experience. Second, it presupposes that those who question or critique assimilation or Americanism dislike America or are unwilling to compromise their ideas or behavior to become "American." Lastly and most importantly, it leaves unquestioned *whose* America or *what type* of America US citizens are supposed to embrace and assimilate.

In the United States, one discovers significant intolerance and condemnation for those who question assimilation and the meaning of what it means to be American, and who offer criticisms of the United States or reject the normative standards of what it supposedly means to be American or Western. The retort by most conservative and many liberal Americans, and especially white Americans, is: "this is the greatest country in the world" (sometimes called "American exceptionalism"). A more aggressive response often is "if you hate America so much, then move." Immigrant groups settling in the United States are often viewed suspiciously if they retain their language, dress, non-Western framing, and non-Judeo-Christian religious beliefs. While certain native-born gatekeepers of "America" might accept incorporation of some immigrant cuisines, they often chastise those who fail to relinquish other more substantial forms of their home cultures, many of which are routinely viewed as suspect. Additionally, many immigrant groups have individuals who wholeheartedly accept the idea of full Americanization and, adopting to white-framed worldviews and structures, become high-profile spokespersons and critics of their respective racial, ethnic, religious, or nationality groups.

Conservative and liberal news media extol the values of one-way assimilation to US society and often avoid critical discussion of the assimilation path, thereby avoiding in-depth analysis of what exactly American identity means. Watching nightly news and reading major newspapers, one periodically witnesses the display of an unadulterated jingoism that identifies the United States as the "best" or "greatest" country and places high value on the assimilation process faced by immigrant groups. On the left, Rachel Maddow has promoted MSNBC's "lean-forward" message by appearing in television commercials speaking one-sidedly about the greatness of US society—for example, focusing on US technological innovations with no discussion of its major racial and other social barriers. In other lean-forward ads, another MSNBC host, Chris Matthews, has noted some of these social hurdles. Yet, problematically, he too has often presented a skewed view of the country as successfully addressing these racial, gender, and class barriers. In one ad he is at Independence Hall in Philadelphia praising the progressive developments of the US "founders" who authored the Declaration of Independence, a sketch that ignores the troubling reality that these individuals were all unelected white property-owning men, and many were major slave-owners.[1] In this commercial and others, Matthews uncritically points to the advances in civil rights and women's rights as examples of the virtues of US society, while avoiding a discussion of racial and gender inequalities that were central in the formation of the nation and are still evident in most segments of US society.

The right-wing talk shows and news media have often called unabashedly for one-way assimilation and Americanization of all US residents, especially immigrants, to a mythical ideal of a now-perfect US society. Serious criticism of that societal myth is also met with reactionary accusations of being an unpatriotic American, often in an effort to silence discussion of societal problems, international misdeeds, persistent inequalities, or power imbalances. Over his terms as president, Barack Obama has been described as anti-American by right-wing radio and television media when he raised questions about social problems. To take another example, arch-conservative talk show host Sean Hannity has called for US authorities to insist that all Muslim Americans assimilate fully to US society and claimed that Muslims living in European societies have actually rejected assimilation there. Failing to consider widespread discrimination against Muslims and Western violence against Muslims, and ignoring the fact that a quarter of US Muslims are African Americans, Hannity and other right-wing commentators have simplistically advanced the notion that most Muslims oppose assimilation to, or fail to assimilate to, supposedly benign Western social norms.[2]

In this context, political discourse among politicians, of all backgrounds, while in office or seeking office must never offer critical assessments of the United States or question the benefits or constraints of assimilating into the "melting pot" and becoming a "real American." Recall the comments of white Representative Mo Brooks (R-AL) who insisted that "We should not be dividing anybody based on national heritage or race. Rather, we should be bringing us all together. That's what the melting pot ideal of America is all about."[3] These views of an ideal America are not limited to white advocates. Thus, President Barack Obama often insisted that the United States is the best country in the world and proclaimed that "we are one people." In his book, *Dreams from My Father*, Obama discussed his own fast-track assimilation as an "American success story."[4] However, as major African American commentators have reminded us, most African Americans do not share the major advantages that Obama possessed, such as the socioeconomic resources discovered in his immediate interracial family background.[5] Louisiana governor and Republican presidential hopeful, Piyush (Bobby) Jindal has represented a much more conservative political viewpoint, but has similar views of the United States as the leader among nations and the greatest land of opportunity. He has cited his success story as an assimilated son of immigrants from India who embraced the idea of the American Dream. However, Jindal's views on Muslim assimilation in Western societies have been stereotyped and problematical.[6] He has stated that certain immigrants "want to come to our country but not adopt our values," and instead hold values "antithetical" to American values. Along with other conservatives, he repeated the white-generated framing of Muslim immigrants as creating "a nation within a nation," asserting without evidence that "in the West, non-assimilationist Muslims establish enclaves and carry out Sharia law as they can without regard for the laws of the democratic countries which provide them a new home." He added, that if immigrants do not "want to be Americans," they should just "stay where they are."[7]

Success in assimilating is often associated with an individual's or group's economic success and adaptation to the US business culture, values, and behaviors. Thus, many studies of assimilation focus on economic success, occupational achievements, and wealth generation, for past and present immigrant groups. Adopting a capitalistic vision of success and a belief in a legitimate class hierarchy, supposedly shaped by meritocracy and hard work, are widely viewed as necessary components of success in the US economy.[8] Rarely is corporate exploitation of the working class, corporate overseas economic imperialism, and corporate deindustrialization acknowledged when addressing this required individual assimilation to the capitalistic culture and economy. Myths of the economic success of self-made individuals and groups persist, despite overwhelming evidence that much individual wealth is socially inherited—that is, across several family generations. Assimilating to the US economic culture and achieving significant economic assets are viewed as part of becoming a successful American.

Challenging the capitalist US business model and culture and challenging notions of what it means to be an economically successful

American—i.e., "achieving the "American Dream"—are often deemed to be inciting class warfare or the bickering of those people jealous of the achievements of the successful who have "earned" their position and wealth.[9] Indeed, most social scientists, politicians, business leaders, mainstream media commentators, and the public generally avoid discussion of contemporary US imperialism or neo-colonialism and explain away or severely misinterpret the foundational and systemic causes of the socioeconomic inequalities observed in the widening gap between the "haves" and "have-nots." To better elucidate how American success and assimilation theory are exalted and embedded in US society, including in educational institutions, we now turn to some of the dominant discourse about assimilation and American success discovered in important recent writings by several academic analysts.

"Triple Package": Assimilation Theorizing in Pop Social Science

Two prominent Yale University law professors, Amy Chua and Jed Rubenfeld, have written a bestselling book on societal assimilation, entitled *The Triple Package*.[10] For a time it generated much fanfare and controversy in social science circles, as well as in the popular media. Their ideas reignited discussion about US assimilation processes, including many of the old biases, misunderstandings, and poorly considered prescriptions of the past and present assimilation theory in the social sciences noted in previous chapters. A central message in the book is that individual success is culturally rooted and achieved through hard work and is therefore not genetically predetermined. Also seemingly appealing is their idea that all racial groups—including African, Asian, and Latino Americans—have within them subgroups that have become successful, acquired positions of influence and respect, and thus have been included in the upper socioeconomic ranks of society. However, their broad perspective is highly problematic in its uncritical notions of US socioeconomic success and of the cultural assimilation necessary for that success.[11]

A key problem with *The Triple Package* argument, and with most other mainstream assimilation theory, is the taken-for granted assumption that societal measures of success and the pressured assimilation to certain US ideals are in fact desirable and righteous. Like many other Americans, Chua and Rubenfeld presuppose that assimilation to capitalistic institutions and exclusive statuses is a good thing and that conventional paths to societal success are worthy. One-way assimilation to core institutions is thereby naturalized and the paths to success go unquestioned. However, they largely ignore major issues and hurdles facing numerous racial and ethnic groups in US society. It is extremely difficult for a group to be successful assimilating in a society defined by major racial discrimination and unjust inequalities. Indeed, should people seek to assimilate and succeed in a society whose economic institutions and government actions are often detrimental to a great many Americans, while greatly benefiting a relatively small few? Is it a good thing to assimilate into a society that promotes, just to take a few conspicuous examples, racialized policing, a growing prison-industrial complex, overseas imperialist wars, and a corrupt criminal justice system?

Chua and Rubenfeld claim that some US individuals and groups "do strikingly better than others in terms of wealth, position, and other conventional measures of success," but they do not explain *who* determines these conventional measures of success and what this success entails on a larger scale. Their view of success in modern societies revolves around "what modern economies reward." Thus, they say they mean success in its "vulgar" meaning of "gaining of money and position," and ridicule non-materialistic and unselfish success.[12] However, those striving for wealth and position may achieve substantial individual success, but, as we read the empirical evidence, their great success is rarely translated into real betterment of society, usually being narcissistic at its base.

According to Chua and Rubenfeld, three cultural commonalities are discovered among successful Americans. This triple cultural package accents (1) a sense of superiority, (2) a sense of personal insecurity, and (3) significant personal-impulse control. Interestingly, they do note the distinctive paradox of successful individuals experiencing both a sense of superiority and a sense of insecurity, but without critically analyzing this human tension. They also recognize in passing that a *superiority* complex, while it might foster success, can inspire "racism, colonialism, imperialism and Nazism." Apparently, the threat of these dramatic societal evils does not stand in the way of individuals aggressively seeking such societal success. *Insecurity* involves an "anxious uncertainty" about one's place in the society, but they fail to critically explain who or what determines one's societal place.[13] Indeed, research demonstrates many anxieties about personal place and worth among people of color are created by the society's systemic racism with its active white racist frame that disparages and subordinates people of color and penalizes whites who do not aspire to capitalist norms.[14] Their discussion of *personal-impulse control* appears to make some sense in judging an individual's potential success. Yet again, one needs to ask what likely rewards, what likely types of success, and what social capital inspire this type of impulse control. For many people the racial, class, and gender barriers regularly prevent access to those widely advertised rewards. Overall, they describe this triple cultural package as involving an "I'll show them mentality" on the part of successful individuals and groups. Yet, one needs to ask, who is it that you are going to show, and why?

While noting the supposed success that comes with the triple package, Chua and Rubenfeld also address some of the negative consequences associated with this triple-package deal. They realize the individual pathologies that can arise from an excessive stride toward their heralded individual "success." However, they fail to examine the societal pathologies that develop from individuals and groups aggressively aspiring to the normative model of social success they propose. In their view, the triple-package sociocultural groups focus, generally successfully, on conventional material and prestige-oriented success. Discussing groups that supposedly lack this triple package, Chua and Rubenfeld argue that *past* forms of oppression have played a role in that social reality, but also suggest that these hindrances are no longer major obstacles that cannot be overcome with much extra personal and group effort. As examples of this, they discuss a few subgroups among certain "cultural groups," such as the Nigerian Americans among black Americans, who are said to have overcome the racially discriminatory hurdles of US society.

This position ignores the fact that subgroups such as Nigerian American immigrants mostly came to the United States as relatively well-off, often well-educated members of African middle and upper classes—the case for a majority of documented immigrants of color. Most have not faced the generations of extensive discrimination and asset deprivation faced by the majority of native-born African Americans as they grow up and develop families within the United States. The Nigerians and other immigrants of color they consider typically migrate with some or many socioeconomic and educational resources that greatly help them to deal with the substantial racial discrimination they too must face. Even their significant resources do not enable them to attain full social success in this racialized society, especially if success is measured by more than simple economic and educational variables.[15] That is, they still cannot avoid facing, over their lives, much white racial discrimination. There is also the question, ignored by Chua and Rubenfeld here, about *who* (i.e., powerful whites) grants this access to avenues of socioeconomic success for some subgroups, but not for others with larger numbers, such as the majority of African and Latino Americans.

As already noted, we consider a very serious deficiency in *The Triple Package* to be Chua and Rubenfeld's materialist perception of success. In our view and that of many other analysts, the true sign of societal success is not how successful an individual or subgroup becomes (i.e., self-serving success) but how an individual or substantial group contributes to the larger success of the whole society. By overlooking this more meaningful, broader understanding of success and by proffering their limited sense of material success, Chua and Rubenfeld demean the individual and group successes of the majority of African Americans and others who supposedly lack this particular triple package, ignoring their often substantial contributions to improving this society and its human relations. These successes include advancing, often against dramatic barriers, civil rights and other human rights throughout the global community.[16] As Stephen Steinberg insightfully observes, most groups that Chua and Rubenfeld

> tout as exemplars of success would not be on American soil but for the 1965 Immigration Act that was passed on the heels of the Civil Rights Movement. Not only that, but thanks to the

black protest movement, immigrants from Asia, Africa, and Latin America entered a nation with far more favorable climate of tolerance than existed in past times.[17]

To ignore the type of societal success that is associated with African Americans' efforts in establishing greater democracy, freedom, human rights, and justice in the United States is to be oblivious to a much larger, more powerful, and expansive understanding of human success.

Assimilation Theory in Contemporary Mainstream Social Science

In Part I of this book, we discussed the rise and subsequent centrality of assimilation theory in the social sciences, particularly in the writings of Robert Park, Gunnar Myrdal, Milton Gordon, Nathan Glazer, and Daniel Moynihan. These and other social scientists perceived acculturation of ethnic and racial groups as a unidirectional pursuit toward a white core culture and a white racial framing of society. Ideas such as American culture or mainstream culture, American values, American society, Americanization, and American were inadequately defined, if at all, by these and other social scientists. Groups such as African Americans and other Americans of color were often disparaged for their supposed inability to fully assimilate. Little attention was paid to US society's major structural barriers, dominant racist framing, national imperialistic narratives and praxis, and historical patterns of systemic discrimination that have greatly inhibited numerous groups' attempts at socioeconomic and other assimilation into major societal institutions. One notable feature of most assimilation theory is its hyper-focus on individual and group agency, while nearly completely evading analysis of major social structural constraints and barriers. Another significant feature of this assimilation theorizing is its unquestioned, uncritical acceptance of one-way assimilation as an ideal process of socialization and social group behavior—and of US society as a model society and form of social organization that all individuals and groups ought to accept and strive toward.

In short, these earlier canonical proponents of assimilation theory failed to describe in significant depth the realities of societal exclusion and inclusion of different racial-ethnic groups, the rigid patterns of social group relations, the great structural inequalities, and the systemic racism targeting all people of color. These failures of assimilation theory are not surprising considering that the key assimilationist theorists were white and perceived this society through the privileged yet limited lens of the white racial frame and from their own white privileged status. The white-centered lens embedded in their flawed theories of assimilation was unable to accurately perceive the dramatic "un-assimilation" in many societal areas of most African, Native, Latino, and Asian Americans, those groups substantially excluded from prized full-Americanization despite their long list of important societal contributions and historical legacies of hard work and commitment to democracy.

Today, problematically, many elements of this conventional assimilation theory have not been discarded by contemporary social scientists, despite conceptual shortcomings, egregious implementation in social policies, and broad incorporation in the racist national narratives of the United States and other societies that maintain systemic racism directed against people of color. In fact, assimilation theory remains a dominant framework in much of the social science assessment of immigration, national belonging, and other aspects of racial-ethnic group constructions and relationships. While noting some problems associated with earlier assimilation theory, a number of influential contemporary mainstream social scientists have attempted to rework or salvage assimilation theory. This unsuccessful attempt to reinvigorate assimilation theory perpetuates a number of major inconsistencies and deep problems in earlier assimilation theory, thereby demonstrating the intellectual insolvency of this outdated and socially damaging theoretical paradigm as a grand theory of racial matters.

Nathan Glazer's Qualified Defense of Assimilation Theory

In the mid-1990s, three decades after publication of his book *Beyond the Melting Pot* (see Chapter 2), Nathan Glazer authored a major journal article titled "Is Assimilation Dead?" There he laments a supposed decline in social assimilation theorizing, but maintains a belief in the perseverance and importance of that process for most groups, with the major exception of black Americans.[18] While Glazer does acknowledge this central deficiency in traditional assimilation theorizing—its inability to explain the exclusion of black Americans in the assimilation process—he maintains that the theory still has significant usefulness in explaining the acculturation and amalgamation of European ethnic groups. Nonetheless, he fails to see how this major discrepancy casts a shadow on the exclusionary societal assimilation of these white groups.

We discover a number of misperceptions and weak arguments in Glazer's discussion there and in other later writings. In the first place, Glazer prematurely announces the death of mainstream assimilation theory. According to him, today we must live with a new conceptual paradigm inside and outside academia that accents multiculturalism and cultural pluralism, one that has supposedly replaced conventional assimilation theory.[19] However, this has not happened, for assimilation theory is thriving in social scientific analyses of immigration, one of the central subject matters of the social sciences. This is particularly true of social science research on racial-ethnic issues and immigration. In contrast, multiculturalism theorizing has come under significant public attack, and "cultural pluralism" remains an ideal concept only in words, not a social reality in practice.

One can sense Glazer's dismay over his view that understandings of multiculturalism have triumphed in racial theory, and his disappointment in conventional assimilation theory's supposed demise because of misunderstandings, "political correctness," and its "singular" flaw of ignoring the plight of black Americans. Yet, he insists that "properly understood, assimilation is still the most powerful force affecting the ethnic and racial elements of the United States," apart from that failure in regard to black Americans.[20] He does provide a solid historical examination of the ways that black Americans were excluded in assimilation theorizing, depicting how the concept was constantly oriented to European immigration. The mainstream assimilation process included or excluded migrant groups at different moments in US history, but eventually incorporated whites and even some immigrants of color, while excluding black Americans.[21]

Unsurprisingly, like most other white social scientists, Glazer overlooks W.E.B. Du Bois' early and astute discussions of cultural pluralism that provide analyses of black incorporation in the US social system and call for an inclusive cultural pluralism involving *all* racial and ethnic groups. Bypassing the work of Du Bois and the writings of numerous other important black social thinkers, Glazer offers the mistaken claim that one-way assimilation into white institutions was what most black leaders and social thinkers have desired. Glazer resurrects Robert Park as the "most important" sociologist who dealt with US racial and ethnic issues and addresses the assimilationist stance of E. Franklin Frazier, one of Park's black students who promoted the idea of substantial assimilation. However, most black social thinkers have realized that their full socioeconomic assimilation was highly unlikely in a racially segregated society. For this reason, many critical black intellectuals and activists have ultimately shunned assimilation theory and asserted alternative theories for understanding racial group relations, including theories of cultural pluralism, black separatism, and black nationalism.[22]

Problematically, these alternative black perspectives are erased in Glazer's poorly researched analysis. Instead, rejecting the idea that black Americans have possessed a distinctive culture that challenges assimilation, he further argues that it is "desirable that they become culturally, socially, economically, and politically assimilated, that they be simply Americans with dark skins."[23] Glazer's perspective demonstrates a rather uninformed one-way or top-down understanding of US culture and society, one in which blacks have had little or nothing to offer US culture or society. Rather, for Glazer, black citizens must obsequiously acculturate to the social world and behaviors of white America. Most dramatically, he fails to realize that important aspects of what is culturally, socially, economically, and politically "American" is often inseparable from black American culture and centuries of black contributions to US society. Moreover, Glazer's distaste for contemporary multiculturalism and his blindness to black cultural traditions and empowerment in the face of discrimination are revealed in another unreflective and even hostile argument that some multicultural education programs represent a "hysterical and irrational Afrocentrism"—even as he demonstrates favorable response to programs of Italian American studies and Jewish studies in higher education.[24]

Concluding his article, Glazer finds that assimilation is not in practice really dead. While the theory may appear to be dead, in his view the ongoing societal reality is one of continuing conventional assimilation. He cites data indicating that the ethnic sense of European American groups such as Italian Americans is weakening, even as the apartness and lack of assimilation for black Americans remain. In addition, he presents the questionable claim that other groups of color such as Latino and Asian Americans have a real choice in how they will be identified and assimilated into US society. For Glazer, it would appear that black Americans' choice in this case is limited to the black leaders opposed to cultural pluralism, those who still attempt to seek full assimilation despite the US history of discrimination. Because Glazer never addresses this long history and the current realities of institutional and systemic racism, one is left wondering if, in the end, Glazer blames black Americans for their significant exclusion from much of the mainstream socioeconomic and other assimilation processes.[25]

Rethinking Assimilation Theory: Richard Alba and Victor Nee's Understanding of Race

Richard Alba and Victor Nee are two contemporary social scientists who attempt to revitalize assimilation theory. They have authored a number of works that address contemporary assimilation processes, including *Remaking the American Mainstream: Assimilation and the New Immigration* (2003) and *Blurring the Color Line: The New Chance for a More Integrated America* (2009).[26] In their analyses, they examine white Americans and Americans of color from a reworked assimilationist perspective that provides more nuanced and critical understandings of assimilation than the canonical accounts of analysts such as Park, Myrdal, Gordon, Glazer, and Moynihan. They document the experiences of new groups of immigrants—especially immigrants of color—who seek socialization and a place in US society. They recognize the intellectual "sins" of ethnocentrism that pervaded much past racial theory. Yet, despite attempts to reconstruct assimilation theory, they actually reproduce some of the problematic assumptions underlying earlier theoretical analyses. They also generally avoid addressing more critical social science research and theory that better explain US racial-ethnic realities, especially the social structural barriers and power hierarchies of a systemically racist society.

A primary aim of Alba and Nee is to reformulate assimilation theory as a dominant social science paradigm. They view this perspective as the best way to understand the "integration into the mainstream" that has taken place for many generations among US ethnic groups. In their assessment, assimilation theory is also essential for understanding larger issues of US ethnic and racial dynamics, including the relationships of "majority and minority groups."[27] Early on, they revert to the older and conceptually problematic concepts of "minority," "majority," and "mainstream integration," concepts that require much more critical analysis than they provide. Mainstream integration generally presupposes a neutral and healthy societal condition and model toward which groups are supposed to assimilate. The minority–majority language and dialectic re-establishes an unquestioned power dynamic that upholds, implicitly or explicitly, the white framing promoting the sanctity of white majority dominance. Like many other social scientists, Alba and Nee utilize "ethnicity" as an all-encompassing concept to cover various ethnic, racial, religious, and national-origin groups. Race is thus subsumed under the rubric of ethnicity, and thus their reconsideration of assimilation theory, unsurprisingly, discards serious consideration of systemic racism and whites' role in its contemporary perpetuation.[28]

Alba and Nee do provide some important critical analysis of the canon of assimilation theory. Reviewing the writings of earlier social scientists, they demonstrate nuances, complexities, and limitations in the canon. They note, for example, that Milton Gordon perceived immigrant group assimilation into the dominant social institutions as more or less inevitable. However, they note that Gordon actually argued that the current and likely future of the United States consisted of several distinctive ethnic sub-societies (for example, Protestant, Catholic,

Jewish) into which immigrants were integrated, at least in social networking and other primary group terms. Still, they find that, despite his more nuanced understandings of seven important dimensions of group assimilation, Gordon did view the acculturation process to the dominant culture to be one-way and generally inevitable.[29] They underscore a gap in Gordon's multidimensional assimilation theory; he overlooks how group assimilation into core economic institutions is a very important dimension of overall assimilation, a point that other social scientists, including the second author, have emphasized since the 1970s. For Alba and Nee, this economic assimilation is important in fostering other types of assimilation as it is said to create equality across ethnic group lines.[30] However, such economic assimilation, and associated occupational mobility, can signal just a limiting type of individual materialistic success in this capitalist society. Such steps by individuals and groups can be problematical, discriminatory, and unhealthy, and they provide no assurance of *equal* status across ethnic and racial group boundaries.

Furthering discussion of the different assimilationist perspectives, Alba and Nee also discuss the straight-line assimilation popularized by W. Lloyd Warner and Leo Srole, Herbert Gans, and others. According to Alba and Nee, this approach, which envisions each new generation pushing their ethnic group closer to full societal assimilation, fails to consider how particular historical events can shift the process out of a straight-line path. They also examine the 1960s work of Tamotsu Shibutani and Kian Kwan, scholars who improve upon Gordon's understanding of assimilation by looking more closely into the broader causal mechanisms that generate the assimilation process.[31] Shibutani and Kwan extend the analysis of assimilation beyond the US context, demonstrating some global dynamics and environmental contexts of ethnic stratification, including population ecology and social distance issues. They thus move beyond Gordon's analysis of assimilation to better explain the links between microsociological social-distance matters among particular groups and the larger macrosociological shifts in society grounded in population ecology and population movements.[32]

Alba and Nee identify several key differences between realities and perceptions of past and present eras of immigration. The older theorizing of assimilation by Park and Gordon addressed specific historical circumstances, mainly the large-scale white ethnic migration from Europe. This migration needs to be distinguished from the more recent migration to the United States of non-European immigrants, such as those from Asia and Latin America.[33] One major distinction between the mass immigration of white Europeans and the more recent immigration by people of color is the hiatus period for European immigrants that allowed different white national-origin groups to loosen ties with their overseas communities. This hiatus was forced on them by restrictive 1920s immigration laws that ended or seriously interrupted the large-scale European migration. Unlike this earlier European migration, the more recent immigration after the reforms of the 1965 immigration act has involved an uninterrupted and less restricted movement of migrant groups, and mostly of groups of color. Without the major historical interruption experienced by European immigrants, these new groups of migrants have experienced a significantly different social context that allows for the maintenance of their ethnic (i.e., racial) communities.

In a significant move from earlier assimilation theory, Alba and Nee make clear that the past and present eras of immigration differ significantly in the racial character of immigrant groups. The fact that today's immigrants are mostly people with distinctive skin colors and other physical characteristics raises the issues of whether they can successfully assimilate and will face problems assimilating because they do not resemble the core ethnic group (that is, whites). However, Alba and Nee are optimistic that the often darker-skinned and non-European immigrants will eventually assimilate fully into the core society like their earlier European predecessors. In their view, racial differences are not as "rigid" and prohibitive to full assimilation as many social scientists believe. As they see it, numerous earlier European immigrants who were temporarily viewed by the established dominant group (e.g., British Americans) as racially distinct were soon able to overcome the discrimination and become a part of the white "American majority." They reason too that, as white baby-boomers retire, new and better job opportunities must become available to Americans of color. They predict that whites' racist views and discrimination will greatly change, thereby allowing people of color to integrate fully into core institutions in the relatively near future. Like other mainstream social scientists and media analysts, they consider the currently white-dominated institutions as becoming much more inclusive as major racial barriers decline.[34] In contrast to this view, we see vast differences between the past white immigrants and the current immigrants of color in the societal process and success in "becoming white."

Discussing new immigrant groups of color who in their view demonstrate ethnic identities that are malleable, Alba and Nee point to certain light-skinned Latino and Asian groups that have significant rates of intermarriage with whites and also to some Asian immigrants and their children who have gained "acceptance in the white community by distancing themselves socially from blacks."[35] However, social scientists who research current adaptation patterns of Latino and Asian immigrants and their children continue to find major structural barriers, including direct and indirect discrimination. Some of these researchers have developed concepts such as "segmented assimilation" to describe more accurately what they find empirically. Certain immigrant groups, such as those of Mexican origin, have significantly different paths in societal adaptation. They adapt to the host society in divergent patterns, including downward mobility for many who are native-born. Thus, children of Mexican immigrants frequently do not move up the socioeconomic ladder as readily as children of earlier white immigrants did, and many are downwardly mobile.[36] Moreover, major field research studies of middle-class Asian and Latino immigrants and their children show that they are not being assimilated into white middle-class society nearly as fast or completely as the optimistic assimilation analysts suggest. They currently face substantial white-racist framing and discrimination in numerous sectors of their lives.[37]

Echoing Glazer's view of the problematical exclusion of blacks from the mainstream assimilation process, Alba and Nee concede that the "most intractable" racial line for assimilation to cross is that between whites and blacks. More strikingly, they argue that it is not darker skin but the "appearance of connection to the African-American group" that is the most difficult racial barrier in US assimilation, giving as evidence the apparent assimilation success of dark-skinned South Asians who gain access to higher-status economic positions and neighborhoods.[38]

In an analysis of socioeconomic attainments, they discuss the educational and economic advantages and often successful assimilation of high "human capital immigrants" like these South Asians, who come in with significant educational and professional skills, immigrants who are contrasted with traditional labor migrants like Mexicans. While analysis of differences between immigrant groups of color is important, their use of the term "human capital immigrants" is misleading, because it clearly suggests that the traditional labor migrants do not possess *real* or *valuable* human capital. They thus accent the "low stock" of human capital of certain immigrants of color. Additionally, they appear to buy into the limiting materialistic notion of group success as just making it into the higher-level economic positions and esteemed occupations of the capitalist system, while overlooking the major human capital and achievements of workers and laborers who do much of the hardest and necessary labor of that economic system. Indeed, in many cases, the human capital of laborers appears more valuable to the rudimentary and essential economic operations of society than the human capital of many professionals. We do not discount the achievements and value of professional immigrants, but aim to emphasize the great economic value of the working-class immigrants who, frequently because of the low-paying jobs they are permitted to hold by dominant-group employers, have more difficulty being assimilated into the upper reaches of major institutions and indeed constantly face being undervalued in this capitalist society.

Alba and Nee address the different experiences of assimilation between immigrants who work in "ethnic economies" and those who work in the general labor market, and they also examine the spatial and settlement patterns of different immigrant groups. What they find is mostly unsurprising. For instance, they discover in the data that darker-skinned immigrants face racial discrimination in US housing, and thus are more isolated in racially segregated neighborhoods.

Conversely, numerous lighter-skinned immigrants, such as some Latin Americans, have an easier time moving into certain historically white neighborhoods. They further demonstrate that, along with lighter skin color, English proficiency and educational levels of immigrants are factors leading to successful assimilation in some areas of US society.[39]

In addition to what we noted above, Alba and Nee recognize other important criticisms of mainstream assimilation theory. They note its "ethnocentric, ideological biases," "conceptions of a static homogeneous American culture," and "Anglo-conformity." Nevertheless, rather than rejecting this problematical assimilation theory, they believe in amending it, arguing that the conventional theory still has "great power for an understanding of the contemporary ethnic scene in the United States."[40] For that reason, social scientists should still use it in making sense of US ethnic and racial group matters, including past and present immigration. They view such assimilation as central to US history and define its ultimate trajectory as the "decline, and at its endpoint the disappearance of an ethnic/racial distinction and cultural and social differences."[41] They fail to underscore, however, that this disappearance involves more or less one-way assimilation into major societal institutions, a process largely controlled by whites, especially powerful whites, and one that will largely dictate the acceptance or rejection of racial-ethnic groups over present and coming generations.

On certain points, we understand their reluctance to abandon a societal adaptation theory as a way of grappling with the past and present forms of immigration and do see assimilation theory's usefulness in explaining certain social phenomena related to social group incorporation in US society. However, we do not believe it should serve as the primary theoretical framework for understanding racial-ethnic group experiences, divisions, and positioning in society. Rather the idea of immigrant and other group *incorporation* (a less-loaded term) into the society's dominant institutions should be retained as a conceptual tool in a much broader and more critical theoretical framework, not as the starting point and dominant framework to understand new and old group relations in society.

Alba and Nee fail to substantially reformulate assimilation theory or correct many problems associated with the earlier canonical accounts. Let us briefly offer a sociological analysis that counters many existing analyses of contemporary assimilation theory. In the first place, a fundamental problem with canonical and contemporary assimilation theories lies in the very concept and term of "assimilation" itself. When this term was developed more than a century ago in its modern sense of immigrant group adaptation, it was *highly racialized* by whites who used it widely in both political speeches and emerging social science analyses. For example, at the turn of the twentieth century, popular and academic analysts directed much hostile framing and rhetoric at Asian immigrants seen as racially inferior and very "unassimilable" to the white core culture and society.[42] Thus, this modern concept of assimilation was clearly born with a *unidirectional* white-conformity assumption at its center. Some assimilation theorists such as Milton Gordon and Alba and Nee have recognized this distinctive unidirectional dimension (Gordon called it "Anglo-conformity"), yet none has analyzed in detail what this central white-conformity bias has meant for particular racial-ethnic groups, for the society as a whole, or for assimilation theorizing. Indeed, most seem to accept this Eurocentric, one-way approach to assimilation as inevitable.

Given this early and built-in racialized bias, consider what this white-conformity assumption means in both theory and societal practice. Most contemporary assimilation theorizing generally portrays *good* group assimilation as a more or less unidirectional adaptation to the white core culture and institutions. Yet, from the perspective of most immigrants of color, some or much of this white-conformity assimilation process is *not good* for them, as it means abandoning important home-culture elements and preferences (for example, language) they value greatly and frequently use to counter the racial oppression and capitalist inequities they face in US society.[43]

Additionally, another problematic feature of most past and present assimilation theory involves its heavy focus on individual and group agency to the exclusion of substantial analyses of social structures and barriers. Most theorists such as Alba and Nee solely or mainly address individuals' or groups' ability or inability to assimilate, and agential factors that contribute to this process. Yet, these analysts mostly ignore or downplay US society's institutional barriers and deeply ingrained ideological forces that greatly inhibit the success of some groups, while promoting the success of certain other groups. Significantly, in a deeply racialized, systemically racist country such as the United States, it is impossible to speak accurately of progressive group assimilation without addressing the structural, institutional, and systemically racist social system that shapes group formations, social relations, and the paths or obstacles toward major societal success.

As we have seen above, a major problem is that many contemporary assimilation analysts envision an immigrant group of color reaching eventual and full societal assimilation to a societal position similar to that of whites. However, becoming truly "white" in societal status and privilege entails considerably more than just certain economic achievements and attempts at successfully mimicking many white norms and folkways. To be even substantially integrated into most key aspects of the white-normed core culture and associated institutions requires acceptance there by whites. The latter control the institutionalized defining processes as to who is really white and white-privileged, and who is not. This society's racialized statuses on the dominant racial ladder, including the premier white status, are *institutionally enabled*. This involves being vetted in overt and subtle ways through institutional procedures maintained by whites, especially those with significant power. In everyday reality, no individual or family gets to position themselves as truly white in racial status and privilege by themselves, but only by means of white-accepted physical appearance, key white-cultural symbols, and accumulated socioeconomic resources recognized by the dominant white group collectively. Such recognition comes by means of well-institutionalized definitional and screening processes in major economic, legal, educational, and neighborhood institutions, and generally over a period of time. Thus, simply conforming via attempted assimilation to the white core culture is just part of this complicated process. People of color and others doing this conforming have to be *vetted* and *accepted* by elite and ordinary whites to even rise significantly in the social hierarchy, and even more so to rise to the level of full or even near-white societal status.[44]

Almost all the mainstream assimilation theorizing conceals in various ways the principal white agents at the top of society who have long created and still control the major social adaptation processes of immigrants and others in this society. Over the long course of US history, elite whites (usually men), together with their white assistants and everyday enablers, have controlled most employment, educational, political, and neighborhood access, and erected the discriminatory barriers restricting major institutional access and success for immigrants of color and their descendants. Immigrants of color, an important focus in contemporary assimilation theorizing, are typically among the least powerful in controlling and shaping these long-term societal incorporation processes. Yet this deep societal reality is not adequately theorized.

When addressing important matters of human social interaction, contemporary analysts such as Alba and Nee re-establish many assumptions of earlier theorists, such as the unquestioned value of assimilating to the white-shaped core culture and conventional materialistic standards that supposedly determine successful societal assimilation.

Rubén Rumbaut: Paradoxes of Assimilation Theory

Sociologist Rubén Rumbaut has also revisited the canon of assimilation theory, discussing theories of Robert Park, W. Lloyd Warner, Milton Gordon, and more recent analysts. He addresses key themes of assimilation crafted by these thinkers, including links between assimilation and upward mobility, and the Anglo-conformity, melting-pot, and cultural-pluralism goals in much assimilation theorizing. Rumbaut astutely reveals certain important problems and paradoxes of assimilation. One involves the significant *social costs* of pressured assimilation and upward mobility for different immigrant groups. He exposes, for example, the rarely discussed reality that highly Americanized "Asian-origin newcomer groups, exhibit higher rates of depressive symptoms and suicidal ideation" than other immigrant groups. Studies of the relationship between health and assimilation demonstrate that increasing cultural assimilation to the core culture often has significant health risks, such as cigarette smoking and drug use. Not surprisingly, one-way assimilation is often a negative and traumatic process.[45] Another important facet of the immigrant assimilation process that Rumbaut explores is the tension between ethnic self-identification and becoming "American," a tension shaped by social-historical forces and contexts, including immigrants' national origins and US immigration policies.

Evaluating some issues that Alba and Nee also discuss, Rumbaut notes the differences between more recent immigration and past immigration. In his view, much greater attention needs to be given to historical contexts, as there have been important changes in society that accompany shifting immigrant groups. He highlights issues related to the socioeconomic assimilation of many new immigrants who come better educated and occupationally prepared than many in the native-born US population. Many have already acquired advantages, including not only educational and occupational attainments and skills, but often English language proficiency and significant monetary resources. There are large social-class differences among different groups of contemporary immigrants, many of which (e.g., low-wage workers with little education) will have to struggle against major socioeconomic and other barriers in the prevailing assimilation process. In contrast, a majority of the affluent new immigrants are significantly Americanized and acculturated before they come to the United States, having already learned the English language, adopted US "consumption patterns, lifestyles, and popular culture," and been prepared for "political assimilation."[46]

In his theorizing and empirical analyses, Rumbaut has pled not only for an acknowledgment of assimilation's contradictory meanings and differential transformative qualities, but also for its continuing usefulness as an analytic social science tool. In his view, a careful study of assimilation processes helps to explain differences in individual and group incorporation into US society as many immigrants now come from the international periphery to the US core, and helps to explain the troubles accompanying this process. Assimilation processes help to illuminate racial and ethnic inclusion or exclusion and deterministic acculturation or "coerced" Americanization. In the ongoing assimilation process, he observes human variety in the intersections of human biographies with societal structures and the "inventiveness of human agency and sheer weight of circumstance." There too, he asserts, the assimilator and assimilated are not "fixed, static things… but permanently unfinished creations," and as a result, the US core society "is ineluctably transmuted, even as it keeps its continental name, America."[47] Thus, Rumbaut tags assimilation as a process of contradictions in which the identity and agency of new immigrants shape US history, and that history in turn shapes immigrant identity and agency.

Rumbaut's case for continuing assimilation theory and empirical analysis is stronger than many other social scientists because he does not frame assimilation as the dominant framework for immigrant and other societal analysis, but rather as an often useful concept. He fully realizes the important contradictions inherent in the concept and accents the continual metamorphosis of actual societal adaptation processes. He addresses important negative impacts of the pressured acculturation process, such as physical health issues and psychological issues associated with identity development in the process of usually coercive Americanization.

While these are clearly important and well-assessed conceptual and empirical concerns, Rumbaut's analysis reveals a few shortcomings noticed in most other discussions of assimilation, such as his focus on individual and group agency at the expense of a full analysis of the relevant structural barriers of a white-racist society and his apparent assumption that successful assimilation is largely rooted in certain socioeconomic achievements in society. Problematically, Rumbaut does not provide a substantial enough discussion of the societally embedded racist meanings, asymmetrically structured racial relationships, and historically deep systemic racism that fundamentally shapes a still white-dominated "America." In our view, he might consider providing a much better analysis of the extensive institutional problems facing immigrants of color trying to assimilate into this nation defined by systemic racism. As he briefly and correctly observes, assimilation for many immigrants—including immigrants of color—often involves a rejection, disassociation, and movement *away from the black community*, but he does not seem to follow up with an in-depth analysis of the implications of this important observation.

As we argue later, those immigrants and their children who are incorporated into the United States are most definitely forced to adapt to a white racial framing of this society, part of which often includes accepting much of its anti-black sub-frame's many negative stereotypes, images, and narratives. They must tacitly accept or actively perpetuate numerous aspects of the centuries-old systemic racism that largely defines and shapes this society.[48] One key question, then, is this: Are the skills necessary for immigrants to fully succeed in US society those that produce a better, more complete and democratic society, or are they skills that reinforce the hyper-capitalistic, systemically racist, and often imperialistic character of the United States? This is just one of the critical questions that, in our view, these assimilation analysts should be actively posing.

Deconstructing Assimilation Theory

As a dominant contemporary framework for understanding the workings of the US and other countries' racial and ethnic relations, most specifically immigration and social group adaptation, assimilation theory powerfully shapes the ways that most social scientists perceive and discuss racial matters. Frameworks of ethnicity, class, and other theoretical perspectives discussed in earlier chapters often incorporate, to some degree, certain ideas and preconceptions that emerge from conventional assimilation theory. Robert Park, the social scientist arguably most responsible for the early development of assimilation theory, is still heralded as one of the most influential social scientists on racial matters, and his theoretical model of assimilation, delineated in the famous racial relations cycle, is still taught to many students of racial and ethnic matters.[49] The lasting influence of Park on the field of racial relations studies has been absorbed by many social scientists who are taught these conventional ideas about social assimilation in Western countries. Rarely are the ethnocentrism and colonialist mentality that support Park's racial relations cycle and his idea of one-way assimilation to a white racial framing of society and to Eurocentric societal institutions fully and critically considered.

Honest assessment of Park's writings on racial matters would entail exploring empirically and more critically the "competition" and "conflict" stages of his racial relations cycle and necessitate further analysis of Park's observation of the exclusion or weak assimilation of black Americans into US society, as well as the extensive exploitation of other people of color in the United States and globally. His race relations cycle and associated assimilation accounts ought not to be viewed as a necessary and positive societal model of social relations and societal socialization, but instead understood as often involving the deleterious racialized management of Western societies that continues to exclude, segregate, or colonize many non-European peoples.

Social scientists who are largely uncritical of the current racial-ethnic status quo will likely continue to laud and promote conventional assimilation theory. In our view, critical social scientists should assertively present the fallacies and ultimate untenability of this traditional assimilation framework. By focusing heavily on the agency of individuals and groups that seek acceptance, benefits, and a place in a racist, classist, and sexist Western society, conventional assimilation theorists will continue to promote a false model of such pathological social adaptation. Of great concern for social sciences, this ideal and often touted social theory of assimilation does not account for the structural constraints and exclusionary tactics of societal oppressions—such as systemic racism, classism, and sexism—that are central to Western societies. As a result, it does not offer a path to a more democratic, egalitarian, and just society. Assimilation theorists since Park have mostly avoided serious critical discussions of the extensive social conflicts that deeply define and shape modern Western societies and their internal and inter-societal relations, and they typically pay too little attention to the positive benefits of a culturally pluralistic and truly democratic society. While recent assimilation analysts acknowledge the barriers of skin color to full assimilation in US society and other Western societies, they offer no penetrating critiques of the deep-lying societal processes that erect and sustain these large-scale racial barriers.

Mostly adhering to dominant US values and Eurocentric folkways, mainstream assimilation theorists often ignore, discount, or demonize the group organizations, home-cultures, and counter-framing that oppose or demonstrate the deficiencies of Western values in regard to group relations and individual behavior. Assimilation theory has a built-in bias, historically often a jingoism, that Western "civilization" is the best model for all people. Focusing almost exclusively on societal changes and historical shifts in Western societies, most assimilation theorists generally ignore the persistent social structures of oppression and exclusion and the maintenance of unbalanced power relations. They usually leave unexplored the societal hegemony of assimilation ideas, the brainwashing and false consciousness of those undergoing assimilation, and the resistance techniques associated with contending with this white-pressured assimilation. Problems associated with assimilation that corrupt a society's ideals are also largely unaddressed. Typically, assimilation theorists ascertain societal "success" as socioeconomic achievements in a hierarchical, inegalitarian capitalist system that provides great socioeconomic opportunities to a relatively small number of people. Additionally, assimilation theorists narrowly perceive successful assimilation as joining the ranks of (mostly white) groups, organizations, and institutions that promote social segregation and racial framing for those not included. Achieving the increasingly exclusive "American Dream" for some often means assisting in maintaining an American nightmare for many others, just as civilization for the West has largely involved the de-civilization, de-development, and de-valuing of people of color across the globe.

Flaws in the common assimilationist model are apparent in the unwillingness of US and other countries' governing elites to fully and fairly incorporate many people of color, as we have seen in the writings of numerous theorists discussed above. In Europe, the governing socio-racial class of countries such as France and Germany has revealed an unwillingness to allow truly egalitarian assimilation of their Arab and other Muslim immigrant populations. Outside Europe, elites of European background, such as in Brazil and Israel, have also shown an unwillingness to fairly assimilate—socioeconomically and in other ways—non-European immigrant groups. Substantial socioeconomic and other assimilation for some and not for others is the reality in numerous societies, but certainly not a model for the way a truly just and democratic society should be constructed. The most pronounced flaw of the assimilation model, as we have noted several times, is the model's underlying and unquestioned logic of people necessarily conforming to a white racial framing of society, and thus to a society produced through, defined by, and operating according to the ideals, laws, and institutions largely created and implemented by whites.[50]

Conclusion

Many social scientists and other analysts have pointed to Barack Obama's election to the US presidency in 2008 and 2012 as a sign of significant transformations in the US racial structure and major institutions. For example, one referee on a paper sent to the *American Sociological Review* asserted that the presence of Obama and his family in the White House demonstrates "fundamental changes in American racial relations." We find this argument to be unreflective and unpersuasive, especially when considering the large numbers of empirical studies demonstrating the still substantially unequal character of US racial relations and the other dimensions of systemic racism chronically affecting Americans of color. This largely vacuous argument sidesteps the data from many recent empirical studies.[51] Only a disproportionately small number of people of color hold positions of significant power in the major institutions of the United States and other Western societies, and those that do often have their hands tied by yet more powerful white elites. For example, the small core of black elites are mostly not afforded the same power, resources, and capital as their elite white counterparts. One example of the clash between an overly optimistic perspective on black middle-class advances and a sounder framing based in empirical research can be seen in sociologist Charles Willie's critique of sociologist William Julius Wilson's emphasis on the apparent socioeconomic gains of the black middle class, discussed in his *Declining Significance of Race*.[52] Using numerous examples and varied empirical data, Willie long ago demonstrated that there are numerous serious vulnerabilities and racialized challenges facing the contemporary black middle class in comparison with the white middle class, an empirical reality that continues to hold true.

Additionally, proponents of the now commonplace "minority success" stories ignore powerful whites' *qualified* accommodation of some people of color who are strategically incorporated into positions of power in order to offset major criticisms of the oppressive societal realities that persist. The effective reproduction of centuries-old systemic racism, especially when challenged by recurring protests over oppression (e.g., in the 1960s), has necessitated a grant by whites of some power, much of it symbolic, to a small fraction of black Americans and other Americans of color. However, the societal reality today remains one where a great many talented people of color are excluded from powerful positions they fully deserve and still face racial discrimination from whites of all backgrounds. Possibly the greatest problem associated with past and present assimilation theory is the failure to acknowledge that in the United States and other societies, the everyday processes of societal assimilation more or less require an unhealthy conformity to a white racial framing of society. Such conventional assimilation entails support or acceptance of a systemically racist society that still causes great harm to people of color across the globe.

Notes

1 "Lean Forward" commercials by Rachael Maddow and Chris Matthews on MSNBC's site: www.nbcnews.com/id/40112039. See Rachael Maddow, "On America Greatness," *MSNBC*, www.nbcnews.com/id/21134540/vp/42705352#42705352 (accessed September 1, 2015); and Chris Matthews, "Liberalism Always Wins Eventually" (MSNBC Promo-Lean Forward Campaign), *YouTube*, July 24, 2014, www.youtube.com/watch?v=F9YcC7qqUrQ (accessed September 1, 2015).
2 Sean Hannity, "Views on Muslim Assimilation," *Salon*, January 15, 2008, www.salon.com/2015/01/08/sean_hannity_responds_to_hebdo_attack_is_the_u_s_making_a_mistake_not_insisting_on_assimilation (accessed September 1, 2015).
3 Paul Gattis, "Rep. Mo Brooks: Democrats 'Dividing America by Race' in 'Waging a War on Whites,'" www.al.com/news/index.ssf/2014/08/rep_mo_brooks_democrats_dividi.html (accessed September 28, 2015).
4 Barack Obama, *Dreams of My Father: A Story of Race and Inheritance* (New York: Broadway Books, 2004).
5 See "In Depth With Tavis Smiley," *CSPAN*, January 5, 2015, www.c-span.org/video/?323064-1/depth-tavis-smiley (accessed September 1, 2015).
6 Alexandra Jaffe, "Bobby Jindal's Slams 'No-Go Zones,' Pushes 'Assimilation,'" *CNN*, January 21, 2015 www.cnn.com/2015/01/19/politics/jindal-no-go-zones-london (accessed September 1, 2015).

7 Jack Jenkins, "Bobby Jindal Doubles Down on Totally Inaccurate Muslim 'No-Go Zone' Comments," *ThinkProgress*, January 28, 2015, http://thinkprogress.org/world/2015/01/28/3616417/bobby-jindal-warns-muslim-invasion-america-doubles-inaccurate-no-go-zone-comments (accessed August 30, 2015).
8 See Joe R. Feagin, David Baker, and Clairece B. Feagin, *Social Problems*, 6th edn (Upper Saddle River, NJ: Prentice-Hall, 2005).
9 For example, after publication of Thomas Picketty's well-researched book, *Capital in the Twenty-First Century* (Cambridge, MA: Harvard University Press, 2014), David Brooks, commentator at the *New York Times*, accused him of being "jealous" of today's wealthy.
10 Amy Chua and Jed Rubenfeld, *The Triple Package: How Three Unlikely Traits Explain the Rise and Fall of Cultural Groups in America* (New York: Penguin, 2014).
11 Many parents overlook the intellectual degeneration of many elite universities. Take Harvard, for example, which recently was headed by a Larry Summers, who disparaged and chased off Dr. Cornel West, a leading US black academic, and who proposed that women are not programmed to be scientists like men. Harvard has also housed the advocate of IQ racism, Richard Herrnstein, and the problematical sociobiologist, Edward Q. Wilson.
12 Chua and Rubenfeld, *The Triple Package*, pp. 6–30.
13 Ibid., pp. 9–10.
14 See Joe R. Feagin, *Racist America: Roots, Current Realities, and Future Reparations*, 3rd edn (New York: Routledge, 2014).
15 See Yoku Shaw-Taylor and Steven A. Tuch (eds.), *The Other African Americans: Contemporary African and Caribbean Families in the United States* (Lanham, MD: Rowman & Littlefield, 2007).
16 See Joe R. Feagin, *How Blacks Built America: Labor, Culture, Freedom, and Democracy* (New York: Routledge, 2016).
17 See Stephen Steinberg, "Tiger Couple Gets It Wrong on Immigrant Success," *Boston Review: A Political and Literary Forum*, March 11, 2014, http://bostonreview.net/books-ideas/stephen-steinberg-chua-rubenfeld-triple-package (accessed September 27, 2015).
18 Nathan Glazer, "Is Assimilation Dead?" *Annals of the American Academy of Political and Social Science* (1993): 122.
19 Ibid., p. 123. We also draw on Nathan Glazer, *We are All Multiculturalists Now* (Cambridge, MA: Harvard University Press, 1998).
20 Glazer, "Is Assimilation Dead?" p. 123.
21 Ibid., pp. 124, 131. See Fred Wacker, "Assimilation and Cultural Pluralism in American Social Thought," *Phylon*, 40(4) (1979): 325–33.
22 Glazer, "Is Assimilation Dead?" pp. 133–4; and see W.E.B. Du Bois, "Conservation of the Races," in Julius Lester (ed.), *The Seventh Son: The Thought and Writings of Du Bois*, (New York: Vintage, 1979 [1897]); W.E.B. Du Bois, *The Souls of Black Folk* (New York: Penguin, 1995 [1903]).
23 Glazer, "Is Assimilation Dead?" pp. 133–4. See also Glazer, *We are All Multiculturalists Now*.
24 Glazer, "Is Assimilation Dead?" pp. 134–5. On blacks' major impacts on US society, see Feagin, *How Blacks Built America*.
25 Glazer, "Is Assimilation Dead?" pp. 135–6.
26 Richard Alba and Victor Nee, *Remaking the American Mainstream: Assimilation and the New Immigration* (Cambridge, MA: Harvard University Press, 2005); Richard Alba, *Blurring the Color Line: The New Chance for a More Integrated America* (Cambridge, MA: Harvard University Press, 2012).

27 Richard Alba and Victor Nee, "Rethinking Assimilation Theory for a New Era of Immigration," *International Migration Review*, 31(4) (1997): 827.
28 Ibid., p. 834; Alba and Nee write: "We view 'racial' distinctions as a type of 'ethnic' distinction... In our usage, then, the term 'racial' is implied in 'ethnic.'"
29 Ibid., p. 832.
30 Ibid., p. 835. For one of the earliest discussions of this, see Joe R. Feagin, *Racial and Ethnic Relations* (Englewood Cliffs, NJ: Prentice-Hall, 1978), pp. 29–30.
31 Alba and Nee, "Rethinking Assimilation Theory," pp. 833, 836; also see Tomatsu Shibutani and Kian Kwan, *Ethnic Stratification* (New York: Macmillan, 1965).
32 Alba and Nee, "Rethinking Assimilation Theory," p. 831.
33 Ibid., p. 842.
34 Ibid., p. 846.
35 Ibid., p. 846.
36 See Alejandro Portes and Min Zhou, "The New Second Generation: Assimilation and Its Variants," *Annals of the American Academy of Political and Social Science*, 530 (1993): 74–9; Joe. R. Feagin and Clairece B. Feagin, *Racial and Ethnic Relations*, 9th edn (Upper Saddle River, NJ: Prentice-Hall, 2011), pp. 226–8.
37 See Joe R. Feagin and José Cobas, *Latinos Facing Racism: Discrimination, Resistance, and Endurance* (Boulder, CO: Paradigm, 2014); Rosalind S. Chou and Joe R. Feagin, *The Myth of the Model Minority: Asian Americans Facing Racism*, 2nd edn (Boulder, CO: Paradigm, 2015); Mia Tuan, *Forever Foreigners or Honorary Whites? The Asian American Experience Today* (New Brunswick, NJ: Rutgers University Press, 1998).
38 Alba and Nee, "Rethinking Assimilation Theory for a New Era of Immigration," p. 846.
39 Ibid., pp. 859–60.
40 Ibid., p. 863.
41 Ibid., p. 863.
42 Feagin and Feagin, *Racial and Ethnic Relations*, p. 286.
43 Feagin and Cobas, *Latinos Facing Racism*, p. 5.
44 We rework here arguments in Feagin and Cobas, *Latinos Facing Racism*, pp. 4–6.
45 Rubén G. Rumbaut, "Paradoxes (and Orthodoxies) of Assimilation," *Sociological Perspectives*, 40(3) (1997): 494.
46 Ibid., p. 501.
47 Ibid., pp. 505–6.
48 See Feagin, *The White Racial Frame*, passim.
49 See Alan Sica, "B.T. Washington and R.E. Park Find the Man Farthest Down," *Contemporary Sociology*, 41(4) (2012): 409; Glazer, "Is Assimilation Dead?" p. 132.
50 See also L. Paul Metzger, "American Sociology and Black Assimilation: Conflicting Perspectives," *American Journal of Sociology*, 76(4) (1971): 627–47.
51 See, for example, recent studies cited throughout Feagin, *Racist America*.
52 William J. Wilson, *The Declining Significance of Race: Blacks and Changing American Institutions* (Chicago: University of Chicago Press, 1978).

CHAPTER 8
A SYSTEMIC RACISM CRITIQUE OF RACIAL FORMATION THEORY

Michael Omi and Howard Winant's *Racial Formation in the United States* (hereafter, *Racial Formation*), first published in 1986, proposed a new theoretical paradigm for race analysis, racial formation theory (hereafter, *formation theory*). They presented this theory as an innovative way of discussing racial matters that challenged many preconceptions and perspectives of the mainstream social sciences' discussion of race and ethnicity. *Racial Formation* presents an extremely well-researched and expansive overview of key themes in racial analysis, providing rich, detailed social and historical examples of racial matters and covering numerous important racial theories, concepts, perspectives, themes, and controversies. The most recent edition of *Racial Formation* (2015) reflects formation theory's staying power and ongoing contributions to racial and ethnic studies. Indeed, many important studies of race and ethnicity continue to incorporate insights and ideas of this innovative formation theory.[1] To celebrate the twenty-fifth anniversary of its initial publication, an edited volume, *Racial Formation in the Twenty-First Century* (2012), drew major race scholars from across the social sciences to reassess the utility of formation theory in explaining developments in the study of racial and ethnic issues.[2] Additionally, when scanning the references of most articles addressing racial matters over the last several decades, *Racial Formation* appears repeatedly, demonstrating numerous ways formation theory is employed to understand an array of different racial and ethnic social phenomena.

Clearly, *Racial Formation*'s impact on the field of racial and ethnic studies is unquestionable and substantial. Focusing on the United States, Omi and Winant critically examine the conventional ethnicity/assimilation and class/stratification perspectives and the less conventional nation/colonialism counter-approach to understanding "race" issues. In their view, with which we agree, the ethnicity/assimilation and class/stratification paradigms significantly downplay racial matters. They show that "race" cannot be mostly limited to matters of ethnicity or class, as in these first two paradigms, but is instead an autonomous field of societal conflicts, organization, and ideological meanings. However, their critique of the third paradigm, which includes what we term the "black radical tradition," is weakly constructed. As we show below, they incorrectly condemn this latter perspective for "essentializing" race in a manner that accents black and cultural "nationalism" and denies improved "racial democracy." Nonetheless, the important theorizing of Omi and Winant has helped to problematize the mainstream social science that still overemphasizes white-framed concepts and theories of "ethnicity" and "assimilation" by providing a perspective that clearly highlights the primary reality of "racial formations" in society.[3]

Racial formation theory, despite its significant contributions to our knowledge of US racial matters, has thus far failed to deliver a comprehensive and critical race-theoretical analysis that explains the complexities and rigidity of racial meanings, racial relations, and well-institutionalized racism in historical or contemporary US society. The latest edition of *Racial Formation* (2015) has done little to correct most of these problems. Despite *Racial Formation*'s attempt to move beyond mainstream race theory, formation theory repeats certain errors of other mainstream theories discussed in previous chapters. Most notably, Omi and Winant neglect examining in detail the ongoing systemic racism in the US and societies across the globe, the extremely unbalanced power relations among certain major racial groups, the persistence of a dominant white racial framing in establishing many societal realities, and the unrelenting obstacles to "racial democracy" and important reversals of what they perceive as racial "progress." Our view of racial matters is less optimistic, addresses institutional persistence in matters of white racism, and argues for a more critical analysis of institutional, structural, and systemic racism, without which one generates distorted understandings of past and present racial realities for the United States and other countries.

In this chapter, we underscore certain limitations of formation theory's understandings of whites and colorblind explanations of racism, specifically their avoidance of addressing whites' well-institutionalized power and dominant white racial framing in shaping systemically racist societies. We expose some significant weaknesses in Omi and Winant's view of the racial state as the "pre-eminent site" for racial group pluralism, contestation, and democratic exchange. We also note formation theory's too idealistic view of racial democracy and the "great transformation" in racial politics that supposedly has taken place in US society.

Formation Theory's Evasion of Systemic Racism Analysis

As with many contemporary mainstream theories of racial matters, formation theory omits a specific upfront, in-depth, and critical discussion of whites' centrality in actively creating and maintaining systemic societal racism in white-run countries such as the United States. Omi and Winant do not analyze the four-plus centuries of history of European American (white) oppression of people of color in the territory that became the United States. Thus, formation theory is ill-equipped to understand or discuss well contemporary racial matters in which whites—and most especially elite whites—play a leading role in sustaining and developing systemic racism, forging asymmetrical racial group relations between people of color and whites, and substantially controlling contemporary meanings about many racial matters. Rarely in *Racial Formation* do Omi and Winant present an explicit and needed critical analysis of "whites" or "European Americans," the group responsible for institutionalizing extensive racially discriminatory practices that have long been central to US society. For decades now, systemic racism theorists and empirical researchers have defined and systematically analyzed both "whites" and "elite whites" as necessary units of empirical and theoretical analysis.[4] As we show in the next chapters, an adequate theory of US racial matters is impossible without forthright discussion of different levels of whiteness and of the multiple strata of white agents in racial oppression. As in centuries past, whites remain the most powerful, resource-laden, and socially, politically, and economically influential US racial group.

Missing in their formation theory is a significant, critical, and thorough discussion of the systemic racist practices and white-framed ideas of the dominant racial group, a serious omission that blurs understanding the well-established racial hierarchy with whites at the top and people of color at the base. Without systematically identifying whites' dominant role in generating and maintaining racial oppression, sharply unequal statuses in racial hierarchies, and white racist framing of these and other oppressive actions, formation theory fails to provide the necessary analysis of the racialized realities central to US society, as well as to other Western societies. Any attempt at theorizing racial matters is incomplete and, indeed, futile without specifically considering how white Americans have become the most powerful US racial group in economic, political, and other social resources, and thus in societal control. While they certainly acknowledge whites' central role in systemically racist societies, Omi and Winant largely avoid a sustained, systematic, and critical analysis of whites, especially the powerful white elite, as the group most responsible for perpetuating systemic racism in the US and the global-wide racial framing and structural racial-group inequalities that substantially result from past and present European imperialism and colonialism.[5]

Nationally, by means of the racialized political and legal systems of the US state, and internationally through imperialist international relations and global economic exploitation of people of color, whites have implemented a series of methods for crudely shaping and constructing racial identities that conceptually distinguish and physically separate whites and people of color. Recall that by the eighteenth and nineteenth centuries, people of European descent had created color-coded categories for distinguishing themselves and people of different skin tones and related physical characteristics (see Chapter 1). This color ranking of human groups created centuries ago by whites still exists, as is evident in contemporary studies of "whiteness" and the establishment of "black" studies programs. Indeed, contemporary debates about the use of term "Redskins" as a name for the National Football League's football franchise in the US capital, as well as the routine use of color-coded racial groupings in books such as Frank Wu's *Yellow: Race in America Beyond Black and White* and Richard Rodriquez's *Brown: The Last Discovery*, illustrate the ways that color-coded racial categories, substantially created by whites, still persist and thus work to create racial group boundaries, discrimination, and identity.[6] As we have observed previously, this color-coding system has also entailed frequent use of other physical characteristics, as well as associated cultural characteristics, to distinguish racialized groups in society's hierarchy.

These well-institutionalized racial identities are perpetuated in an array of societal norms and institutions, including scientific and medical categorization, residential and occupational segregation, racial images in the mainstream media, and throughout popular culture. They are also expressed in official and unofficial sources of demarcation, such as the US Census and job applications, and often determine access to or exclusion from educational opportunities. While increases in mixed-race racial categories and self-chosen forms of racial identity challenge society's established racial hierarchy to some degree, white racial stereotypes and other racial framing continue to forcefully and arbitrarily pigeonhole people into persisting racial groups based on skin color and other physical characteristics. For example, President Barack Obama's mixed-race heritage has made little difference in how he has been racially coded in a white-framed society like the United States, which has labeled him from childhood as black and thus regenerated the mentality of the infamous "one-drop-of-blood-rule" strategically developed by whites centuries ago. This is just one example of rigid color-coded racial categorizations created and recreated by whites and embedded in white-framed societies in an effort to maintain asymmetrically arranged racial group divisions that empower whites and disempower people of color, prop up white privilege, and sustain power and a "property interest" in other valuable aspects of whiteness.

The formation theory of Omi and Winant does not provide a systematic analysis of the tremendous power and persistence of the racial hierarchy created by whites or of whites' continuing and central role in creating salient racial-group divisions and conflicts grounded in that old racial hierarchy. As previously noted (see Chapter 6), one striking example of whites' perpetuation of racial categories and a racial hierarchy is discovered in the contemporary resurgence of biosocial/socio-genomic explanations of differences in human group behavior. Other examples are discovered in commonplace Eurocentric mappings of "intelligence" and pathologies among different racial groups, and in the way groups are constantly categorized and arranged hierarchically according to their different skin tones and associated physical characteristics delineated by the white-framed racial hierarchy. Differences in incarceration rates attributed by some researchers to racial group genetics and test-score research that purports to explain "IQ" differences that exist between blacks, whites, Asian Americans, and Latino Americans in biological terms remain a central activity of some in the race-relations academic industry. For more than a century, these racialized theories about the higher "IQs" of certain groups have been funneled through prestigious academic journals, institutional reports, books, and lecture circuits by major scientists of different fields. One important example of this mainstream scientific perspective on racial-group differences in intelligence can be seen in the 1994 letter, "Mainstream Science on Intelligence," that appeared in the most important US business newspaper, the *Wall Street Journal*. It was drafted by Linda Gottfredson, an educational psychologist funded by the white supremacist Pioneer Fund, and signed by no fewer than 51 other scientists who research "intelligence" tests.[7]

The primary message of the letter was a defense of Herrnstein and Murray's *The Bell Curve* (see Chapter 1) and further claims that whites have higher "IQs" than black and Latino Americans. They claimed that the "bell curve for whites is centered around IQ 100; the bell curve for American blacks [is] roughly around 85; and those for different subgroups of Hispanics roughly midway." Other racialized claims in the letter include: "intelligent tests are not culturally biased"; "there is no persuasive evidence that the IQ bell curves for different racial-ethnic groups are converging"; and "black 17-year-olds perform, on average, more like white 13-year-olds." Not surprisingly, all the scientists who signed the letter were white and deeply embedded in the conventional white framing of racial group differences.

Nowhere in their racial formation analyses do Omi and Winant substantially address the critical ways that elite and ordinary whites have developed a persisting US racial hierarchy that has for centuries worked to institutionalize and regularly reinforce white social, political, and economic power. They do not fully address how that enduring racial hierarchy is routinely rationalized, today as in the past, by white claims of intellectual and moral superiority. Instead, racial formation offers limited portraits of whites and mostly focuses on certain micro-processes of racial identity and stereotyping. For example, they explain how various US citizens internalize and act upon some racial stereotypes, such as the "black banker harassed by [presumably white] police while walking in casual clothes" or whites "who assume that the non-white colleagues are less qualified persons hired to fulfill affirmative action guidelines, indeed the whole gamut of racial stereotypes."[8] These forms of white racial stereotyping, while significant in reproducing racial hierarchies, are only a small part of the problem of systemic racism, and especially its white racial framing. These micro-level actions reveal the attitudes of white groups and individuals who are operating in a much larger, centuries-old system of racial oppression. Such understandings of white stereotyping will appear theoretically much less significant unless one examines and understands how a *broad array* of such white racialized prejudices, stereotypes, narratives, images, and emotions operate in upholding a systemically racist social system. That is, such micro-level racial actions are embedded and routinized in white-framed social institutions and other macro-level racist structures. Indeed, racialized attitudes and human behaviors often seem hard to understand when divorced from their larger context of a dominant white racial frame that is discovered by a close examination of society's racial institutions and historical legacies.

By substantially locating contemporary race and racism issues primarily among the stereotyped attitudes and micro-actions of human beings ("different types of human bodies"), Omi and Winant generally avoid a deeper analysis of the foundational, institutional, and systemic racism created and maintained by whites to the present.[9] As we show in the next chapters, our understanding of systemic racism as created and guided by whites, especially elite men, is significantly different from the perspective offered by Omi and Winant, who have claimed "there is nothing inherently white about racism." They rhetorically ask, "Is all racism the same, or is there a distinction between white and non-white versions of racism?" Responding to their question, they state, "We have little patience with the argument that racism is solely a white problem, or even a 'white disease.'" They argue that "whites can at times be victims of racism—by whites and or non-whites" and oppose viewing whites as "the racist group."[10]

The racial formation presentations of Omi and Winant have thus offered a pluralist view of racism, one in which racism can be generated by any and all racial groups. This misguided logic ignores many centuries of field research on racism and dominant whites, and it illustrates the problems associated with focusing too much on micro-level forms of racism such as individual or small group stereotyping and prejudice. This results in bypassing the necessary analysis of whites' racism as a macro-level reality foundationally, systemically, and institutionally embedded throughout society, and seen in all types of everyday human behavior. This unfortunate error becomes more pronounced when Omi and Winant at one point attempt to contrast and roughly equate "black supremacy" with "white supremacy," a move that also limits the concept of racism to racial stereotypes and prejudices, thereby again overlooking the fact that in the US and other societal cases racism—grounded by white ideas and actions—is foundational and systemic. Significantly, this perspective bypasses a full analysis of the huge institutionalized power inequalities long ago established, and still perpetuated by whites in Western societies.[11]

Clearly, a serious problem in their work, one found in other mainstream sociologists dealing with racial matters, is to limit much discussion of racism to individual and small group prejudices or ethnocentrism. With their substantial focus on racial prejudices and individual and group agency, Omi and Winant fail to develop more comprehensive understandings of racism as fully systemic and involving not only prejudices and ideas but also a quite broad white-racist framing, well-institutionalized racist practices, and an enduring system of racial oppression. Major analyses of foundational, institutional, and systemic racism, such as empirical investigations of whites' macro-level forms of power in society, are missing. Indeed, as Omi and Winant suggest, all racial groups can possess viewpoints—attitudes and beliefs—that are ethnocentric and prejudicial. However, as we stress, only whites possess the necessary power, socioeconomic resources, and social capital to operationalize, put into action, and fully institutionalize their racial ethnocentrism and prejudice, and have for centuries developed and refined a system of racial oppression that does just that. Additionally, as we show in the next chapters, whites have also created a broad and well-institutionalized white racial framing that includes much more than racial prejudices and ethnocentric beliefs, for it also includes racialized images, emotions, and many narratives of white supremacy that profoundly shape contemporary societies.

White racial attitudes and biases are significantly different from those of other racial groups in their development and extraordinarily powerful influence over several centuries, including in how they substantially affect social practices and institutionalized structures of many contemporary societies across the globe. Whites are set apart from other US racial groups in that they do not experience numerous negative impacts of systemic racism—the racial oppression, marginalization, discrimination, exclusion, and inequalities facing people of color in virtually all major institutions. Even poor and working-class whites, with fewer socioeconomic resources than affluent and elite whites, still possess the privileged racial capital and racial positionality not extended to people of color. Moreover, as we demonstrate throughout, a broad white racial frame justifies, especially in white eyes, the systemically racist practices and social systems that have been created by whites now for centuries.

Limitations of Formation Theory's State-Centered View

Problematically, when Omi and Winant do address larger racialized institutions such as "the state," they fail to demonstrate the ways this far-reaching and powerful institution has helped to create a white-framed and systemically racist country from its earliest days to the present. In the United States particularly, any discussion of government is incomplete without an analysis of the ways this influential political institution is controlled by, and functions according to, the framing and norms of elite whites at its helm. White economic and political elites founded and have run the US state since its inception. Even the election of the first African American president and incorporation of a few high-level black government officials have done little to offset this ingrained white power at the highest level of society. Today, as in the past, individuals of color usually must operate in a political-economic system shaped fundamentally by a white political and economic elite; the latter have largely dictated the well-institutionalized norms, functions, operation, and boundaries of this centuries-old system.

For example, in the first decade of the twenty-first century, Eric Holder, the first black attorney general, was regularly vilified and periodically disempowered by the mostly white officials of the US justice system and other officials of the US state, such as leading Republican members of Congress. In his attempts to create a more equitable criminal justice system, Holder faced great resistance and unbending long-established rules that limited his ability to implement significant changes. Similarly, despite being the US president, Barack Obama's power to realize social reforms and enact government programs that might create greater racial, class, and gender equality has frequently been blocked or weakened by highly placed white officials in the US legislative and judiciary branches, officials who are usually part of the white power elite. Even when he has been successful in generating some progressive changes in the racialized social system that benefited working-class Americans, including many Americans of color (e.g., in health care and the criminal justice system), these changes have been continually challenged, weakened, and in some cases reversed.[12]

In defining race and laying out their main concepts—such as racial projects, racialization, and racial formation—Omi and Winant present only a partial view of racial meanings, racial relations, and racism. They do emphasize the way that "race" is socially constructed. As they see it, race is "an unstable and 'decentered' complex of social meanings." Their concept of "racial formation" thus represents the "socio-historical process by which racial categories are created, inhabited, transformed and destroyed." The concept of racialization is defined as the extension of these racial meanings "to a previously racially unclassified relationship, social practice, or group."[13] Yet their formation theory does not offer a thorough explanation of the ways that racial matters operate beyond this social construction and extension of race "meanings." For the US case, it fails to address how foundational and systemic racism, with its broad white racial framing, persists for centuries, aggressively resisting major transformations and evading destruction. Omi and Winant thus emphasize struggles over racial meanings much more than individual and organized struggles over the dominant racial hierarchy, racist social institutions, racially segregated networks, and the massive racial inequalities in many societal resources. They usefully highlight how race concepts shape racial identities, but spend relatively little time on the ways that this racialization process shapes major societal institutions—and on the ways that these institutions, despite temporary or modest modifications, defy fundamental and foundational changes. As we have expressed in an earlier critique of racial formation theory:

> While "race" is indeed socially constructed, the empirical realities of the racial social-historical world, past and present, are not adequately represented with this heavy emphasis on contending racial meanings. Indeed, these meanings reflect the tangible reality of materially oppressive racial structures. The central issue that in our view should be addressed is what racial group wins these (often fixed) contests over concrete resources most of the time, and what racial group, fundamentally and usually, has the power to impose most central racial meanings and structures of oppression on less-powerful racial groups.[14]

Realities of White-Racist State Formation

In contrast to Omi and Winant's understanding of the US state as the pre-eminent site of mediating racial conflict and promoting racial democracy, we view the state as constantly a major perpetrator of white racial oppression, as a substantially white-racist state that mediates racial group conflict in a strategically progressive direction only when necessary. Much empirical data sustains this conclusion. When pressured by outside forces, such as protests by those oppressed, state officials (all white until recently in US history) have sometimes responded and reluctantly agreed to important racial changes, but only in ways that ultimately have not challenged most of whites' power and control over the society. The US state has certainly not been a political institution whose major goal is real racial democratization, nor is this state a pluralist meeting ground that more or less impartially addresses disputes among various racial groups, as racial formation theorists Omi and Winant have long suggested. Instead, the state remains one whose *foundation* was created by an all-white-male elite at an undemocratic constitutional convention and one that has been maintained and reinforced at the top by mostly white elite officials in its still substantially undemocratic legislative, judicial, and executive branches.

Important critical racial analysis demonstrates that the US state is a substantially white-controlled and white-interest-oriented government complex that "regularly generates racial conflict, enforces racial divisions, and attempts to exploit, exclude or eliminate certain racial groups through homogenizing or marginalizing processes."[15] People of color who do not conform to the structural and operational realities of the white-controlled state—at its various local, state, and federal levels—are routinely marginalized, disempowered, dispossessed, or imprisoned. Considering that full democratic representation and real social justice are still often denied to them, it is not surprising that African Americans, Asian Americans, Native Americans, Latino Americans—all Americans of color—still feel the need to form their own special interest groups to challenge state policies and organize large-scale protests to seek the proverbial US ideals of "liberty and justice for all."

How racially democratic are contemporary US political institutions? Elsewhere, Joe Feagin has demonstrated in detail how major US political institutions are not democratic, even in the twenty-first century. The US Senate was originally established to keep full control of legislation in the hands of the white male elite, as one can see from the fact that it was not directly elected by voters until the early twentieth century and, with two exceptions, had only elite white men as senators until the mid-twentieth century. Today, it remains overwhelmingly white and male. The US Supreme Court is even more undemocratic in its structure. It is, in effect, the highest "legislative" body in the country, yet all of its members have been unelected, to the present day. (All were white men until the late 1960s.) Additionally, most members of other important government bodies, including the US House of Representatives, have been overwhelmingly or, more recently, substantially and disproportionately composed of affluent or elite whites.[16] Unsurprisingly, these political organizations routinely make decisions in the interest of some portion of the white (male) elite.

For example, the US Supreme Court's early twenty-first century reversals of much of the 1965 Voting Rights Act protecting voters of color in many areas and its late twentieth century and early twenty-first century blocking of affirmative action policies have had major negative effects on the representation of African Americans and other Americans of color in numerous political bodies and in historically white educational institutions. Legislatively, the US Congress's unwillingness to pass comprehensive and sensible immigration reform policies in the early twenty-first century has so far resulted in the mistreatment and/or deportation of numerous Latino workers who have been indispensable to much day-to-day functioning of US economic institutions.

One can see from just these brief examples the fragility of Omi and Winant's belief that the US state is becoming a relatively democratic arena where Americans of color now have a major say in contention with increasingly less powerful whites. Racially democratic inclusion in the oversight and decision-making operations of major US government agencies remains relatively weak. Elite whites and whites who back them continue to rule and dictate political realities very disproportionately to their advantage, and thus to the disadvantage of people of color. For instance, African Americans face such current discriminatory realities as legislatively generated hyper-incarceration in the prison-industrial complex and significant disenfranchisement in numerous geographical areas, usually because of hyper-incarceration and/or voting barriers. Many Latino Americans have reduced political rights because of their status under white-generated immigration law or policy and, in addition, are hurt by voting barriers established by powerful white officials to reduce black voting. Both groups are seriously underrepresented in numerous areas of US politics and routinely face arbitrary injustices at the hands of white local and federal officials. Moreover, within major federal government institutions, Asian Americans, one of the more economically integrated groups of color, and Native Americans, one of the most marginalized and racially segregated groups of color, are on the whole even less represented than African and Latino Americans, especially in the federal legislative and judiciary branches and in the upper levels of the federal executive branch. Presently, and unmistakably, the US state remains as in the past racially undemocratic, maintaining undemocratic racial group relations largely favoring whites and substantially restricting or marginalizing most groups of color.

Since its earliest days, the US state has largely promoted the ideas, inclinations, and institutions preferred by the white ruling elite, thereby ensuring the oppression of people of color, especially those who do not accommodate the bidding of that elite. Omi and Winant's portrayal of the contemporary US state as a site of pluralist contestation of "racial projects" and a somewhat even playing field where different racial groups have the ability to contend for power is severely flawed in a number of specific ways. Moreover, even when a certain segment of the US state attempts to correct some power imbalances between whites and people of color or to amend a few racially oppressive practices, one soon sees significant white resistance or blockage by other segments of the state.

For example, in the past and in the present day, legislative or judicial attempts to rehabilitate important aspects of the racist criminal justice system have typically received lip service with little reform from those in command of that system, even given its high profile and well-documented abuses. Some modest laws to reduce racial discrimination are well-written, but are often weakly enforced. Systemically racist framing and actions of powerful whites at the helm of the criminal justice system persist despite the periodically large numbers of protesters who organize against the patterns of law enforcement abuse directed at people and communities of color. We see this repeatedly in this country. The deaths of black Americans at the hands of (mostly white) police officers recur so often that civil rights protests seeking to ensure that, as one recent movement put it, "Black Lives Matter," never cease. In such cases, black protesters must expend much energy, much time, and many resources of still perpetually oppressed black communities. As some in the US Justice Department during Barack Obama's presidency recognized and attempted to remedy nearly 50 years after the 1960s civil rights movement, the racial oppression facing black and brown Americans is still systemic in policing and in the laws, courts, and prisons of the US state. Problematically, this realization and documentation of the racially oppressive actions of the state's institutions has so far brought few significant changes. If the US state were a political site where major racial conflicts are often truly resolved and where racial groups are able to successfully contest the state's political imbalances and abuses, one would expect to witness much greater racial changes in US society.

Overall, Omi and Winant's focus on the state is too narrow and thus insufficient as an explanatory principle. Research across social science disciplines demonstrates that the US economy is equally as important a site of racial conflict and contestation—and racial group interaction in general—as the US state.[17] Indeed, in its major shaping and continuance the state is often substantially a product of the economic decisions and power exercised by the dominant racial group. Omi and Winant do not explain how the highly racialized economy, with its extensive exploitation of people of color and routine wealth generation for a majority of whites, regularly shapes the US "racial state." They neglect fully addressing the ways that the US state often acts as a facilitator and implementing tool for the white capitalist elite and as a regulator and obstacle for working people, those in the working and middle class. The latter group of workers and their families includes both people of color and whites, who compete in a US economy that still is racially segregated and generally favors whites.

The US state was intentionally set up to ensure an asymmetrical relationship of political-economic resources, power, and capital along racial lines. This state has helped greatly to create and maintain the dominant racial hierarchy, including the sharply unbalanced socioeconomic relationship between the mostly white ownership class and a large group of workers of color. Additionally, in this unbalanced racial group arrangement, workers of color are routinely denied certain rights, protections, and/or privileges (e.g., W.E.B. Du Bois' "public and psychological wage of whiteness") afforded to white workers in a systemically racist capitalist system. This is particularly evident in the ways in which US government officials allow the callous economic abuse and exploitation of the many workers of color who largely undergird the service economy and other low-wage economic sectors.

US elites, overwhelmingly white even in present times, have long created government practices and institutions that generally favor their political-economic interests. In contrast to ordinary workers, they receive excessive tax breaks and, are able to manipulate the economic and political-legal system in their interest and dictate government rules, regulations, and legal loopholes allowing them to exploit the economy and control its main productive source, the large working and middle classes. Indeed, Omi and Winant seem to miss the point that systemic racism and modern capitalism are co-reproductive and wedded together in this rigged political-economic system—and that they are perpetually reproduced by leading white officials in the US state, as well as by major white business leaders.

Contestation of State and State-Facilitated Oppression

Resistance by people of color to the white racist state and their conflict with white racial oppressors occurs on a regular basis, but this resistance is usually stymied or quelled with major assistance from government agencies such as the police or military forces. The state has great resources to offset such citizen resistance. Even the more profound historical challenges to, and occasional victories against, the racialized US state (e.g., the *Brown v. Board of Education* case and the Civil Rights Acts of 1964, 1965, and 1968) are eventually weakened, diluted, or met with newer forms of racial discrimination and domination, such as those termed "colorblind racism."[18] We see much evidence on this point, for example, in the historical reality of slavery being replaced by Jim Crow segregation, and then with Jim Crow segregation being replaced by contemporary racist structures such as informal workplace discrimination, hyper-policing of communities of color, and aggressive racialization of the prison-industrial complex. Yet again, these "new Jim Crow" patterns centrally involve the actions of the leaders of powerful US state and federal governments, most of whom at the top are elite whites.[19]

To locate the activity of racial group contestation primarily within state institutions, as Omi and Winant generally do, downplays many other significant sites of racial group conflict. As we noted above, economic conflict over jobs, resources, and capital between whites and people of color is equally as important and sociologically revealing as operations more directly involving the state. Moreover, conflict in the economy is usually entwined with the state's structure and operation. Just as elite whites mostly control the state, elite whites such as top bankers and other top corporate executives largely control and shape the economic realm of a systemically racist society such as the United States. Below them are the disproportionately white acolytes and enablers, such as the middle-class managers and supervisors in the upper tiers of the working class, while the lowest tiers of US workplaces remain primarily or disproportionately workers of color.

The societal significance of whites' privileged access to socioeconomic resources and the immense imbalance of economic power between whites as a group and subordinated groups of color is hard to overstate. Social scientists, including Omi and Winant, who analyze this societal power asymmetry between whites and people of color often imply that conflict and contestation over socioeconomic resources involves a mostly legitimate, fair, or unrigged competition for resources, property, capital, and other political-economic power. The latter includes the power to influence the state and public policy and public opinion. Yet, like the state itself, the economies of systemically racist states are not only substantially white-run but also aggressively white-framed. That is, they are operated and structured according to well-established white-framed ideas and institutionalized practices that leave little room for fair economic competition, contestation, and conflict-resolution.

In contrast to Omi and Winant's optimistic vision of the state as a site where racial groups and their racial projects compete for political power in an arena that apparently allows for fair competition, we suggest that the state arena does not in fact allow for much fair competition or truly just and effective avenues of political contestation.[20] Similarly, the modern US capitalistic economy—to a substantial degree initially established and long maintained by whites as a slavery-based socioeconomic system—is one that is still mostly controlled at the top by elite whites with dominant economic power. Neither the white-run US state nor the white-run US economy are sites that allow for true or fair racial group contestation.

Significantly, two other sites of racial group contestation in systemically racist societies, where competition among groups cannot be as thoroughly constrained or blocked by whites, are the critical realms of knowledge and culture. Certainly, whites do attempt to dominate, and often succeed in dominating, societal knowledge and culture; they do so in aggressive efforts to hegemonize white-framed knowledge and marginalize or destroy the cultures of people of color. Nonetheless, people of color are more easily able to construct counter-cultures and counter-knowledge systems than establish alternative polities and economies. Historically and today, one often observes a more active or successful contestation among racial groups over matters of group knowledge, societal framing, and cultural meanings and practices.

One example of this reality, addressed more fully in the next chapter, involves different ways that social scientists and other social analysts from different racial, class, and gender groups explain and critique important social realities of the modern world. Thus, analyzing racial theory from its earliest days with the birth of social sciences, one clearly sees competing views and contestation between the dominant racial group and subordinated racial groups with regard to racial meanings, the organization of racial and class relations, and the structure and operation of the racialized social systems of slavery, colonialism, Jim Crow, and contemporary oppression. For example, African American social thinkers and activists early advanced black counter-framing with major counter-narratives and adopted important modes of resistance to the dominant white racial framing that used science, religion, and the dominant culture to intellectually and morally justify whites' oppression of people of color. A critical black epistemology, social scientific worldview, and policy-oriented perspective challenged much eighteenth- and nineteenth-century white framing of society's racial hierarchy and other racial matters, including the Eurocentric knowledge systems that justified white supremacy and the extensive oppression of people of color, on both a national and global scale.

Persisting Systemic Racism: Hurdles to Racial "Democracy" and "Progress"

Two primary tenets of formation theory supporting a more optimistic view of the state as a facilitator to resolving racial group conflict are the notions of racial "democracy" and the "great transformation" in US racial matters over the past half century. As indicated above, the idea of a racially democratic US state is not grounded in empirical reality, as it ignores elite whites' historic establishment and current control of the state and economy.[21] The undemocratic nature of US society in regard to racial matters is evident when considering such realities as the persistence of large-scale residential segregation in towns and cities, an economy with jobs substantially arranged according to the racial hierarchy and with vast economic disparities across the color line, and a corporatist state whose laws and policies still heavily and disproportionately favor whites as a group. The "racial project" of the dominant white group is far from egalitarian, pluralistic, and democratic in nature.

The *dominant* racial project of white subjugation of people of color has long been substantially successful and one largely oriented to the exploitation and related oppression of people of color—thereby routinely favoring white group interests. In contrast, the racial projects of groups of color have involved constantly battling the persisting tyrannies of systemic white racism and have been blocked much of the time from achieving *real* racial democracy and egalitarian group pluralism. Therefore, it is difficult to agree with Omi and Winant's position: "Rather than envisioning a single, monolithic, and dominant racist project, we suggest that racist projects exist in a dense matrix, operating at varying scales, networked with each other in formally and informally organized ways."[22] While numerous racial projects of people of color exist, they presently exist in relation to a dominant white-framed racial project of systemic racism.

Formation theory narratives of the "great transformation" in the US racial state and racial progress in US society since World War II reflect hard-fought group struggles by Americans of color. However, Omi and Winant neglect to analyze thoroughly the constant, significant, and regularly organized white resistance to much racial progress, and especially the major political-economic reversals of 1960s racial progress since the 1970s. White racial framing and other elements of systemic racism persist, albeit sometimes in modified forms, despite the great struggles and sacrifices made by Americans of color in trying to expand democracy in US political and economic institutions. Emphasizing the "historical flexibility of racial meanings and categories," "race as an unstable and decentered complex of social meanings constantly being transformed by political struggle," and the "way race structures society... changed enormously over time," Omi and Winant avoid analyzing the stable, less-flexible, substantially unchanged patterns of systemic white racism—and thus the many important ways that white-framed racist realities persist in many sectors of the society.[23] Thus, they can claim that "racial rule can be understood as a slow and uneven historical process which has moved from dictatorship to democracy, from domination to hegemony" and that US society has witnessed a significant "transition from a racial dictatorship to a racial democracy," as well as that "without question there has been significant progress toward racial democracy."[24] According to Omi and Winant, and many other racial relations scholars, the eclipse of overt Jim Crow in the 1960s signaled a major new era of racial progressivism, major changes in the racial landscape, and the demise of substantial racial oppression by whites.

Indeed, the 1960s civil rights victories over Jim Crow segregation and toward greater racial opportunities generated by large-scale organized black protests and supported by members of other racial groups, including some whites, are highly significant, awe-inspiring episodes in the history of US racial group struggles and of US movements for greater social justice. Tragically, however, the efforts, sacrifices, and gains of those who fought long and hard for these human rights victories and racial progress, then and later, were regularly countered by significant white challenges that have resulted in major setbacks, reversals, and lack of fulfillment of liberty and justice goals. In contrast to Omi and Winant's claim that the US has made great progress toward real racial democracy, we see a vastly different picture of racial matters, earlier and now. Our empirically based view observes a largely unrealized racial democracy at present, recurring white obstacles to substantial racial progress, the persistence of extreme racial inequalities, segregated residential areas and job divisions, and greatly imbalanced political and other social struggles throughout society. These are just a few of the contemporary examples that reveal a major and persisting racial hierarchy and other power divisions separating white Americans from Americans of color that are more like the racial-oligarchic past than some mythical racial-democratic present.

To acknowledge the perpetuation of systemic racism and white-framed societies is *not* to belittle or reduce the many historical achievements of civil rights movements and intellectual and physical resistance to systemic racism by people of color over the past several centuries. Indeed, institutional and systemic racism analysts have often been in the forefront of those accenting the importance of this resistance and also the numerous positive impacts on this society of Americans of color—unsurprisingly, many have been involved in organized resistance movements themselves.[25] The counter-framing and counter-actions by black Americans and other Americans of color seeking greater racial democracy and challenging white supremacy have led to many of the greatest strides toward freedom and advances in democracy this country has witnessed. Nonetheless, this fact does not discount a more powerful reality: that advances in freedom and democracy have not yet outweighed or trumped the many white set-in-place barriers to full freedom, democracy, and equality that still massively confront Americans of color.

Omi and Winant's premature announcement of real racial democracy and a great transformation away from a racially oppressive US society neglects the ongoing social reality that whites, especially those in the top power positions, are largely the architects of past-and-present racial oppression, while people of color are by-and-large the subjects of that continuing oppression. This large-scale, centuries-old, white-framed societal organization of racial groups severely restricts major moves to thoroughgoing democracy and reflects whites' regular regeneration of control over political, economic, and other social structures. Without acknowledging and systematically theorizing whites' central role as the active creators and maintainers of systemically racist societies such as the United States, Omi and Winant's racial formation theory fails to address a still vivid racist empirical reality and to advance numerous key theoretical understandings of contemporary racism matters.

Conclusion

Omi and Winant have argued that systemic racism theory's accent on the ubiquitous societal power of systemic racism and its white frame is too strong and offers no room for people of color and anti-racist whites to combat these racist social structures and forces.[26] Often they ask either/or questions that allow no room for theoretical nuance, such as "Is white racism so ubiquitous that no meaningful political challenge can be mounted against it?" A nuanced response to Omi and Winant's question would be that systemic racism, and the whites who perpetuate it, can both be ubiquitous and at the same time "meaningfully challenged." For Omi and Winant, a vague abstract concept of "race," one that is constantly shifting, supersedes the empirical, concrete, and often enduring realities of systemic racism and white oppression demonstrated in numerous field studies of US society conducted by researchers who have developed institutional, structural, and systemic racism theory. They also claim that "race" somehow "exceeds and transcends racism—thereby allowing resistance to racism. Race, therefore is more than 'racism.'" Oddly enough, while critical of systemic racism theory's arguments of whites' substantial racialized power in society and its critical assessments of notions that racial democracy and racial progress are unrealized ideals at present, Omi and Winant do sometimes indicate that they agree with a less optimistic view of US racial matters.[27]

Omi and Winant chide systemic racism theorists for supposedly arguing that resistance to systemic racism is "futile." While the white racial frame is extremely powerful and the other aspects of white-imposed systemic racism are pervasive and persistent, at no point have systemic racism theorists argued that individual and group resistance is "futile." Indeed, systemic racism analysts have spent much research effort empirically assessing and fully theorizing the important agency of people of color, and of a modest minority of progressive whites, who have worked for centuries to reduce white-racist practices and institutions.[28] Additionally, many developments in contemporary systemic racism theory are grounded in the theorizing and empirical fieldwork on issues of institutional racism done by African American and other analysts of color for more than two centuries. As we demonstrate in the chapters that follow, we ourselves locate the true spirit of and strides toward freedom, justice, human rights, and equality substantially in the societal goals and liberation movements of African Americans, other Americans of color, and progressive whites who have challenged systemic racism and other oppression over centuries. Moreover, we observe that many of the more useful conceptual tools in the study of racial matters today have emerged or been developed within a critical black tradition of knowledge and action, a tradition of thought and action that is basic to the development of systemic racism theory.

It is difficult to understand why formation theory neglects a systematic analysis of the far-reaching, persisting societal effects of whites' control and abuse of political, economic, and cultural power and of the intellectual and psychological dominance of white racial framing that runs deep among the white and other members and groups of racist societies. Despite the deeply engraved social realities associated with the historic white racial frame, social change regarding racial matters and challenges to the white racial frame have long occurred and are occurring, although we have not yet witnessed the major paradigmatic shift or great transformation to a true "racial democracy" that racial formation theory insists upon. The long dominant white racial frame is not absolute or omnipotent; the frame is constructed by human beings and therefore it can be changed or discarded. However, much of the current white frame has so far been remarkably enduring and more than potent enough to withstand most major challenges to it or to repair any significant damage to it. Having vast socioeconomic resources and economic domination, and with control of most state politics and the dominant sociocultural narratives, whites continue to exert great influence and power in systemically racist societies such as the United States.

However, as we detail in the next chapter, even with the disadvantages of little or lesser resources and power, the ideas and actions of racially subordinated peoples have created a consciousness and program that promotes real ideals of freedom, justice, democracy, and equality that contrast with the mostly rhetorical ideals with similar names that have long been articulated by most whites. These real ideals of freedom and justice have fueled many critical social movements, movements that have helped to expand human rights and have generated some moral and intellectual advancements for all residents of the United States and, indeed, of the globe.

Notes

1 For example, Thomàs Alamaguer, *Racial Fault Lines: The Historical Origins of White Supremacy in California* (Berkeley, CA: University of California Press, 2008); Claire Jean Kim, *Bitter Fruit: The Politics of Black-Korean Conflict in New York City* (New Haven, CT: Yale University Press, 2003).
2 For a summary, see Sean Elias, "Book Review" of Daniel Martinez HoSang, Oneka LaBennett, and Laura Pulido (eds.), *Racial Formation in the Twentieth First Century* (Berkeley, CA: University of California Press, 2014) in *Ethnic and Racial Studies*, 37(10) (2014): 219–21.
3 In this chapter and the next we further develop Joe Feagin and Sean Elias' analysis, "Rethinking Racial Formation Theory: A Systemic Racism Critique," *Ethnic and Racial Studies*, 36(6) (2013): 1–30.

4 See W.E.B. Du Bois, *Darkwater: Voices Behind the Veil* (New York: Humanity Books, 2003); Joe R. Feagin and Eileen O'Brien, *White Men on Race* (Boston: Beacon, 2003); Leslie H. Picca and Joe R. Feagin, *Two-Faced Racism: Whites in the Backstage and Frontstage* (New York: Routledge, 2007).
5 Whites are most responsible for perpetuating systemic racism, yet numerous people of color have participated in upholding it. See Feagin and Elias, "Rethinking Racial Formation." See also Michael Omi and Howard Winant, "Resistance is Futile? A Response to Feagin and Elias," *Ethnic and Racial Studies*, 36(6) (2012): 963. The claim that Omi and Winant take analysis of white agents and elites seriously is not backed up in *Racial Formation in the United States*, 3rd edn (New York: Routledge, 2015), which has little discussion of whites and no critical analysis of whites and their specific means of upholding systemically racist societies.
6 Frank Wu, *Yellow: Race in America Beyond Black and White* (New York: Basic Books, 2003); Richard Rodriquez, *Brown: The Last Discovery* (New York: Penguin, 2003).
7 See Linda Gottfredson, "Mainstream Science on Intelligence," *Wall Street Journal*, December 13, 1994; also see a letter making similar claims about whites' superior intelligence, signed by 50 distinguished scientists, including Arthur Jensen, in *American Psychologist*, 21 (1972): 973–5.
8 This quote appears in the second edition of Michael Omi and Howard Winant's *Racial Formation in the United States: From the 1960s to the 1990s*, 2nd edn (New York: Routledge, 1994), p. 59.
9 Omi and Winant, *Racial Formation in the United States*, 3rd edn (2015), p. 110.
10 Omi and Winant, *Racial Formation in the United States*, 2nd edn (1994), pp. 72–3.
11 Feagin and Elias, "Rethinking Racial Formation Theory," p. 943.
12 See Adia Harvey-Wingfield and Joe R. Feagin, *Yes We Can: White Racial Framing and the Obama Presidency*, 2nd edn (New York: Routledge, 2013).
13 Omi and Winant, *Racial Formation in the United States*, 3rd edn (2015), pp. 110–11.
14 Feagin and Elias, "Rethinking Racial Formation Theory", p. 944.
15 Ibid., p. 945.
16 See Joe R. Feagin, *White Party, White Government: Race, Class, and US Politics* (New York: Routledge, 2012).
17 Though not his exact intent, William J. Wilson's work reveals the embedded, deeply rooted racial conflict, contestation, and competition rooted in the economic realm.
18 Joe R. Feagin, *Racist America: Roots, Current Realities, and Future Reparations*, 3rd edn (New York: Routledge, 2014).
19 See John Hagen, *Who Are the Criminals? The Politics of Crime Policy from the Age of Roosevelt to the Age of Reagan* (Princeton, NJ: Princeton University Press, 2010).
20 The current majority-conservative Supreme Court's biases on racial relations often demonstrates an institutional stumbling block to true political contestation for some groups. See Feagin, *White Party, White Government*, passim.
21 Ibid.
22 Omi and Winant, *Racial Formation in the United States*, 3rd edn (2015), p. 128.
23 Ibid., pp. 109–10.
24 Omi and Winant, *Racial Formation in the United States*, 2nd edn (1994), pp. 66–7.
25 See especially W.E.B. Du Bois, *The Gift of Black Folk: The Negroes in the Making of America* (Garden City Park NY: Square One Publishers, 2009 [1924]); Stokely Carmichael (Kwame Ture) and Charles Hamilton, *Black Power: The Politics of Liberation* (New York: Vintage, 1994 [1967]). See also Feagin, *How Blacks Built America*.
26 See Feagin and Elias, "Rethinking Racial Formation Theory" and Omi and Winant, "Resistance is Futile?" See also Omi and Winant, *Racial Formation in the United States*, 3rd edn (2015), p. 130.

27 Ibid.
28 See, for example, Louwanda Evans, *Cabin Pressure: African American Pilots, Flight Attendants, and Emotional Labor* (Lanham, MD: Rowman & Littlefield, 2013); Joe Feagin and José Cobas, *Latinos Facing Racism: Discrimination, Resistance and Endurance* (New York: Paradigm/Routledge, 2014); and Feagin, *How Blacks Built America*.

PART III
SYSTEMIC RACISM THEORY
BACKGROUND AND OVERVIEW

CHAPTER 9
CRITICAL BLACK THEORY: FOUNDATIONS OF SYSTEMIC RACISM THEORY

Significant knowledge and research about racial matters is not limited to the ideas and methods of mainstream social scientists. A long tradition of counter-mainstream African American activists and social analysts have developed theoretical perspectives of racial realities and other social realities contrasting sharply with those of the mainstream social scientists of European descent. Systemic racism theory builds substantially on this counter-mainstream approach, what we identify as a *critical black tradition of social thought* or *critical black theory*. Adequately understanding US racial history and social context is impossible without knowledge of the insights, theoretical approaches, and empirical research of this long-marginalized critical tradition developed by black Americans. Since the 1700s, critical black theorists have developed many concepts and theoretical perspectives essential for better understanding racism issues, in both the past and the present.[1]

The following analysis reviews important ideas of pivotal critical black theorists and demonstrates how their key concepts and perspectives provide an alternative depiction of racial phenomena than the mainstream social sciences and supply intellectual fuel for today's black social scientists, other sociologists of color, and white sociologists who challenge dominant narratives of racial matters in mainstream social sciences. Without question, contemporary systemic racism theory, like many other critical social scientific perspectives, rests to a substantial degree on the shoulders of past and present critical black theorists who have provided a very rich tradition of theorizing white-racist societies.

Key Features of Critical Black Theory

Critical black theory is a centuries-old way of describing and theorizing the social world that exists mostly on the margins of intellectual history and the social sciences, largely unknown and under-studied. Despite its range of powerful insights, critical black theory has so far contributed modestly to mainstream social scientific knowledge, primarily because it faces marginalization or exclusion by whites, who dominate societal distribution of that knowledge. Critical black perspectives often stand in opposition to social science knowledge created by whites, offering significantly different viewpoints on human behavior and the social world. Critical black theory presents epistemological counter-frames to numerous ideas generated by mainstream scientists by providing counter-narratives that debunk many of the dominant white-framed narratives and perspectives on racial matters. Indeed, development of black counter-frames remains a longstanding activity and central form of black resistance to systemic white racism.[2]

A number of key features delineate and distinguish critical black theory, elements of theoretical strength that contemporary systemic racism theory seeks to emulate. To begin with, this black theory is "critical," that is, theory that challenges or responds strategically to disingenuous and damaging "master" narratives, dominant perspectives, and hegemonic belief systems about human beings and societal realities in many cases created by whites. The initial primary focus of critical black theory was a critique of Western slavery and European colonialism and a rejoinder to early extensive proclamations of white supremacy. Later, after the demise of formal slavery and colonialism, critical black theorists shifted to analyzing new social systems of white oppression, such as Jim Crow, apartheid in Africa, and neo-colonialism, as well as new forms of white racial framing legitimating such oppressive systems. A primary aspect of critical black theory, one also central to current systemic racism theory, is an ongoing critique of the ideas and methods of mainstream social science.

As these critical theorists and others have documented, mainstream social science work on racial issues is frequently uncritical or a-critical, thereby producing research and knowledge that directly or indirectly upholds and legitimates systemically racist societies. Mainstream social scientists generally misperceive the degree to which white racist framing and practices shape and define numerous aspects of contemporary Western societies, including the social sciences.

In addition to focusing on racial matters, critical black theory often addresses issues and social realities that closely relate to or somehow intersect with racial matters, such as class and gender oppression. Critical black theory also frequently focuses on the economy, polity, religion, culture, science, and international relations, among other topics. Early on, critical black theorists explored how racial matters shape global relations among nations and among different racial and ethnic groups within nations. Astute critical theorists such as W.E.B. Du Bois and Oliver Cox authored lucid descriptions, explanations, and critiques of Western colonialism, thereby directly or indirectly providing some conceptual tools for later theories such as world systems theory, dependency theory, and modernization theory. Today, as often in the past, much critical black theory is multidimensional, incorporating class analysis, political studies, or feminist perspectives, promoting social-justice perspectives such as critical public sociology, and aggressively and critically questioning the social worlds, ideologies, and institutions known as "Western civilization."

Additionally, critical black theorists frequently utilize diverse research methods, including ethnography, historical and literary analysis, biography, philosophy, cultural studies, and statistical analysis. Frequent use of historical analysis allows for contextualized understandings of social phenomena and knowledge of social practices and structures that precede and shape present-day social realities. Thus, understanding the significance of the past socio-racial realities and present-day effects of slavery systems and Jim Crow segregation has sharpened critical theorists' analyses of contemporary systemic racism. Critical black theory is generally more pragmatic than idealistic, centered on explaining empirical social realities as opposed to abstractly describing ideal social realities, and focused on delivering accurate if harsh empirical truths as opposed to overly optimistic versions of social reality. Critical black theorists have deconstructed democracy, freedom, equality, social progress, and other Western ideal types of social arrangements that typically do *not* fit much of the actual social reality faced by black Americans and other people of color. Additionally, critical black theorists tend to dissect the white-constructed social structures and macro-level phenomena that restrict or enable human agency when they study racial matters, whereas the majority of mainstream social scientists studying racial matters mostly focus on individual human agency, micro-level to meso-level social phenomena, or group statistics.

Differences between the theories of the mainstream social sciences and critical black theory appear in yet other areas of social analysis. The mainstream social sciences have a long history of developing intentionally biased theories that glorify whites, their intelligence, morality, physical appearance, or social organization (e.g., white society, culture, civilization). Simultaneously, they often pathologize people of color and their social organization ("dangerous ghettos," "underdeveloped Third World"). Critical black theory, on the other hand, has long offered much more balanced views of the social pathologies, social contributions, and positive and negative social actions of whites and blacks.[3] Indeed, mainstream social scientists of racial matters have a habit of avoiding critical and systematic analyses of whites as a still-controlling racial group, whereas critical black theorists investigate whites' moral and intellectual hypocrisy, power abuses, and enduring control of the economy, politics, and culture industry. In contrast to many mainstream social scientists who attempt to theorize "race" as intangible, unstable, or in decline, critical black theorists frequently analyze the tangible and continuing empirical realities of well-institutionalized "racism" created by whites. Conventional "race" theory is a product of mainstream social science, whereas *racism* theory with its critical central analysis of whites is more the product of the critical black theory tradition.

In opposition to the idea that the social sciences are colorblind and post-racial, critical black theorists, other critical theorists of color, and critical white theorists have formed organizations and authored research presentations that regularly address issues of institutional and systemic racism. Mainstream social scientists who espouse post-racial and colorblindness notions often seem unaware of the reality or significance of racial divisions within their own disciplines. For example, the field of sociology reflects well the persistence of the color line and concern with racial matters.[4] The American Sociological Association (ASA) stands as the primary professional organization of US sociology and to a large degree represents the mainstream. Within the ASA, however, several sections have developed along racial and ethnic lines. Sections on Asia/Asian-American and Latino/a sociology exist in the ASA, with an indigenous peoples section being considered. Outside the ASA, black sociologists have formed their own Association of Black Sociologists (ABS), with a journal devoted to the study of racial matters. Other social scientists also recognize contemporary racial-ethnic divisions within their disciplines. In an edited volume, *African American Perspectives on Political Sciences* (2007), black political scientists recount many concerns expressed by black sociologists, including academic segregation and marginalization, whites' power in dictating the subject matter, and the persistence of a-critical analyses of racial matters.[5]

For the most part, the mainstream social sciences tacitly accept, justify, or overlook the functionality and structure of extant racialized systems, major institutions, and dominant cultural narratives of contemporary societies. In contrast, critical black theory much more often demonstrates the dysfunctionality of these systems for many groups in contemporary racist societies and raises major concerns about persisting structural inequalities in human group relations. Mainstream social scientific approaches tend to view social problems as solvable in practice and US society as generally decent, improving, and operational, if in need of occasional reform. In contrast, critical black theory views certain US societal problems as being central issues and presently insurmountable, and society as being largely inegalitarian and exploitative—so much so that revolutionary or drastic social change, not reform, appears to be the only means of transforming such a society. We now turn to an intellectual-historical review of critical black theory.

Pre-Civil War Critical Black Theory

While any breakdown of critical black theory by period is artificial, to simplify the following analysis we divide critical black theory into two major periods: pre-Civil War theory and post-Civil War theory. Within these periods are important sub-periods, as we make clear below. Critical black theory originated around the same time as the emergence of the European social sciences (late 1700s to mid-1800s) in an effort to present a black perspective on societal realities and a pragmatic plan to counter growing white-racist framing and practices and challenge white power structures built on enslavement and colonization of people of color. Early black critical analysts present substantially different portraits of society and human relations than their white counterparts, especially when analyzing racial issues. Black social theorists, many of them also activists, identified the inhumane and immoral arrangements of slavery and colonialism by which whites exploited people of color, explaining the negative consequences of these racist systems for human beings and societies. In contrast to white analysts who early shaped social scientific thinking, black theorists challenged whites' dominant framing of their racial superiority and the racial inferiority of people of color. Indeed, the blueprints for institutional and systemic racism theory discovered in early black theorizing appear to us to provide some of the best early sources for contemporary social scientists to use in developing a sound theory of racial matters in Western societies, past and present.

Long before the term "critical theory" was coined to describe the analyses of Europe's Frankfurt School of social theorists, US black social analysts in the late 1700s and 1800s had developed truly *critical* social theories of socio-racial matters. These black theorists produced the first analytical critiques of the ways that racial oppression had become fully *institutionalized* and *systemic*. They critically assessed, often in depth, Western slavery and colonial systems and described how racial matters substantially shaped the colonial society that became the new United States. Critical black analysts offered alternative explanations of racial matters that challenged white-framed racial theories developed by white political and intellectual leaders, including early social scientists.

It is impossible to represent fully the breadth and depth of this early black theory. Much of the earliest critical black analysis was oral and not historically preserved, and during the period of US colonization and slavery, the writings of black Americans usually faced great difficulties in finding publishing outlets and historical preservation.

Despite these odds, numerous critical writings of black social thinkers have survived. These take the form of protest pamphlets, autobiographical narratives, sermons and speeches, and articles in the first black newspapers, as well as in a few white journals in the US and overseas. In the pamphlets are powerful calls for social justice, abolition of slavery, and the demise of colonialism, as well as broader analyses of human practices, group relations, ideologies, and social institutions in the slavery-based US and other societies. Pamphlets were the most widespread, effective, and accessible form of written communication by early black analysts. Some of the earliest pamphlets that exhibit critical black thought were Absalom Jones and Richard Allen's "A Narrative of the Proceedings of the Black People during the Late Awful Calamity in Philadelphia" (1794) and Prince Hall's "A Charge" (1797).[6] Jones and Allen's narrative provides a critique of the white supremacist views of black inferiority and the white supremacist practices of the slavery system. They challenge whites to "try the experiment of taking a few black children, and cultivate their minds with the same care, and let them have the same prospect in view, as to living in the world, as you would wish for your own children, you find them, upon trial, they were not inferior in mental endowments." Speaking of slavery's evil and the fate of racial oppressors, they write, "how hateful slavery is in the sight of that God who hath destroyed kings and princes for their oppression of poor slaves."[7] Often, in an effort to appeal to human beings' sense of right and wrong, the pamphlets of critical black thinkers summoned the reader's moral consciousness and sense of social justice by referencing religious and democratic ideals as well as the principles of humanity.

The first half of the nineteenth century witnessed a flurry of pamphleteering by critical black thinkers, men and women such as James Forten, Russell Parrott, Elizabeth Wicks, Maria Stewart, Mary Ann Shadd, and David Walker, to name just a few.[8] Noticeable here is the cadre of black women theorists writing pamphlets and organizing social movements, many of whom were early founders of US feminist thought and practice. They addressed social concerns of women and of society in general, and of black feminist and community issues in particular. These often forgotten social thinkers were frequently anti-racism activists, and early proponents of activist scholarship.

Early black women theorists such as Wicks, Shadd, and Stewart discussed the hardships and strides of the black community in spite of oppression, argued for social justice and black liberation, and further illuminated the injustices of systemic racism. Shadd believed the liberation of black Americans required denouncing US citizenship and migrating to Canada, noting that there has been an "increasing desire on the part of colored people" to learn about Canada, "since passage of the odious fugitive Slave Law has made a residence in the United States to many of them dangerous to the extreme."[9]

In a major 1833 Boston speech the country's first black female political analyst, Maria Stewart, instructed members of the black community to seek self-empowerment sapped by years of enslavement, and in a defiant tone, wrote a critical sociological analysis:

> The unfriendly whites first drove the Native American from his much loved home. Then they stole our fathers from their peaceful and quiet dwellings, and brought them hither, and made bond-men and bond-women of them and their little ones; they have obliged our brethren to labor, kept them in utter ignorance, nourished them in vice, and raised them in degradation; and now that we have enriched their soil, and filled their coffers, they say that we are not capable of becoming like white men, and that we never can rise to respectability in this country. They would drive us to a strange land. But before I go, the bayonet shall pierce me through. African rights and liberties is a subject that ought to fire the breast of every free man of color in these United States, and excite in his bosom a lively, deep, decided and heart-felt interest.[10]

Among numerous critical black male theorists in this early period, James Forten addressed the need to uphold the ideals and laws of equality, insisting that the "same power which protects the white man, should protect the black." Russell Parrott's pamphlet "An Oration on the Abolition of the Slave Trade" delivers an uncompromising critique of Europeans' "universal desire of gain" that led to enslavement of Africans. Parrott observes that the "discovery of the new world; which, to one portion of the human family, has afforded such advantages, to the unfortunate African, has been the source of the greatest misery; it was the precursor of his sufferings… and it removed him many ages from that state of civilization, which his natural genius entitled him to enjoy."[11]

One of the most impressive and widely circulated anti-racism pamphlets was David Walker's *Appeal*, a scathing critique of chattel enslavement of Africans and European American two-facedness about liberty and justice ideals. A young Boston scholar and printer, Walker explicitly condemns whites who created and maintain slavery systems, points out the hypocrisy between whites' words of democracy, Christianity, and civilization and contrasting deeds of racial oppression, immorality, and barbarity; and he outlines a program for actual black liberation. He specifically identifies whites as the creators, benefactors, and perpetuators of systemic racism in Western slavery societies. Of the critical black works of this period, Walker's *Appeal* is the most direct, unwavering, and brutally honest critique of systemic racism. He provides an analytical breakdown of the dominant white racist framing of black Americans and the first methodically delivered counter-frame challenging that dominant white frame.[12] His writings represent an early model for critical "whiteness studies" that would much later be developed by W.E.B. Du Bois, and then by other black and white scholars.

Throughout the *Appeal*, Walker delineates whites' oppression and dehumanization of blacks, black labor's enrichment of whites, and slavery and colonialism as the underbelly of modern Western civilization and society. He offers critiques of the dominant white racial frame, especially dismantling whites' beliefs in their superior beauty, intelligence, moral standing, and social value, and he vigorously opposes white arguments of black inferiority. He addresses the social ills associated with white "avarice," condemning the money generated by the enslavement and exploitation of black Americans. He identifies whites' obsession with racialized power and the contradictions in whites' sociopolitical system and ideology of democracy and whites' moral system grounded in Christianity.

Along with his critique of whites, Walker offers several global messages "to the coloured citizens of the world" and, "in particular, and very expressly, to those of the United States of America."[13] He addresses and touts the importance of black education, self-direction, and self-worth. For Walker, black Americans are as "American" as white Americans and hold a well-earned stake in the new US society. They also deserve recognition and reward for building the wealth and societal infrastructure of the United States and other white-led nations that have become rich on the coerced labor and unimaginable sacrifices of people of color. Demonstrating the revolutionary side of his critical theory, Walker suggests that blacks have every right, indeed a duty, to rebel against this white tyranny—that is, to use ideas to battle white misinformation as well as to employ physical force, if necessary, to offset oppressive white violence.

The origins of social-justice-oriented social science and the critical social thought underlying numerous social movements advancing positive social change, such as the broad international sociology of human rights, largely begin with these early examples of critical black theory. Pamphlets by African American social thinkers appearing throughout the first half of the 1800s developed pronounced critiques of slavery systems, and its main features of white oppression, black subjugation, conflictual human relations, and excessive wealth generation for whites. In addition to those mentioned, numerous other theorists contributed to the pamphleteering and other social movements for black liberation and the betterment of society, astute analysts such as Robert Purvis, Henry Highland Garnet, Martin Delany, William Wells Brown, Alexander Crummell, and Frederick Douglass. Many of these thinkers, from this era to the early Jim Crow years, wrote other important works in addition to these pamphlets and tracts. They wrote for black newspapers and penned historical and sociological analyses, anthropological studies, novels, poetry, spirituals, and autobiographies.

As noted earlier (Chapter 4), African American scholar Rutledge Dennis has argued that autobiographical narratives can advance sociological theory. Autobiographers with a critical eye are often exemplary social theorists, and W.E.B. Du Bois in particular stands as one of the great examples of biography-grounded critical theory.[14] Before Du Bois, numerous black Americans with firsthand knowledge of slave and "free" societies wrote accurate accounts of these contrasting social worlds and various experiences of oppression. In contrast to early white social scientists' uncritical, indeed often positive, portraits of black enslavement, early critical black autobiographical narratives painted a different picture—an unsavory image of the inhumanity and inegalitarianism of black enslavement. Broad critical insights about the slavery society are found in autobiographies such as James Pennington's *The Fugitive Blacksmith* (1849), Frederick Douglass' three autobiographies (1845–81), and Harriet Jacobs' *Incidents in the Life of a Slave Girl* (1861), the latter one of very few by a black woman.[15] All describe the operation of an essentially totalitarian and systemically racist society. These critical black autobiographical analyses clearly document the white social pathologies linked to slavery. They show that this oppression involved more than occasional negative racial framing and brutal actions of a few whites, for it represented the ongoing ideas and well-institutionalized actions of many millions of white individuals and families that benefited greatly from a systemically racist US society.

Most of these black autobiographies demonstrate that during slavery whites were not as valorous (i.e., superior) and blacks not as passive (i.e., inferior) as was then depicted in dominant white narratives by social scientists and others. Their ethnographic detail is convincing, especially when considering the restrictive contexts of slavery and absence of fieldwork training. One notable autobiographer who brought the social world of slavery to light was Frederick Douglass, who wrote three probing narratives, *Narrative of the Life of Frederick Douglass* (1845), *My Bondage and My Freedom* (1855), and, *Life and Times of Frederick Douglass* (1881).[16] A vast amount of critical analysis appears therein. As historian C. Vann Woodward observed, Douglass "does not stop at recording the sufferings and his protest [of slave societies], as most slave authors do. He analyzes perceptively what slavery did to children, mothers, and fathers of slave families, and what it did to drivers, overseers, masters, and their families."[17] These sociologically insightful narratives of Douglass are only a few samples of the numerous informatively rich autobiographical accounts provided by enslaved and formerly enslaved black Americans.

Along with pamphlets and autobiographical writings, another key location of early critical black thought was the black newspaper, a primary organ of information in the black community. More than 20 black newspapers appeared in northern states before the Civil War, with *Freedom's Journal*, edited by Samuel Cornish and John Russwurm, being the first (1827–9), and Frederick Douglass' *North Star* (1847–1860) being probably the most influential. In addition to various articles, editorials, and community announcements, these early black newspapers published excerpts from books, sermons, speeches, autobiographies, and pamphlets of critical black social thinkers.

The African American newspapers offered unique perspectives and counter-narratives on society not discovered in white-owned papers. Their central tasks included pushing for slavery's abolition, exposing slavery's evils, promoting community educational issues, and providing coverage of local and national news of especial interest to blacks. *Freedom's Journal* noted that for "too long have others spoken for us, too long has the public been deceived by misrepresentations."[18] William Lloyd Garrison's white-run paper, *The Liberator*, offered an outlet for the concerns of white abolitionists, but Douglass and others believed that a black-run newspaper was necessary for fully presenting black perspectives on societal realities. On one level, Douglass' *North Star* proclaimed "truth is of no color," yet, more pragmatically, the underlying goal of the paper was to expose myths about slavery and about blacks told by whites and, in contrast, to present the truths about society revealed in critical black thought.[19]

The pre-Civil War writings of black theorists forcefully articulated black perceptions of society and served as inspiration for countering the extreme oppression that defined southern slavery, as well as the slavery and Jim Crow segregation then in the north. As these theorists remind us, a good portion of northern industry profited from slavery and most northern whites were not welcoming toward "fugitive" blacks migrating north. Most early critical black social thought contradicts the social perspectives of early white social scientists. For instance, Auguste Comte's social evolutionary theory and theory of organicism established justifications for racial hierarchies and assigned different worth to human beings (i.e., racial groups), while Benjamin Banneker argued (in a letter to Thomas Jefferson about his racist views) that it was necessary "to eradicate the train of absurd and false ideas and opinions [about black inferiority], which so generally prevails with respect to [blacks]." According to Banneker, "one universal Father have given being to us all; and that he hath made us all one flesh… and endowed us all with the same faculties."[20] Similarly, David Walker challenged the famous Alexis de Tocqueville's openly racist views that the "European is to the other races of mankind, what man is to the lowest animals," that the Negro "admires his tyrants more than he hates them, and finds joy… in the servile imitation of those who oppress him," and that the "power of thought appears to him a useless gift of Providence."[21] For Walker, those whites who enslave blacks exhibit barbarity, cruelty, and deceit. In contrast to de Tocqueville's understanding of whites as "superior in intelligence, in power, and in enjoyment," Walker bluntly finds whites who perpetuate systemic racism to be "an unjust, jealous, unmerciful, avaricious and bloodthirsty set of beings, always seeking power and authority."[22]

The critical black theoretical writings of Douglass, Harriet Jacobs, Maria Stewart, and others intellectually challenged the kinds of prominent pro-slavery arguments constructed by early white US sociologists George Fitzhugh and Henry Hughes, which asserted that societies need to be organized along unequal racial lines or risk disorder, that blacks were inferior to whites, and that nature and religion condone or necessitate black enslavement (see Chapter 1). Hughes' *Treatise on Sociology* (1854) argued that slave societies were divinely sanctioned and natural, operating according to God's handiwork and the laws of nature. In contrast, according to Frederick Douglass, the social system of slavery represents "a grand aggregation of human horrors" and the "very accompaniments of the slave system stamp it as the offspring of hell itself."[23] Countering Fitzhugh's and Hughes' theoretical defense of black inferiority, the ever-sharp Maria Stewart argued forcefully that "it is not the color of the skin that makes the man, but it is the principles formed within the soul."[24]

In our view, contemporary social scientists studying US racial matters would do well to spend much time examining the socially and historically significant concepts and sophisticated theoretical perspectives in these pre-Civil War black writings. Early on, these critical black social theorists developed important concepts such as *racial oppression* and significant theories of white supremacy and related social matters, thereby illuminating the fundamental elements of systemic racism and whites' associated oppression of people of color, then and now.

Critical Black Theory since the Civil War

Post-Civil War critical black theory reveals a trend of criticisms of racial matters similar to the critical pre-war perspectives. Not long after that war and the short and failed era of federally pressured Reconstruction in the south, one detects a cautionary and pessimistic tone about racial matters among late nineteenth-century critical black theorists.[25] While the war emancipated enslaved Americans, these critical theorists documented the persistence of a systemically racist society and dramatically unequal (termed "Jim Crow") racial group relations still organized in terms of a white-framed racial hierarchy.

Those who witnessed the slavery and post-slavery eras, such as Frederick Douglass and Martin Delany, demonstrated the close linkages between the two, specifically the ongoing racial segregation, vast socioeconomic inequalities, and advancement of white power and control of resources and socioeconomic capital. As they pointedly explained, slavery was dead, but systemically racist structures—the government, economy, dominant culture, educational system, and much of civil society—were still firmly in place, guided by the same white supremacist framing of the earlier slavery society.

Still some critical black social thinkers expressed cautiously optimistic visions of a future more egalitarian society and of the role of black agency in this potential transformation. Douglass, who believed in black assimilation into white institutions, oscillated between optimism and pessimism about the future, although in his last decade he spoke pessimistically of the firmness of the US color line. In contrast to Douglass' assimilationist goals, Martin Delany, often called the father of black nationalism, and Edward Blyden, called the father of Pan-Africanism, argued that whites would likely long remain hostile toward and oppressive of black Americans. They contended that whites would continue to degrade and exclude blacks, denying black knowledge, contributions, and talents. Therefore, blacks should shun unifying with white oppressors and consider emigrating to Africa or other friendlier lands overseas.

Numerous other critical black social analysts wrote about human relations and societal organization in these oppressive eras, including William Wells Brown, Henry Highland Garnet, Alexander Crummell, Henry M. Turner, Charlotte Grimké, and George Washington Williams, to name a few. Several saw the necessity of integrating a critical history with critical social theory and empirical analysis, thereby pioneering work in historical sociology and historical-theoretical social science. Henry Highland Garnet's *The Past and Present Condition, and Destiny of the Colored Races* (1848), William Wells Brown's *The Rising Son: Antecedents and Advancement of the Colored Race* (1874), and George Washington Williams' *History of the Negro Race in America, 1619–1880* (1883) develop historically oriented critical sociological analyses.[26] They advance a historical social science that moves beyond surface-level descriptions and social investigation toward more theoretically developed critical analyses that probe more deeply into socio-historical realities.

Writing in the late nineteenth century, many of these black social analysts recognized that the post-war Reconstruction had failed, a clear sign that the federal government continued to uphold a white-dominated, systemically racist society, and that the economy was firmly controlled by a white elite that persisted in large-scale exploitation of emancipated black workers and newly arrived immigrants of color. The systemically racist system known as "Jim Crow segregation" replaced slavery. In this system, white domination was still visibly stitched into this new societal fabric. Jim Crow racism was still overt on many levels, yet some whites were increasingly concerned to appear less blatantly exploitative and power abusive than under slavery. For example, early white twentieth-century social scientists accented a supposed objectivity or value neutrality, frequently in a move toward an early version of "colorblindness" in research on racial matters. At the same time, most whites in the social sciences and other avenues of knowledge production expressed strong beliefs in the great societal and social scientific progress assumed to be observable in the "civilization" and "modernization" of people of European descent.

The new generation of critical black theorists further questioned the taken-for-granted white narratives of freedom, democracy, globalization, civilization, capitalism, science, and social progress. They viewed the growing white sciences as fallible and often racially biased, white practice of Christianity as often racist religiosity, and white administration of the government as generally racist state control. Many clearly understood how and why Jim Crow's systemic racism was not much different from that of the slavery era. After more than two and a half centuries of extreme white oppression, black Americans were still cut off from the fruits of real social justice and democracy, and their societal advancement and freedoms were severely restricted.

Experiencing ongoing white oppression, and at the same time faced with the challenges of new technological and other societal developments largely occurring in the "white world," post-Civil War black theorists developed innovative social theories and analytical techniques. Many noticeably oscillate between optimism and pessimism about the character of US society and its general population, demonstrating the epistemological challenges of pinpointing and confirming certain socio-racial realities. Some viewed black assimilation to white institutions as the optimum path, others envisioned a new society defined by real cultural pluralism, and yet others perceived black separatism and nationalism as the solution for oppressed African Americans. These post-war theorists developed keen observations about how capitalism remains a social system invested heavily in the perpetuation of systemic racism. Even major theorists who exhibit some Eurocentrism, such as Alexander Crummell and W.E.B. Du Bois, are quite cognizant and critical of white racism and expose the major limitations of white knowledge and morality, of white-structured societies, and of white-controlled international relations.[27]

Consider the central themes surrounding racial matters discussed by the critical black theorists of the late nineteenth and early twentieth century, many of which have become commonplace in contemporary critical analyses of racial matters while others remain severely neglected. These include critiques of Western imperialism, colonialism and related wars, science and capitalism, extreme racial group inequalities, and weak democracy. These theorists repeatedly link these topics to the dominant white supremacist worldview of their era. Emerging from their critiques of the new forms of white supremacy were the fields later known as "whiteness studies" and "black studies." With insightful regularity, these black theorists delineated white power structures and abuses and noted the significance of the well-institutionalized residential segregation, lack of job opportunities, poor educational facilities, and inadequate health care that damaged black families and communities. In addition to honestly addressing black pathologies, they discussed positive aspects of black culture and resistance to oppression, frequently outlining plans for empowerment and liberation—including bold views of black nationalism and Pan-Africanism. Often demonstrating a broad global perspective, they also discussed links between US oppression of people of color and oppression of people of color worldwide, including the marginalization of people of color throughout the Western colonial empires.[28]

Another important contribution by these critical thinkers to social scientific analysis generally, and racial matters particularly, is their understanding of social intersectionality, a way of explaining intersecting social worlds pioneered by pre-Civil War black theorists such as Maria Stewart and Harriet Jacobs. In the nineteenth century they thoroughly explored what has come to be called the *intersectionality* of racial, gender, sexuality, and class issues. Later on, social science theorists such as W.E.B. Du Bois, Oliver C. Cox, and Anna J. Cooper also illuminated the importance of intersectionality, specifically that of racial and class issues and racial and gender issues.[29] A century ago, Du Bois explicitly analyzed the topic of intersectionality and determined that these oppressions can vary socially and historically but are of equal social weight at different times and social contexts.[30] He and others accented how individuals negotiate the intersecting social structures and form identities reflecting these intersections. Cox perceived the interrelation of race and class in his intersectional analyses of racism and capitalism, and Cooper particularly examined gender, race, and class issues in education.

Many black social thinkers, especially those associated with the 1920s–1930s Negro Renaissance, which was a cultural and intellectual revolution, emphasized the idea that social knowledge is discovered in the arts and humanities as well as the sciences. These perceptive analysts demonstrated that one can discover important truths about society in literature, plays, philosophy, and music—including truths about social reality not readily revealed by social science. During the first decades of the twentieth century, art, social critique, and resistance ideas combined forces in the work of a long list of black women and men of great talent and genius, including Langston Hughes, Jean Toomer, Claude McKay, Countee Cullen, Helene Johnson, Sterling Brown, Paul Dunbar, Zora Neale Hurston, Richard Wright, Nella Larsen, and Jessie Fauset, among many others. Numerous black leaders in this era were very politically oriented, such as Alain Locke, T. Thomas Fortune, Carter G. Woodson, Monroe Trotter, Ralph Bunche, and A. Philip Randolph. While many optimistically celebrated the birth of a new black community, others retained skeptical, critical, and admonitory outlooks directed at white-racist institutions. Some adopted a revolutionary tone stressing active resistance and counter-actions toward oppression—for example, Claude McKay, who wrote an important poem that begins, "If we must die, let it not be like hogs hunted and penned in an inglorious spot, while round us bark the mad and hungry dogs, making their mock at our accursed lot."[31]

Early African American Sociologists

In the early decades of the twentieth century, an important group of black social scientists emerged, notably in sociology. Like their white counterparts, this group was almost exclusively male, a sign of the heavy gender segregation existing alongside the pervasive racial segregation in early twentieth-century academia. This group included such University of Chicago sociologists as Oliver Cox, Charles Johnson, E. Franklin Frazier, Bertram Doyle, St. Clair Drake, and Horace Cayton. Highly constrained by a professional social science field determinedly controlled by whites, most largely avoided critical analyses of the white racist society around them. They mostly engaged in descriptive social research, often on the neglected problems of black communities, but typically avoided probing analyses of the racial causes of these community problems. Under the tutelage of all-white professors, these early black sociologists were pressed to utilize white-framed ideas and research plans for their field studies on their own communities.

Nonetheless, some did periodically suggest important critical insights about US society that detoured from their descriptive approaches and challenged white-framed perspectives on the country's racist realities. For example, Johnson's *The Collapse of the Cotton Tendency* (1935) addresses the "age-old custom in the South" of whites keeping blacks in peonage, a common impoverishment practice in rural areas from the 1930s to at least the 1960s. In *Patterns of Negro Segregation*, Johnson notes that the "dominant society" (his code for whites) is the root cause of racial segregation, inequality, and racial group unrest, writing that "there can be no group segregation without discrimination."[32] Doyle's important essay, "The Etiquette of Race Relations—Past, Present, and Future" relates the disturbing observation that "over three hundred years, an etiquette of race relations has governed the association of Negroes and white persons."[33] Additionally, Drake and Cayton's masterpiece study *Black Metropolis* (1945), documents the dynamics of color-coded racial relations, especially the power of the white racial frame in creating and maintaining a "hierarchy of color" even within black communities.[34]

As discussed earlier, Oliver Cox was one of these Chicago-trained sociologists who set himself apart from others by delivering highly critical analyses of whites' historical development of anti-black racism in their pursuit of capitalistic profit, societal power, and dominant control over nature and other human beings. His deeply insightful and prescient analyses explore subjects now central to contemporary racial analysis and to many understandings of critical race and systemic racism theories—patterns of institutional racism, racial-group exploitation, effects of industrialization on racial relations, and the inseparable relationship between modern capitalism and institutionalized racism. Additionally, Cox critically surveyed an array of still current research topics including black migration, job discrimination, black employment and business, urban and rural black communities, and the black family. He also pioneered in probing analyses of policing, the law, and role of the white ruling class in establishing and intertwining capitalism and racial oppression.[35] Importantly, he was an early, often lonely critic, of major white social theorists of racial matters of the mid-twentieth century such as Robert Park and Gunnar Myrdal (see Chapter 1).

Along with the more noted black sociologists who studied at Chicago, numerous others outside of this flagship university contributed to the development of social knowledge concerning turn-of-the-century societal transformations. These included sociologists such as George Haynes, Ira Reid, Kelly Miller, Butler Jones, Walter Chivers, Charles Gomillion, Joseph Himes, Allison Davis, Anna J. Cooper, and Wilmoth Carter.[36] Reading the works of these mostly forgotten or marginalized African American sociologists reveals a distinctive tradition of trenchant social thought and pioneering social analysis on a range of vital social topics, from the education of black women and applied sociology for changing unjust racial relations to the distinctive concerns of the black family model and importance of researching and cultivating racial consciousness. Today, sociologists of knowledge might well ask why these critical black sociologists' understandings of US society frequently counter much of the white-framed analyses of white social scientists of their era and of the present era.

Ida B. Wells-Barnett, W.E.B. Du Bois, Booker T. Washington, and Marcus Garvey

In the late nineteenth and early twentieth centuries, two African American sociologists were especially important in laying the foundations for much subsequent critical black social thought and action—Ida B. Wells-Barnett and W.E.B. Du Bois. Wells-Barnett and Du Bois pioneered critical public sociology aimed at promoting social justice, and they frequently exposed pressing societal issues that mainstream social scientists avoided. Aware of how powerfully white racism routinely shaped the United States, Wells-Barnett and Du Bois devoted much of their social science research and writings to explaining the various structural and institutional components of this white oppression. This difficult task included investigating societal problems stemming from unequal racial group relations and the ways that whites manipulated the meanings of "race" to justify the subjugation of people of color and position themselves atop the society's entrenched racial hierarchy. Both combined critical scholarship with much social action. Wells-Barnett operated as both a journalist writing sociologically and publicly about the white racial brutalities directed toward the black population and as a social activist and early public sociologist who led dangerous anti-lynching campaigns. A scholar-activist for social justice like Wells-Barnett, Du Bois was both a sociologist who critically analyzed US colonialism and institutionalized racism and an activist for racial justice on numerous fronts: as an intellectual shaping public knowledge, as a founding member of the NAACP (and long-term editor of its paper, *The Crisis*), and as an overseas "racial diplomat" assiduously working for social justice and change globally.

While we do not have space here to dig deeply into the sociological work of Wells-Barnett and Du Bois, we can briefly highlight some of their key theories and approaches to producing valuable social knowledge. Wells-Barnett's greatest attribute as a sociologist was probably delivering straightforward and readable public accounts of harsh social realities and human brutalities associated with the systemic racism of the Jim Crow era. Risking white violence, she detailed the lynching, mutilation, rape, and other forms of abuse directed at blacks by whites who typically acted with impunity for their racist, illegal, and immoral actions. Faced with death threats, destruction of her business, and forced violently from her hometown, Wells-Barnett nevertheless continued her campaign to educate the public about the sociology of lynching and other forms of white violence used to maintain white power over black communities. She was thus a courageous pioneer in critical public sociology, a social science practitioner empirically correcting mistruths about society while promoting social justice.

In her important books, *Southern Horrors: Lynch Laws in All Its Phases* (1892) and *A Red Record* (1895), Wells early documented the white racist framing, immorality, and hypocrisy of the US criminal justice system.[37] She demonstrated how the white policing system mostly ignored white lynch mobs murdering black men for fictional or actual violations of Jim Crow norms, while routinely exonerating white men who had murdered black men, raped black women, or stolen black property. She collected and presented data dispelling exaggerated myths about black men who rape white women. Instead, Wells demonstrated how white mob violence often targeted hardworking blacks competing with whites in the economy, black men having consensual relationships with white women, and blacks who failed to relinquish their property or services to whites. She found that lynchings and other white acts of violence were rooted in the white desire to terrorize blacks into a subordinate racial position. Along with her analysis of white violence directed at the black community, Wells examines racial and gender/sexuality intersectionality issues, especially the white racist stereotype of the purity of white woman as opposed to the racist stereotype of black women as sexually wanton.

W.E.B. Du Bois stands as a central figure of critical black social theory and analysis, writing extensively over decades about human beings and the social world. Using various innovative research methods, he researched important racial matters affecting the black community, including the white oppression of black Americans and other people of color. Du Bois was a scholar-activist, a critical public sociologist who campaigned for human rights over a long lifetime. He addressed black American oppression, the oppression of blacks and other people of color overseas, and even working-class whites oppressed by modern capitalism. From his writings, many critical analysts have drawn key insights about racial matters, including those about the color line, double consciousness experienced by people of color in white-dominated societies, racism and colonialism, exclusion of people of color from democracy, diversity of the black community, the character of the white world and its pathologies, and whiteness generally. He headed the Atlanta Sociological Laboratory, one of the first sociology departments, and conducted some of the first multi-methodological sociological research in the field. His research book, *The Philadelphia Negro* (1899), is the first major field study of urban racial matters and a model of ethnographic fieldwork predating the famous Chicago School of urban ethnography by nearly a quarter of a century.[38] One of the mainstream social sciences' greatest intellectual sins is neglect of Du Bois' pathbreaking works,[39] and neglect of the works of other forward-thinking critical social theorists such as Oliver Cox.

In *The World and Africa* (1946) and *Color and Democracy* (1945), Du Bois analyzes the destructive behavior associated with global colonization by whites. In *The Souls of Black Folk* (1903) and other works, he outlines a theory of cultural pluralism and of racial egalitarianism. As we noted, Du Bois periodically used the autobiographical method in theorizing larger social realities, including systemic racism and whites' power structures. An important way of "elucidating the inner meaning and significance of that race problem" is "by explaining it in terms of the one human life that I know best. I have written then what is meant to be not so much my autobiography as the autobiography of a concept of race."[40] Like Frederick Douglass, he wrote multiple autobiographical narratives that critically described racial matters discerned through his vast array of life experiences, including *The Souls of Black Folk* (1903), *Dusk of Dawn* (1940), and *The Autobiography of W.E.B. Du Bois* (1969). Through this extensive personal experience with systemic racism, Du Bois famously discerned that "the problem of the twentieth century is the problem of the color line."[41]

Booker T. Washington and Marcus Garvey, two important post-Civil War critical social thinkers and contemporaries of Du Bois, deserve mention. Despite numerous criticisms that have been made of his life and work in the past and present, Washington was the most important black leader of his era (1890–1915). What is less well-known today is that he was in his time an influential critical black thinker. He led in the large-scale construction of black schools, in training blacks in employable trades, and in philosophical pursuits of black self-development and self-sufficiency. Washington was a strategic accommodationist to Jim Crow segregation, one whose cunning accommodation was pragmatic in that it avoided overt racial group conflict and insured important financial assistance from some white philanthropists. Additionally, he quietly funded court cases fighting against black voter disenfranchisement and other Jim Crow segregation.[42] His critical social theory is discovered in his autobiography, *Up From Slavery* (1901), and in later writings such as "Is the Negro Having a Fair Chance?" (1912). There he, albeit tactfully and subtly, condemns white supremacy and white privilege. Toward the end of his life, he strongly criticized white suppression of black voters, the defunding of black schools, and unjust imprisonment of black men to supply convict labor for white businesses.[43]

Another remarkable activist of this era, Marcus Garvey, also advocated black self-sufficiency and separatism. Like Washington, he was one of the most powerful black leaders of the first half of the twentieth century, heading the largest black social movement in US history. In writings and speeches, he argued that Afrocentrism and black pride were foundational and necessary for black survival and social advancement. Following in the footsteps of earlier black nationalists, Garvey proclaimed that black Americans needed to migrate to Africa and pronounced that Africa was for Africans, not for European colonialists. He led the Universal Negro Improvement Association (UNIA) whose multilingual newspaper, *The Negro World*, disseminated widely his message of African unity, the need to develop a large African nation controlled by black people, and ideals of black self-worth and consciousness. The newspaper exposed in detail white racism's many injustices, including white deceptiveness and well-institutionalized exploitation, and called for concerted black agency. In "'Crocodiles' As Friends" (1923), Garvey wrote that "We must realize that upon ourselves depend our destiny, our future; we must carve that future, that destiny."[44]

The writings of Wells-Barnett, Du Bois, Garvey, Washington, and other critical black analysts of the first half of the twentieth century anticipate and shape many central ideas and theoretical approaches in contemporary black theory and research. Wells-Barnett's understanding of the two-tier criminal justice system, Du Bois' concept of the global color line, Garvey's idea of healthy black pride and independence, and Washington's vision of black self-sufficiency are still key themes current in contemporary black thought and social action. These early figures were not just social theorists but also organizational activists who realized their ideas in actions. This is evident in Garvey's concern with promoting black consciousness and group unity (black nationalism), Wells-Barnett's activist fight to end lynching and reconstruct the criminal justice system, Du Bois' focus on advancing human rights for blacks and other oppressed people, and Washington's lifelong effort to ensure black self-reliance and agency. To borrow the language and thought of Wilson Moses, the "creative conflict" of ideas defines much critical black theory. Whereas Du Bois examined institutional and systemic racism and colonialism, Washington addressed black agency and immediate concerns of southern black communities. In contrast to Wells-Barnett's concern for organizing against violent white racism, Garvey organized a major movement to unite blacks. No one approach can be proven more important than the next, but rather they worked in different but related ways to uplift the black community and battle white racism on many fronts.

After the two world wars of the twentieth century, some years passed with less accessible publication of critical black social theorizing, aside from the writings of the work of a few lingering giants of the previous era such as Du Bois and some general social essayists. Numerous senior African American social scientists left research and writing to assume new positions as organizational leaders at United Nations agencies, as college and university presidents, and as leaders of businesses or non-profit organizations.[45] Persisting institutional discrimination in historically white universities was also a significant factor in the dearth of critical work by black social scientists of this period, for few held posts that allowed for productive scholarship on racism issues. By the 1960s only three African American social scientists were senior professors in major white universities.[46]

Still, critical black social theorizing persisted in the 1950s and increased over the 1960s, much of it coming in the speeches and writings of maverick essayists and civil rights leaders. Had we more space, we would discuss more fully how a few major black essayists carried some of the critical analysis load. Usually described as an essayist and novelist, one of the most famous was the sharp critic James Baldwin, who wrote key social-analytical books in the 1950s and early 1960s. He provided race-critical assessments of new urban redevelopment programs then destroying numerous black communities, for which he coined the term "Negro Removal," and provided penetrating analyses of much institutionalized racism. In his book *The Fire Next Time*, he developed a critical social analysis of black protests, explaining how the "black man has functioned in the white man's world as a fixed star... and as he moves out of his place, heaven and earth are shaken to the foundations."[47] Writing just before official desegregation began to crumble in the south, he also explained how white subjugation regularly created valuable resistance knowledge for African Americans:

> That man who is forced each day to snatch his manhood, his identity, out of the fire of human cruelty that rages to destroy it knows, if he survives his effort, and even if he does not survive it, something about himself and human life that no school on earth—and, indeed, no church—can teach."[48]

Additionally, if we had the space we would discuss the speeches of major civil rights leaders, especially Dr. Martin Luther King, Jr. and Malcolm X, who contributed significantly to maintaining the critical black tradition. Both oriented their speeches and writings to the goals and strategies of the 1950–1960s civil rights *movements*. King spoke of a movement of "creative dissenters" who sought to actualize old liberty-and-justice goals. In his book published a year before his assassination, he reached a verdict on the social reproduction of racial inequality still accurate today: "When the Constitution was written, a strange formula to determine taxes and representation declared that the Negro was 60 percent of a person. Today... Of the good things in life he has approximately one-half of those of whites; of the bad he has twice those of whites." There thus remains a huge "gap between existing realities and the goal of equality." Moreover, African Americans have operated from a "premise that equality means what it says, and they have taken white Americans at their word when they talked of it as an objective."[49]

Similarly, Malcolm X was a major figure in the 1950s–1960s black rights movements, and for years his critical speeches and writings delivered a more radical vision of black action than those of leaders emphasizing cooperation and integration. Accenting black nationalism, he foregrounded black consciousness, great appreciation of black culture, and more aggressive actions against white oppression. He spoke and wrote more about forcing whites to dismantle institutional racism, constantly pressing the white-run government to reign in racist attacks on black Americans and to expand democracy. For years he was critical of the lack of a radical change perspective among mainstream civil rights leaders, but over time, as Dr. King became more openly radical, Malcolm X was moving in the direction of King's concern with multiracial coalitions and insistence that the old liberty-and-justice ideals were indeed worth implementing. In his last year of life he was calling himself a "Pan-Africanist" (no longer "black nationalist"), even as he continued his insistence on black political-economic power and self-determination.[50]

Additionally, from the late 1940s to the 1960s, critical black theory work expanded from its US base and took firm hold overseas in the writings and activism of black anti-colonialists. During this period, a growing international cast of critical black theorists emerged as African and Caribbean movements began to further shake the foundations of Western colonialism. These included Frantz Fanon, Aimé Césaire, George Padmore, Kwame Nkrumah, Eric Williams, and C.L.R. James.[51] By the mid-1960s and 1970s, critical black social theory again increased significantly in the United States, substantially responding to the revolutionary and transforming social movements of that civil rights era.

Black Power and the 1970s Renaissance in Critical Black Thought

In the early 1970s, several important works by black social scientists presented major critiques of mainstream social science analyses of racial issues. Joyce Ladner's pathbreaking edited volume *The Death of White Sociology* (1973), James Blackwell and Morris Janowitz's edited volume *Black Sociologists* (1974), and Robert Staples' *Introduction to Black Sociology* (1976) highlighted major deficiencies in white-framed social science understandings of racism issues and resuscitated or introduced important concepts and theoretical views of these issues from the perspectives of African Americans and other people of color.[52]

Inspired by Stokely Carmichael (Kwame Ture) and Charles Hamilton's revolutionary work *Black Power* (1967) and other powerful black critical thought in the 1960s (for example, the race-critical books of James Baldwin and the speeches and writings of Malcolm X), a new generation of black (and a few white) critical social thinkers reinvigorated sociological analysis of racial power imbalances between whites and blacks, including sociopolitical and epistemological power imbalances. The late 1960s and 1970s black cultural-intellectual revolution was a battle against *both* intellectual and social segregation in academia and the larger society. Following Carmichael and Hamilton's lead, critical black social theorists of the 1960s–1970s era shifted racial analysis away from conventional social science study of *individual racial prejudice* toward more insightful theoretical and empirical analyses of *institutional racism*.[53]

Carmichael and Hamilton's *Black Power* soon became a central handbook for critical black social thought in this period, indeed to the present day. In this extraordinarily important work they tackled numerous themes about US racism that have become essential in critical black thinking and the study of racial matters. Here they explore deeply the very meaning of US racism and reveal that it is centrally a means of "subordinating a racial group and maintaining control over that group." For Carmichael and Hamilton, US racism is rooted in white power and authority, as seen in the "white power structure" that oversees "control over black lives." An extension of centuries of slavery and European imperialism, contemporary institutional racism operates overtly and covertly in the social, political, and economic colonialism of blacks and other people of color (both internal and external colonialism). For them, and for subsequent critical analysts of diverse backgrounds who have been influenced by their thought, institutional racism and the colonialism associated with capitalism have long been intimately and structurally intertwined. As they note, "Most whites participate in economic [and other forms of] colonialism," for institutional racism benefits the whole white community.[54]

Carmichael and Hamilton argue that perceptions of US society are shaped profoundly by institutionalized oppression. A major intellectual divide exists between the perspectives of the racially oppressed and of the white oppressor. "We cannot emphasize too much this relatively simple idea: that the two groups operate from different vantage points and different concepts of what constitutes legitimacy."[55] Recalling Du Bois' understanding of African Americans' "second sight," they illustrate blacks' heightened awareness about social realities that stems from knowing well two different social worlds: The "victim of continued societal oppression brings to the situation a wholly different set of views of what is legitimate for change," regularly offering "sharpened insights" and "increased sensitivity" about the social structure.[56]

According to Carmichael and Hamilton, years of white racial framing and dehumanizing blacks have produced serious social psychological problems for black individuals and communities—such as self-hate, despair, wishing to be white, and other individual and social pathologies that are the direct result of centuries of white oppression. Indeed, institutional white racism and its privileges and power have enabled powerful whites to co-opt significant numbers of black individuals into substantially accepting, even buttressing these structural arrangements of racial discrimination. In their view the co-opted "black bourgeoisie" disassociate, at least in part, with their blackness and their relationship to the working-class members of black communities and seek assimilation to whiteness and the material rewards of buying into the institutionally racist system. This co-opted black group, "hand-picked blacks resting on a white power base" who are "responsive to white leaders," frequently help exploit the black working class by means of "indirect rule."[57] For example, like all politicians in a government system defined significantly by institutional racism, to a varying but substantial degree the black politicians become corrupted in established political offices because they mostly uphold, rather than critique and counter, the dominant values and institutions that perpetuate a system of racial oppression.

Carmichael and Hamilton further explain that, in order for black Americans to contend with the individual and community pathologies generated by institutional racism, black Americans should focus on developing a strong racial consciousness and self-determination. Here they are reflecting the older black tradition of leaders such as Marcus Garvey. Blacks especially must redefine themselves in opposition to the many negative images of black Americans that whites have constructed. Moreover, the goal "must *not* be to assimilate" to white folkways and culture.[58] Even social integration into US society is problematic, for whites and blacks have different views of racial integration in areas such as the economy and education, with blacks normally wishing to fairly access the potential opportunities of integration and most whites threatened by significant and egalitarian integration of people of color. Echoing earlier critical black theorists, Carmichael and Hamilton also highlight the hypocrisy of supposed US political democracy, for it is a system that offers major political influence to whites. They further question white humanity and morality for ignoring the severe and continuing white-imposed difficulties facing black communities, observing that there exists *no* "American dilemma" on racial matters because most whites have no problem with white privilege and persisting discrimination against Americans of color. Like earlier African American thinkers, they view active rebellion and revolution, not traditional reform, as a legitimate means of overturning well-institutionalized racism. They also extend the older pan-Africanist view that black people from different geographical areas, such as the US and the Caribbean, should focus on the development of a globally interconnected black community.[59]

Along with shifting the analytic focus toward macro-level structures of racism and whites' power in shaping these racialized social structures, many critical black theorists developed and sharpened theoretical perspectives that have helped to shake the theoretical foundations of mainstream social science, much in the way that post-modernists have forced a reworking of dominant theoretical perspectives in the humanities. Like post-modernists, 1970s-era critical black analysts questioned the notions of objectivity and scientific validity and debunked the narrowness and authority of Western knowledge. As the authors in Joyce Ladner's edited volume make clear, objectivity is impossible in a system of racial oppression and is usually a disguised term for acceptance of a white framing of society. Like the 1920s–1930s black Renaissance, the 1970s renaissance of critical black theory spurred renewed interest in black cultural studies and intellectual history and inspired a more social-activist type of social science, the latter still today in need of full consideration of racial justice issues and of uncensored and forthright explanations of US and global white racism. For decades, critical black theorists have perceived mainstream social sciences as white-normed and white-framed. Whiteness typically becomes an unspoken standard in mainstream social sciences and humanities and across society more broadly. Unsurprisingly, given this white-framed social scientific outlook, white social thinkers rarely focus upon their limitations or the social pathologies created by whites.

A Brief Overview of Recent Critical Theory

Clearly, a strong tradition of critical black thought has existed in the US from the late 1700s to the present. Critical black thought involves different approaches focused on an array of issues and with varying degrees of criticality, yet several themes link the varied forms of this critical thought. One concern is with the welfare of the black community, which demands vigilant scrutiny of white ideas and practices that have long threatened that community's welfare. Exposing the relationship between systemic racism and capitalism, dismantling the practices of white supremacy, and presenting new knowledge and an alternative vision of the social world and human relations are other major concerns of critical black thought that have now spanned several centuries.

Contemporary critical black thought continues to produce perceptive understandings of human beings and their social worlds, especially the ways that well-institutionalized white racism remains a fundamental feature of contemporary societies such as the United States. Yet, since the 1970s, critical black theory has been under attack, often ignored, discounted, or marginalized in mainstream social science. This is obvious, for example, in the disparagement, defunding, and elimination of numerous African American studies programs established soon after civil rights victories of the 1960s and 1970s. Even moderate voices in African American studies have been degraded or silenced.

Nevertheless, new critical black theorists and ever-new concerns of critical black theory continue to materialize. We only have space here to underscore the contributions of just a few of these theorists, who deserve a major book just on their work. For example, since the 1980s the critical sociologist John Stanfield has actively deconstructed the operations of white-framed social sciences in works such as his *Black Reflective Sociology* (2011). He demonstrates the workings of racist framing in social science, including its frequent ethnocentric basis and the role of white epistemological considerations in the use of prevailing research methods, including those dealing with racial matters in this society. Another critical black social scientist, Ann Morning, has challenged the renewed socio-genomic and biosocial theory in the social sciences.[60] For example, Morning's *The Nature of Race* (2011) presents a social constructionist view to understand new perspectives and practices in the field of socio-genomics research.[61] In *The Racial Contract* (1997), the influential black social philosopher Charles Mills seeks to "bridge two areas now largely segregated from each other: on one hand, the world of mainstream ethics and philosophy… on the other, the world of Native American, African American, and third and fourth world political thought historically focused on issues of conquest, imperialism, colonialism… race and racism, slavery, jim crow [*sic*], reparations."[62] The black philosophers George Yancy and Lucius Outlaw explore the relationship between racism and philosophy and argue that Du Bois' understanding of "race" remains important to contemporary social analysis.[63]

The African American historian Lerone Bennett has critically deconstructed whitewashed histories of the United States. In *Forced into Glory: Abraham Lincoln's White Dream* (1999), Bennett demonstrates that this most esteemed US president on racial matters actually harbored a racist perspective on numerous issues and had once promoted his vision of an idealized white society devoid of blacks. Scholars Derrick Bell and Michelle Alexander have done much to ensure that critical black theory informs legal analysis and assessments of the criminal justice system. These critical race analysts, along with several other legal scholars such as Kimberlé Crenshaw, Ian Haney-López, Richard Delgado, and Gary Peller form an interracial group of analysts who have focused on the numerous ways that systemic racism shapes the US criminal justice system. Cheryl I. Harris, for example, developed the important idea of whiteness as "property," which provides an array of legal and other societal rights only for whites.[64] Derrick Bell, a founder of critical race theory, penned penetrating analyses of legal cases such as *Brown v. Board of Education* (1954) and developed innovative and influential critical concepts such as "interest convergence" and "racial realism." Following in the path pioneered by Angela Davis, Alexander has written in great detail about the ways that the US prison-industrial-complex represents a new type of "Jim Crow segregation," a damaging government vehicle threatening the vitality of many black communities.[65]

The contemporary black sociologist Patricia Hill Collins has produced much innovative research and writing, including in her pathbreaking *Black Feminist Thought* (1990), that serve as a guide for a renewed black feminist epistemology and a model for current research studies on the intersectionality of race, class, gender, and sexuality (see Chapter 10 for details). Indeed, she has been an important pioneer in criticizing both white feminist theory and mainstream racial theories for not examining more forcefully both white racism generally and, most particularly, racism in regard to black women and other women of color. Collins demonstrates the diversity of contemporary critical black theory, probing and revealing some of its very important gender and gendered racism aspects.[66]

Rutledge Dennis's work (1996, 2003) addresses the persistence of a dual US society, one still divided by the color line, one that generates the dual marginality experienced by black Americans caught between, and existing partly within, black and white social worlds. Other examples of contemporary critical black theory's diversity and deep explorations can be seen in Tukufu Zuberi and Eduardo Bonilla-Silva's provocative edited volume, *White Logic, White Methods* (2008), a book in which these prominent sociologists of color aptly defend their critical research methodologies and theoretical logics to skeptical (white) mainstream colleagues who espouse a different social science worldview.[67] An examination of important non-Western critical black social theorists such as Yosef Ben-Jochannan, Ivan van Sertima, and Cheikh Anta Diop goes well beyond the space we have here, but they too have been influential on US theorists working in the areas of institutional, structural, and systemic racism.

In addition, several important journals publish much critical black theory—for example, *Souls: A Critical Journal of Black Politics, Culture, and Society*; *Du Bois Review: Social Science Research on Race*; *Journal of Black Studies*; and *Issues in Race and Society: An Interdisciplinary Global Journal*, the journal of the Association of Black Sociologists (ABS). As we have noted previously, the ABS is one of several black social science organizations functioning as an important outlet for disseminating the research and alternative social scientific perspectives of black social scientists often marginalized in the social science mainstream. The many difficult realities faced by critical black thinkers, publication outlets, and professional organizations demonstrate that many of the racially oppressive characteristics of earlier slavery and Jim Crow social systems persist in contemporary white-dominated societies such as the United States.

Despite numerous handicaps, critical black social theorists have influenced many other theorists of color, as well as some critical white theorists such as the authors of this book, to better understand empirical and conceptual truths about institutional and systemic white racism, specifically the oppressive social worlds long rationalized and obfuscated by centuries of white racial framing inside and outside the social sciences. Since the 1970s, several white social scientists and non-black sociologists of color have astutely and critically investigated various white-racism issues, including the social sciences' historic mistreatment and neglect of racial matters. For instance, Stanford Lyman's *The Black*

American in Sociological Thought (1972), James McKee's *Sociology and the Race Problem* (1993), and Stephen Steinberg's *Race Relations* (2007) explore racial segregation and weak social science analysis of racial matters, as well as the inherent white biases of mainstream social science. Expanding beyond the US context, George Steinmetz's edited volume, examines the ways the social sciences have avoided critical racial analysis and supported Western colonialism.[68]

Conclusion

Critical black social theory and its offshoots have developed and periodically expanded substantially, and in the process have challenged white-dominated mainstream social sciences' historical and contemporary inability to address and research matters of systemic white racism adequately and critically. The critical tradition of black social thinkers has greatly advanced social scientific knowledge about matters of racial oppression, as well as many other facets of social reality, yet much of this social scientific knowledge remains unknown, marginalized, or unheeded by mainstream social scientists. If the mainstream social sciences were to fully incorporate the critical insights, penetrating concepts, and sophisticated theoretical perspectives of many critical black social scientists and other critical social scientists, mainstream social scientific knowledge would be revolutionized and much more advanced than it now is. There is an urgent need to discover, or rediscover, and implement the copious critical ideas and insightful theoretical perspectives about racism matters that have been generated by critical black thinkers. Our outline of systemic racism theory in the next chapter is one effort to aggressively foreground and build on the insights of a long, wise tradition of critical black theorists.

Notes

1 Defining "theory" and positing certain individuals as "theorists" can be controversial enterprises. Questions concerning what counts as theory and who counts as theorists often get in the way of the knowledge being produced, and tend to create divisions that legitimate some theories/theorists, while discounting others. We view theory as explanation of human behavior and the social world backed by empirical realities and sharp observations, and theorists as those who provide such explanations.

2 See, for example, Joe R. Feagin's works: *Systemic Racism: A Theory of Oppression* (New York: Routledge, 2006); *The White Racial Frame: Centuries of Racial Framing and Counter-Framing*, 2nd edn (New York: Routledge, 2013); and *How Blacks Built America: Labor, Culture, Freedom, and Democracy* (New York: Routledge, 2015). Also see Sean Elias, *Black and White Sociology: Segregation of the Discipline* (Doctoral Dissertation, Sociology Department, Texas A&M University, 2009); Sean Elias, "W.E.B. Du Bois, Race, and Human Rights," *Societies Without Borders*, 4(3) (2009): 273–94.
3 See, for example, Du Bois' criticisms and complimentary portraits of black Americans in *The Philadelphia Negro: A Social Study* (Philadelphia: University of Pennsylvania Press, 1996 [1899]) as well as both his praise of white culture in *The Souls of Black Folk* (New York: Penguin, 1995 [1903]) and critique of white culture in *Darkwater: Voices from Within the Veil* (Mineola, NY: Dover Publications, 1999 [1920]).
4 See Sean Elias' forthcoming work, *Drawing the Sociological Color Line*.
5 See *African American Perspectives on Political Science*, ed. Wilber Rich (Philadelphia Temple University Press, 2007). Especially see Charles Hamilton's "Foreword," pp. ix–x.
6 Absalom Jones and Richard Allen, "A Narrative of the Proceedings of Black People During the Late Awful Calamity in Philadelphia (1794)," in Richard Newman, Patrick Rael, and Phillip Lapansky (eds.), *Pamphlets of Protest: An Anthology of Early African American Protest Literature, 1790–1860* (New York: Routledge, 2001), pp. 32–42; Price Hall, "A Charge (1797)," in Newman et al. (eds.), *Pamphlets of Protest*, pp. 44–50.
7 Jones and Allen, "A Narrative of the Proceedings of Black People During the Late Awful Calamity in Philadelphia," pp. 41–2.
8 See the early works of these and other critical black social thinkers in Newman et al. (eds.), *Pamphlets of Protest*, and in Thomas Frazier (ed.), *Afro-American History: Primary Sources* (Belmont, CA: Wadsworth, 1988); George Ducas (ed.), *Great Documents in Black American History* (New York: Praeger Publishers, 1970); Howard Brotz (ed.), *African-American Social and Political Thought, 1850–1920* (New Brunswick, NJ: Transaction Publishers, 1997).
9 Mary Ann Shadd, "A Plea for Emigration, or Notes of Canada West," in Newman et al. (eds.), *Pamphlets of Protest*, p. 199.
10 Maria Stewart, "An Address Delivered at the African Masonic Hall" (Boston, February 27, 1833), in Marilyn Richardson (ed.), *Maria Stewart, America's First Black Woman Political Writer: Essays and Speeches* (Bloomington, IN: Indiana University Press, 1987 [1831]), pp. 63–4.
11 Russell Parrott, "An Oration on the Abolition of the Slave Trade," in Newman et al. (eds.), *Pamphlets of Protest*, p. 75.
12 David Walker, *Appeal: In Four Articles With A Preamble, To the Coloured Citizens of the World, But, in Particular, and very Expressly, To Those of the United States of America* (Baltimore, MD: Black Classic Press, 1993 [1830]). See also James Turner's informative "Introduction," pp. 9–19.
13 Ibid.
14 Rutledge Dennis, "W.E.B. Du Bois: The Autobiographer as Sociological Theorist," *Perspectives*, 29 (2006): 3–5.
15 James W.C. Pennington, *The Fugitive Blacksmith; or, Events in the History of James W.C. Pennington, Pastor of a Presbyterian Church, New York, Formerly a Slave in the State of Maryland, United States* (Cornwall: Dodo Press, 2009 [1849]); Frederick Douglass, *Narrative of the Life of Frederick Douglass* (Mineola, NY: Dover Publications, 1995 [1845]); Frederick Douglass, *My Bondage, My Freedom* (New York: Penguin Classic, 2003 [1855]); Frederick Douglass, *Life and Times of Fredrick Douglass* (Mineola, NY: Dover

Publications, 2003 [1881]); Harriet Jacobs, *Incidents in the Life of a Slave Girl* (Mineola, NY: Dover Publications, 2001 [1861]).
16 See previous endnote for full references of Douglass' autobiographies. For a more critical take on Douglass' thinking and life work, see Bill E. Lawson and Frank M. Kirkland (eds.), *Frederick Douglass: A Critical Reader* (Malden, MA: Blackwell Publishers, 1999).
17 Quoted in Philip Foner, "Introduction," in Frederick Douglass, *My Bondage and My Freedom* (Mineola, NY: Dover Publications, 1969 [1855]), p. ix.
18 Samuel Cornish and John Russwurm, "To Our Patrons," *Freedoms Journal*, 1(1) (1827): 1, https://web.archive.org/web/20150209163534/http://www.wisconsinhistory.org/pdfs/la/FreedomsJournal/v1n01.pdf (accessed September 2, 2015).
19 On the masthead of the *The North Star*, Douglass notes, "truth is of no color." See Library of Congress website, www.loc.gov/exhibits/odyssey/educate/norths.html (accessed September 2, 2015).
20 Benjamin Banneker, "Letter to Jefferson," in George Ducas (ed.), *Great Documents in Black American History* (New York: Praeger, 1970), p. 24.
21 Alexis de Tocqueville, *Democracy in America* (New York: Vintage Books, 1945 [1835]), p. 345.
22 Walker, Article 1, *Appeal*, p. 37.
23 Douglass, *My Bondage, My Freedom*, p. 430.
24 Maria Stewart, "Religion and the Pure Principles of Morality, the Sure Foundation of Which We Must Build," in Richardson (ed.), *Maria Stewart, America's First Black Woman Political Writer*, p. 29.
25 See, for example, Kenneth Stampp, *The Era of Reconstruction, 1865–1877* (New York: Vintage, 1967).
26 Henry Highland Garnet, *The Past and Present Condition, and Destiny of the Colored Races*, ed. T.R. Frazier (New York: Harcourt, Brace, and World, 1970 [1848]); William Wells Brown, *The Rising Son: Antecedents and Advancements of the Colored Race* (Boston: Anti-Slavery Office, 1874); George Washington Williams, *History of the Negro Race in America, 1619–1880* (New York: Arno Press, 1968 [1883]).
27 See Wilson Moses, *Creative Conflict in African American Thought: Frederick Douglass, Alexander Crummell, Booker T. Washington, W.E.B. Du Bois, and Marcus Garvey* (Cambridge: Cambridge University Press, 2004). Specifically note Moses' analysis of Crummell's deep appreciation of European culture, to the point where he partially embraces white framing of the European civilizing process.
28 Note that, like their white counterparts and other theorists of color, some black theorists are critical with regard to certain subject matter and acritical with regard to other subject matter. There are also degrees of criticality.
29 See, for example, W.E.B. Du Bois, *Black Reconstruction in America, 1860–1880* (New York: Free Press, 1998 [1935]), which addresses intersections of race and class, and Oliver C. Cox's *Capitalism as System* (New York: Monthly Review Press, 1964), which explores the relationship between race and class on a global scale.
30 Elias, "W.E.B. Du Bois, Race, and Human Rights," pp. 277–8.
31 Claude McKay, "If We Must Die," David L. Lewis (ed.), *The Portable Harlem Renaissance Reader* (New York: Penguin Books, 1995), p. 290.
32 C. Johnson, E.R. Embree, and W. Alexander, *The Collapse of the Cotton Tendency* (Chapel Hill, NC: University of North Carolina Press, 1935); Charles Johnson, "Excerpts from *Patterns of Negro Segregation* (1943)," in John Bracey, August Meier, and Elliott Rudwick (eds.), *The Black Sociologists: The First Half Century* (Belmont, CA: Wadsworth, 1971) pp. 136, 149.

33 Bertram Doyle, "The Etiquette of Race Relations—Past, Present, and Future," in Bracey et al. (eds.), *The Black Sociologists*, pp. 121–2.
34 St. Claire Drake and Horace R. Cayton, *Black Metropolis* (Chicago: University Of Chicago Press, 1993 [1945]).
35 See Oliver C. Cox, *Caste, Class, and Race* (Garden City, NY: Doubleday, 1948); Oliver C. Cox, *Race Relations: Elements and Social Dynamics* (New York: Philosophical Library, 1976); Oliver C. Cox, *The Foundations of Capitalism* (New York: Philosophical Library, 1959).
36 See Bracey et al. (eds.), *The Black Sociologists*; James Blackwell and Morris Janowitz (eds.), *Black Sociologists: Historical and Contemporary Perspectives* (Chicago: University of Chicago Press, 1974); Robert Washington and Donald Cunnigen (eds.), *Confronting the American Dilemma of Race: The Second Generation Black American Sociologists* (Lanham, MD: University Press of America, 2003); Mary Jo Deegan, *Race, Hull-House, and the University of Chicago: A New Conscious Against Ancient Evils* (New York: Praeger, 2002). Also see Pierre Saint-Arnaud, *African American Pioneers of Sociology: A Critical History*, trans. Peter Feldstein (Toronto: University of Toronto Press, 2009).
37 Ida B. Wells, *Southern Horrors and Other Writings: The Anti-Lynching Campaign of Ida B. Wells, 1892–1900*, ed. Jacqueline J. Royster (Boston: Bedford/St. Martin's, 1997).
38 See Elijah Anderson, "Introduction" in W.E.B. Du Bois, *The Philadelphia Negro: A Social Study* (Philadelphia: University of Pennsylvania Press, 1996 [1899]), p. xviii; Aldon Morris, "Sociology of Race and W.E.B. Du Bois: The Path Not Taken," in Craig Calhoun (ed.), *Sociology in America: A History* (Chicago: University of Chicago Press, 2008), pp. 503–34; Earl Wright II, "The Atlanta Sociological Laboratory, 1896–1924: A Historical Account of the First American School of Sociology," *Western Journal of Black Studies*, 26(3) (2002): 165–74.
39 See Aldon Morris, *The Scholar Denied: W.E.B. Du Bois and the Birth of Modern Sociology* (Berkeley, CA: University of California Press, 2015); Sean Elias, "W.E.B. Du Bois's Position in Sociological Theory," *Perspectives*, 28(4) (2006): 10–16.
40 W.E.B. Du Bois, *Dusk of Dawn: An Essay Toward an Autobiography of a Race Concept* (New York: Harcourt, Brace, and World, 1968 [1940]).
41 W.E.B. Du Bois, *The Souls of Black Folk* (New York: Penguin, 1995 [1903]); W.E.B. Du Bois, "W.E.B. Du Bois, Dusk of Dawn: An Essay Toward an Autobiography of a Race Concept," in N. Huggins (ed.), *W.E.B. Du Bois Writings* (New York: Penguin, 1986 [1940]); W.E.B. Du Bois, *The Autobiography of W.E.B. Du Bois: A Soliloquy of Viewing My Life from the Last Decade of Its First Century* (New York: International Publishers, 1997 [1968]).
42 Louis R. Harlan, "The Secret Life of Booker T. Washington," *Journal of Southern History*, 37(2) (1971): 393–416; August Meier, "Toward a Reinterpretation of Booker T. Washington," *Journal of Southern History*, 23(2) (1957): 220–7.
43 Booker T. Washington, *Up From Slavery* (New York: Oxford University Press, 1995 [1901]); Booker T. Washington, "Is the Negro Having A Fair Chance?" *The Century Magazine*, November 1912.
44 Marcus Garvey, "'Crocodiles' As Friends," in David L. Lewis (ed.), *The Portable Harlem Renaissance Reader* (New York: Penguin Books, 1995), pp. 22–3.
45 John Stanfield II, "Introduction," in John Stanfield II (ed.), *A History of Race Relations Research: First-Generation Reflections* (Newbury Park, CA: Sage, 1993), p. xv.
46 Ibid., p. xv.
47 James Baldwin, *The Fire Next Time* (New York: Dell, 1963), p. 20.
48 Ibid., p. 134. See also James Baldwin, *Nobody Knows My Name* (New York: Dell, 1961).
49 Martin Luther King Jr., *Where Do We Go from Here?: Chaos or Community* (New York: Bantam Books, 1967), pp. 7, 9.

50 Peniel E. Joseph, *Waiting 'Til the Midnight Hour: A Narrative History of Black Power in America* (New York: Holt, 2007), p. 14; Manning Marable, *Malcolm X: A Life of Reinvention* (New York: Viking, 2011), Kindle loc. 9142–7.
51 See, for example, Franz Fanon, *The Wretched of the Earth*, trans. Constance Farrington (New York: Grove Press, 1963); Aimé Césaire, *Discourse on Colonialism* (New York: Monthly Review Press, 2001); George Padmore, *How Britain Rules Africa* (New York: Negro Universities Press, 1969); Kwame Nkrumah, *Neo-Colonialism: The Last Stage of Imperialism* (New York: International Publishers, 1966); Eric Williams, *From Slavery to Castro: The History of the Caribbean, 1492–1969* (New York: Vintage Books, 1984 [1970]); C.L.R. James, *The Black Jacobins: Toussaint L'Ouverture and the San Domingo Revolution* (New York: Vintage Books, 1989 [1963]).
52 Joyce Ladner (ed.), *The Death of White Sociology* (New York: Random House, 1973); James Blackwell and Morris Janowitz (eds.), *Black Sociologists: Historical and Contemporary Perspectives* (Chicago: University of Chicago Press, 1974); Robert Staples, *Introduction to Black Sociology* (New York: McGraw-Hill, 1976).
53 Stokely Carmichael (Kwame Ture) and Charles Hamilton, *Black Power: The Politics of Liberation* (New York: Vintage, 1994 [1967]), Kindle loc. 164, 175, 185.
54 Ibid., Kindle loc. 460.
55 Ibid., Kindle loc. 2711.
56 Ibid., Kindle loc. 2704.
57 Ibid., Kindle loc. 216, 269, 275.
58 Ibid., Kindle loc. 727.
59 Ibid., Kindle loc. 2903.
60 John Stanfield II, *Black Reflective Sociology: Epistemology, Theory, and Method* (Walnut Creek, CA: Left Coast Press, 2011); Ann Morning, "Does Genomics Challenge the Social Construction of Race?" *Sociological Theory*, 32(3) (2014): 189–207.
61 Ann Morning, *The Nature of Race: How Scientists Think and Teach about Human Difference* (Berkeley, CA: University of California Press, 2011).
62 Charles Mills, *The Racial Contract* (Ithaca, NY: Cornell University Press, 1997), p. 4.
63 See Lucius T. Outlaw's defense and Anthony Appiah's critique of Du Bois' understanding of race in Bernard Bell, Emily Grosholz, and James Stewart (eds.), *W.E.B. Du Bois: On Race and Culture* (New York: Routledge, 1996), pp. 15–38. See also George Yancy, *Look, a White! Philosophical Essays on Whiteness* (Philadelphia: Temple University Press, 2012).
64 Cheryl Harris, "Whiteness as Property," *Harvard Law Review*, 106(8) (1993): 1707.
65 Michelle Alexander, *The New Jim Crow: Mass Incarceration in the Age of Colorblindness* (New York: The New Press, 2012).
66 Patricia Hill Collins, *Black Feminist Thought: Knowledge, Consciousness, and the Politics of Empowerment* (Boston: Unwin Hyman, 1990).
67 Rutledge Dennis, "Continuities and Discontinuities in the Social and Political Thought of W.E.B. Du Bois," in Rutledge Dennis (ed.), *W.E.B. Du Bois: The Scholar as Activist* (Greenwich, CT: JAI Press, 1996), pp. 3–23; Rutledge Dennis, "Towards a Theory of Dual Marginality: Dual Marginality and the Dispossessed," *Ideaz*, 2(1) (2003): 21–31; Tukufu Zuberi and Eduardo Bonilla-Silva (eds.), *White Logic, White Methods: Racism and Methodology* (Lanham, MD: Rowman & Littlefield, 2008).
68 Stanford Lyman, *The Black American in Sociological Thought* (New York: G.P. Putnam's Sons, 1972); James McKee, *Sociology and the Race Problem: The Failure of a Perspective* (Urbana, IL: University of Illinois Press, 1993); Stephen Steinberg, *Race Relations: A Critique* (Stanford, CA: Stanford University Press, 2007); George Steinmetz (ed.), *Sociology and Empire: The Imperial Entanglements of a Discipline* (Durham, NC: Duke University Press, 2013).

CHAPTER 10
SYSTEMIC RACISM THEORY

The mainstream social sciences remain unable to develop a comprehensive, meaningful theory of matters of white-imposed racism, as we demonstrate in previous pages. Therefore, we agree with Mustafa Emirbayer and Matthew Desmond's recent intimation that no grand theory of these racial matters presently exists.[1] However, unlike Emirbayer and Desmond, who search out principles for race theory by turning to the conceptual schemes of white European social theorists, many of whom *never* seriously studied racial matters, we suggest that contemporary social theorists of Western racial matters would do much better to evaluate and build on the work of the many critical and insightful black theorists and other theorists of color. Social theorists of color, particularly African American social thinkers, have experienced and documented social reality from the front lines of systemically racist societies and have not been as subject to the white racial framing that shapes the perceptions of a great many white social scientists and other social analysts.

Even the most radical (Karl Marx), theoretically rich (Max Weber), and innovative (Pierre Bourdieu) European social thinkers often exhibit a white racial framing in their social thought and fail miserably in assessing the significance of racial matters in shaping the social world, including their own societies and life-worlds. This cannot be said about critical black social theorists, such as those examined in the last chapter, whose analyses of the realities of "race" present more than 200 years of insightful racial theorizing and thus can serve as the starting points for a more sound theory of racial matters, especially in regard to Western countries.

The following outline for a theory of racial matters, systemic racism theory, builds substantially on social knowledge about racial issues generated by critical black thinkers. Contemporary critical race theories produced by non-black critical race analysts, including white critical race analysts, are frequently extensions and reworkings, directly or indirectly, of critical black epistemologies and investigations of racial matters, which have a long productive history of producing critical sociological insights. The intellectual importance and fruits of centuries of critical black social thought deserve much more contemporary recognition, and we believe such considered recognition is an initial and important step toward implementing critical insights of blacks in current social science theories of racial matters, something most mainstream social scientists fail to realize. Along with centering critical black thought in the study of racial matters, systemic racism theory integrates knowledge from a number of other critical theoretical perspectives and from the theory-influenced pursuits of much contemporary empirical research on racism.

Important Theoretical and Empirical Influences

Before outlining systemic racism theory's key concepts and perspectives, we should note several theoretical influences in addition to the critical black thought discussed in the previous chapter, and also note numerous empirical-research studies that support and complement systemic racism theory. Considering the profound structural interrelatedness of race, class, and gender—and the interweaving dynamics of racial, class, and gender power and exploitation—systemic racism theory is a natural ally of both critical feminist thought and critical class analysis. Systemic racism theorists understand the importance of borrowing ideas and conceptual language from these other important theoretical perspectives. For example, Marx's concept of "class consciousness" offers perceptions of consciousness in the context of oppression (oppressor and oppressed) that can be applied to understanding "racial consciousness." Additionally, Marx's concept of "class conflict" reflects interactions of groups in opposition that aid understanding "racial conflict." Critical class analyses by writers from Karl Marx and Thorstein Veblen to contemporaries such as Thomas Piketty and Mark Mizruchi offer analyses and knowledge useful for understanding some racial matters, just as critical racial analysis presents ideas and research projects useful for understanding social class dynamics.[2]

Critical feminist thought—such as the work of Catharine MacKinnon, bell hooks, Dorothy Smith, Patricia Hill Collins, and Angela Davis—presents insightful analyses of gender oppression, specifically patriarchy and sexism, which reveal parallels to and intersections with racial oppression and class oppression.[3] Critiques of patriarchy, heteronormativity, and male sexism expose insights about gender and power that can be useful for analyses of racial group power, white supremacy, whiteness, and white racism. For instance, the critical feminist argument that the state is typically male-controlled is quite true. Then, too, is the argument that the state is controlled mostly by white men of the capitalist elite. These intersecting racial/gender/class understandings should be considered when theorizing and researching the contemporary power elite that has the greatest power to generate and perpetuate racial, class, and gender inequalities. This leads to intersectionality analysis, a closely related theoretical influence on systemic racism theory and field research.

Race-Gender Intersectionality: Black Feminist Scholars

Intersectionality theorizing in the past and present has frequently highlighted the intertwining of racial, class, and gender identities as well as the interrelatedness of racialized, classed, and gendered social institutions throughout the social world. Adequate social analyses of contemporary societies cannot ignore this recurring intersectionality and the ways major identity markers and associated buttressing structures interact and intertwine. Systemic racism and other race-critical theorists have been particularly interested in mapping the intersections of racial and gender oppression, as well as in demonstrating ways in which class oppression serves an interactive function in maintaining racial oppression and gender oppression.

Numerous black women scholars have played a very important role in developing ideas and empirical analyses probing the intersection of racism and sexism, thereby directly influencing systemic racism theory. Social philosopher Angela Davis has analyzed how enslaved black women have faced distinctive gendered oppression—exploited like black men for productive labor as workers, but also for reproductive labor as women "breeding" enslaved children.[4] Sociologist Yanick St. Jean has examined the "double burden" of everyday racism and sexism woven together in the lives of middle-class black women.[5] Humanities scholar bell hooks has provided sociological analysis of the racist imaging of female beauty, which portrays black women as non-attractive and deviant—thereby revealing how white perspectives get precedence in views of US women.[6] Similarly, sociologists Elizabeth Higginbotham, Louwanda Evans, and Brittany Slatton have demonstrated empirically and theoretically the great importance of studying the racial, gender, and gendered-racist stereotypes and discrimination regularly faced by black women in contemporary social worlds.[7]

Systemic racism analysts, including the authors, have made very substantial use of the extraordinary theoretical and empirical work of black sociologist and former American Sociological Association president Patricia Hill Collins. Her astute, often pathbreaking black-feminist analyses of intersectionality issues have informed many contemporary scholars about how racial oppression intersects with gender, sexuality, and class oppression, and how accurate understanding of intersections involves a distinctive epistemological perspective. In her view, a black-feminist framework has been essential to developing meaningful sociological understandings of women of color in society. For example, Collins has traced out in detail the gendered-racist character of major stereotypes of black women—such as the docile mammy and irresponsible welfare mother—and how such brutally racist imagery is perpetuated by white-dominated mainstream media, and thus greatly shapes discrimination faced by black women.[8]

In addition, Collins has contributed significantly to epistemological and methodological considerations in researching racism. She has developed the idea of the "outsider within" in researching and understanding racial, gender, and intersectionality issues in everyday life. Both black women and men must operate within historically white institutions as outsiders without the racial/gender privileges of whites, especially of white men, the classical "insiders."[9] In her provocative book *Fighting Words*, Collins critically discusses bias in social science theory: "Social theory in particular can serve either to reproduce existing power relations or to foster social and economic justice." She adds that "elite groups routinely minimize the workings of their own power in what counts for theory... As a result, prevailing definitions of theory portray it as an ahistorical, static system of abstract logic, reason, of science."[10] White elites do not necessarily produce more important knowledge than others, but do have the power, as we have argued throughout this book, to make their knowledge the most legitimate conceptual framework. For example, the white dominance of US sociology from the 1890s to the 1960s meant there was almost no research published on black women from a critical black viewpoint in any major journal. In her critical epistemological analysis, Collins has influenced systemic racism theory and helped to move the social sciences in the direction of understanding the moral foundations of social theory: "Because the search for justice has been central in African-American women's history, I emphasize an ethical framework grounded in notions of justice as specific cultural material for exploring this more general question of moral authority for struggle."[11]

This ethical emphasis links to another important theme in Collins' analytical work, one that has also influenced systemic racism theory and research: that one must recognize and thoughtfully consider black and other resistance to white oppression. Indeed, in her research she has shown how African American women have been a constant and integral part of the country's civil rights movements. Unsurprisingly, too, Collins has been a leader in emphasizing the concrete and material character of black culture: the important values of a racial group "have concrete, material expression: they will be present in social institutions such as church and family, in creative expression of art, music, and dance, and, if unsuppressed, in patterns of economic and political activity."[12]

Systemic racism theory has regularly examined the interrelationship of racial, gender/sexuality, and class oppression, and, additionally, revealed how racial oppression intersects with yet other large-scale forms of social structural oppression such as religious and ethnic oppression. Not all oppressions are of equal significance and weight in a given historical era or society, yet all are similar in their construction stemming from power relations that pit an oppressor group against an oppressed group. Systemic racism theory is committed to this intersectionalist analysis, but with a central focus on systemic racial oppression.

Socio-Historical Analyses

Systemic racism theory relies on a long line of critical social-historical analysis about racial matters. As we demonstrated previously, critical social historians and historical sociologists have long been at the forefront of the empirical and theoretical analysis of well-institutionalized racism. We see this in the socio-historical writings of important early African American analysts such as Henry Highland Garnet, Martin Delany, George Washington Williams, and William Wells Brown. African American analysts during and after the turn of the twentieth century, such as Ida B. Wells-Barnett, Carter G. Woodson, Anna J. Cooper, and W.E.B. Du Bois sustained this tradition of crucial socio-historical analysis. We observe this clearly in W.E.B. Du Bois' writings from the 1890s to the 1950s, such as *The Suppression of the Africa Slave Trade, Black Reconstruction in America, 1860–1880*, and *Black Folk: Then and Now*.[13]

Since the time of Du Bois' groundbreaking historical writings, numerous critical social historians and historical sociologists have continued to explicate US and global realities in ways that strengthen systemic racism theory's historical accounting of essential matters of racial oppression. For example, there is John Hope Franklin's classic, *From Slavery to Freedom*, first published in 1947 and currently in a 2010 revised edition.[14] Franklin was the brilliant, leading African American historian, and historian of African Americans, for a generation. During the 1950s–1970s era, moreover, a racially diverse array of historians such as C. Vann Woodward, C.L.R. James, Kenneth Stampp, Winthrop Jordan, Eric Williams, John G. Jackson, Lawrence Levine, and Edward Said did much to provide critical analysis of US and global racial histories.[15]

Moreover, in the 1980s–2000s era, the historical writings of Angela Y. Davis, Aldon Morris, Chancellor Williams, Martin Bernal, Paul Gordon Lauren, John Henrik Clarke, and Lerone Bennett, Jr., among many others, have further deepened and sharpened our understandings of these highly racialized histories.[16] Important critical historical writings since 2000 have included the works of Ronald Takaki, Juan Gonzalez, Ramón Gutiérrez, George Frederickson, Ira Katznelson, Molefi K. Asante,[17] as well as Nell I. Painter, Jenny Irons, Sven Beckert, Roxanne Dunbar-Ortiz, and Edward Baptist, again among numerous others.[18] Additionally, critical biographical narratives in the tradition of Frederick Douglass and W.E.B. Du Bois, such as activist-theorist Stokely Carmichael's *Ready for Revolution* (2003),[19] have also been an important source of historical information for systemic racism and other race-critical theorists.

Other Contemporary Influences

Systemic racism theory is also deeply rooted in liberation social science and critical public sociology and similar social science, which focus on developing knowledge and social practices promoting social justice, human rights, and more egalitarian human relations.[20] Thus, systemic racism theory is a type of critical public social science with the pragmatic aim of developing a more just society. In this pursuit, a deconstruction of the white racial framing and racialized practices of systemic racism and other intersecting forms of societal oppression are a top priority. Additionally, systemic racism theory endorses the interdisciplinary incorporation of philosophy, literary studies, and biography, as well as new social media in the social science analysis of contemporary racial matters.[21] Keeping up with current events and contemporary social issues in society and across the globe that reflect the machinations of systemic racism are further essential tasks of systemic racism theory.

Several other key theoretical perspectives on racial matters are influential in much systemic racism theorizing. These include critical race theory, post-modernist and post-structuralist critiques of Western thought, and anti-colonialist literature. The critical race theory and analysis of legal scholars, the earliest being mostly scholars of color, has aggressively exposed structural and systemic racism in the US legal and criminal justice system, presenting very important conceptual understandings such as "interest convergence," "racial realism," and "property interest in whiteness." Critical race theorists of color have also provided important counter-framed analyses that critique dominant narratives about the US legal system, such as Derrick Bell's critique of the *Brown v. Board of Education* Supreme Court decision and Michelle Alexander's exposé of racial oppression in the prison-industrial complex we noted previously. Critical race theory is one of the few critical theories of racial matters that possesses an interracial task force of scholars of color and a few whites working, usually as law school scholar-teachers, to dismantle the legal and other systemic racism of the United States. In contrast, there is a largely white-group enterprise termed "post-modernist thought," which utilizes the ideas of theorists such as Martin Heidegger, Michel Foucault, and Jacques Derrida to problematize and deconstruct many central ideas of Western thought, including objectivity, the authority of science, societal progress, and ethnocentrism.[22] Anti-colonialist critics, such as Frantz Fanon, Aimé Césaire, Edward Said, Albert Memmi, and Raewyn Connell, have developed similar criticisms of Westernism and a distinctive non-European perspective in their deep and extensive anticolonial critiques.[23]

Two contemporary theories of racial matters that complement systemic racism theory are Eduardo Bonilla-Silva's structural racism theory and Michael Omi and Howard Winant's racial formation theory, both of which centralize US racial matters. Publishing on his structural framework since the mid-1990s, Bonilla-Silva directs analysis to matters of "racialized social structures" often obscured in mainstream social sciences' hyper-focus on framing racial matters from the perspective of individual agency and white Eurocentricity and supremacy. In his influential empirical and theoretical work he has substantially addressed whites' current role in perpetuating the contemporary racialized social system by means of "colorblind racism," the latter a complex white attitudinal framework that presents, as he puts it, "racism without racists."[24] Our minor criticism of Bonilla-Silva's important perspective on racial structures and white attitudes questions his emphasis on the predominance of colorblind racism, presented as more subtle and covert attitudinal racism. Numerous recent field research studies demonstrate that much current white framing of society still involves blatantly racist framing that perpetuates not only old racist attitudes but also old white-framed racist narratives, interpretations, ideologies, and emotions, as well as blatantly racist actions based on that framing (see below).[25] More subtle or disguising colorblind attitudinal racism is just one important variety of the contemporary manifestations and machinations of contemporary systemic racism. Additionally, researchers using a white racial frame approach (see below) in contemporary field research studies have regularly found that much of the "colorblind" perspective of whites today is only a variation of much earlier white attempts to *knowingly* put a good face (i.e., white virtuousness) on overtly racist commentaries and other actions.[26]

Despite our previous critique of racial formation theory on a number of fundamental conceptual and empirical points, we find that Omi and Winant's analyses of racial matters supply a number of rich concepts and perceptions that have helped keep some contemporary social science discussions focused directly on analysis of racial matters and avoided the "ethnicity turn." Their ideas have inspired analytical use by social scientists, including concepts of racial projects, racial group formations, racial rule, and the racial state. Their historical and critical breakdown of several conventional race-theoretical perspectives and analyses of US racial issues is often detailed and informative. Yet, as noted previously, this theory's key concepts—such as racial formation and racial projects—are developed in a too ahistorical, decontextualized, and relativistic form, one that underplays the early *foundational* and continuing *systemic* depth of white racial (most especially, white-on-black) oppression in US society and its major institutions. Their theory becomes much more accurate, especially in empirical terms, if it is reworked to recognize that the specific racial projects and formations they emphasize are nested within a much bigger "societal box"—that is, the larger societal context of a longstanding *system* of white-designed racial oppression that always surrounds and greatly shapes the racial projects and formations they emphasize.[27]

In addition to the assorted theoretical perspectives noted above, systemic racism theory rests substantially on numerous conceptual advancements and a growing and diverse array of empirical studies on matters of US and overseas racism conducted by Joe Feagin and numerous colleagues since the early 1970s. Among Feagin's key works are *Ghetto Revolts* (1973, with Harlan Hahn), *Discrimination American Style* (1978, with Clairece Feagin), *White Racism* (1995, with Hernán Vera), *Systemic Racism* (2006), *Racist America* (2000, 2014), *The White Racial Frame* (2010, 2013), and *How Blacks Built America* (2016), which examine and develop many of the themes central to systemic racism theory that we discuss below.[28] These books and many others, including co-authored works with colleagues and students, provide numerous theoretical insights, conceptual developments, historical examples, and empirical documentations concerning matters of US and global racial oppression.[29] These conceptual and empirical research books paint a detailed and nuanced picture of the interrelated structures and operations of four centuries of systemic racism in the United States. Among the important concepts explored below are the dominant "white racial frame," foundational and "systemic racism," and the extensive "home-culture frames" and "counter-frames" developed by Americans of color in resisting centuries of racial oppression, concepts briefly introduced at the beginning of this book (see Introduction).

A Brief Outline of Systemic Racism Theory

In the following outline, we first present some basic definitions of systemic racism theory and the theory's two principal conceptual understandings: *systemic racism*, and the *white racial frame*. Next, our analysis focuses on elaborating other important characteristics and distinctive perspectives of systemic racism theory. Before concluding our discussion, we deliver two brief sections on the centrality of racism analysis and of analyzing whites that allow us to further craft our understandings of systemic racism and its major dimensions.

Systemic Racism, the White Racial Frame, and Counter-Frames

Systemic racism theory strives to be a historically and empirically backed, epistemologically rigorous social theory of racial oppression and related matters that generates important knowledge about human beings and their social worlds. Knowledge about systemic racism intellectually counters the dominant white racial framing in the United States and other Western societies, as well as in their social sciences. For that reason, it can pragmatically help to dismantle systemic racism in these societies. As noted previously, systemic racism theory is substantially a child of critical black thought and other critical perspectives of social reality that do not shy away from decisive analyses of societal oppressions and power hierarchies that were set in place during the founding of the United States and of other slavery and colonial societies. In the following discussion we focus primarily on the United States, but much of what we discuss is applicable to other Western societies.

Systemic racism refers to the foundational, extensive, and inescapable hierarchical system of US racial oppression that has been devised by whites to subordinate people of color. Systemic racism is a concrete material and social reality, and thus is well embedded in all major institutions of US society. It involves racial oppression that unjustly enriches, materially and socially, the oppressor racial group (whites) and thereby unjustly impoverishes, materially and socially, subordinated racial groups (people of color). A central feature of systemic racism—largely ignored in mainstream theories and some critical theories—is that over *many generations* its white enforcers' actions have routinely *reproduced* the major social networks and institutions that incorporate the asymmetrically structured material and social relations among racial groups. Although rarely noted or analyzed, this critical societal reproduction of unbalanced racial power and privilege persists by means of an important array of intergenerational social inheritance mechanisms supported by most societal institutions.[30]

Individuals, social groups and organizations, and societal institutions are materially and socially structured, and operate to uphold a systemically racist society that benefits whites as a group. Unsurprisingly, US educational institutions, the justice system, and the economy have been well documented as key sites of systemic racism by critical social scientists. However, these are not the only major sites. Systemic racism involves white-devised oppression that runs throughout the entire US social system, reflected not only in these aforementioned institutions but also in the dominant culture and subordinated cultures, in various knowledge paradigms, and in the collective consciousness of dominant and subordinated racial groups. We note too that the major societal institutions are, if necessary, gradually reshaped and refurbished by powerful whites, especially the white elite, as the country faces new international, demographic, and social-historical changes.[31]

To rationalize and defend US society's extensive racial oppression and its associated inequalities over the centuries, whites, especially the most powerful whites, have collectively constructed and maintained an essential and pervasive *white racial frame*. This still-dominant white frame involves much more than racial stereotypes and prejudices—the conventional concepts in mainstream theories—for it is a powerful white worldview that has become embedded in the mostly white-constructed social structures of the United States and many other societies. In this manner, it has become a concrete and determinative force in society with effects much like material forces. The white racial frame is a meta-structure that includes not only broad and persisting racial stereotypes and prejudices, but also racialized narratives, ideologies, images, emotions, and inclinations to discriminate. It racially rationalizes, pervades, and shapes all major institutions, including state, economic, and civil-society institutions. For centuries, this pervasive white frame has routinely implemented and protected US society's inegalitarian structure of material resources and its central racial-power hierarchy dominated at the top by whites.[32]

When viewing the broad scope and power of the rationalizing and action-shaping white racial frame, one can see just how extensively operational it continues to be in shaping everyday sociocultural realities. White-framed racist imagery and propaganda frequently sculpt the racially defined dominant cultural norms and unquestioned dominant narratives about US society, as well as the racialized narratives, national myths, and "imagined communities" of other systemically racist societies.[33] Thus, one sees its heavy impact rather conspicuously in the mainstream media, from the first Hollywood blockbuster film, *Birth of a Nation* (1915), to the day-to-day blatantly racialized discourse of the white radio talk-show hosts and commentators on numerous television shows, especially on the more conservative networks. Their blatantly racialized commentaries are obviously white-framed, but the race-related discourses of others in the mainstream media are very frequently white-framed as well, if often more subtly or covertly framed. This white racial framing demonstrates and reinforces a key aspect of systemic racism, in the past and present. Constantly reiterated, white framing justifies the US racial hierarchy, routinely positioning Americans of color beneath whites, white racial power generally, and the major and unjust inequalities sharply dividing whites from oppressed racial groups.

Another major feature of this pervasive white racial framing in the mainstream media is complete silence about well-institutionalized white racism and a failure to criticize whites' collective role in negatively shaping the broad US racial landscape, including hierarchical racial group relations.[34] Unlike the conservative media, the more "liberal" mainstream media do periodically address attitudinal racism issues and present some criticisms of, usually very localized, white racial discrimination. Yet, even these media present their own version of white-framed understandings of human relations and the social world and remain generally uncritical about broader matters of systemic racism and the general white abuse of racial power. They often remain ignorant or dismissive of the more critical counter-framing of racial matters by African Americans and other Americans of color.

Beyond the mainstream media, recent research studies by increasing numbers of critical social scientists, many of them developing aspects of systemic racism theory, demonstrate the extent and effectiveness of the dominant white racial frame and other aspects of systemic racism. We do not have space for the necessary book-length review of these studies, but can illustrate the powerful racialized reality they demonstrate, including why there is a need for systemic racism theory. Consider one major research study involving 626 white college students at two dozen US colleges and universities. They recorded, in six- to 12-week diaries, some of the racial events in their daily lives. One white male student at a Midwestern college provides a typical account from about 7,500 overtly racist accounts in the diaries. He writes of recurring party joking with other white males:

> [W]ith the full group membership present, anti-Semitic jokes abound, as do racial slurs and vastly derogatory statements... Various jokes concerning stereotypes... were also swapped around the gaming table, everything from "How many Hebes fit in a VW beetle?" to "Why did the Jews wander the desert for forty years?" In each case, the punch lines were offensive, even though I'm not Jewish. The answers were "One million (in the ashtray) and four (in the seats)" and "because someone dropped a quarter," respectively. These jokes degraded into a rendition of the song "Yellow," which was re-done to represent the Hiroshima and Nagasaki bombings. It contained lines about the shadows of the people being flash burned into the walls... A member of the group also decided that he has the perfect idea for a Hallmark card. On the cover it would have a few kittens in a basket with ribbons and lace. On the inside it would simply say "You're a nigger."... Supposedly, when questioned about it, the idea of the card was to make it as offensive as humanly possible in order to make the maximal juxtaposition between warm and ice hearted... Of course, no group is particularly safe from the group's scathing wit, and the people of Mexico were next to bear the brunt of the jokes. A comment was made about Mexicans driving low-riding cars so they can drive and pick lettuce at the same time. Comments were made about the influx of illegal aliens from Mexico and how fast they produce offspring.[35]

These diaries were written down by well-educated whites who are supposed to be the least racist generation in US history. The thousands of recorded racist events reveal openly the still-dominant white racial framing that is often downplayed or weakly portrayed in mainstream research. There is much more to their racist framing than obvious stereotypes. Note the vivid racist images, emotion-laden performances, and underlying racial narratives—and how well these young whites have learned from friends, relatives, and other sources about white superiority and the racialized others' inferiority. We observe here how the dominant white frame structures everyday events and recurring performances by whites, which in turn reinforce that dominant frame. At the center of this dominant frame is a pro-white sub-frame accenting white privilege and power, including a racialized arrogance and sense of entitlement.

Like the media, many mainstream social scientists working on racial matters are often invested in a version of this dominant white frame, as can be seen when they often pathologize, scapegoat, or devalue people of color and overtly or subtly normalize, glorify, or idealize whites—a pattern of misinformation and disinformation that systemic racism theory and field research attempts to dissect, deconstruct, and correct.

Importantly, systemic racism theorists and researchers have followed black critical thinkers in emphasizing the central importance of the active and covert *resistance* to systemic racial oppression by African Americans and other Americans of color. Two fundamental frames suggested by systemic racism theorist Joe Feagin are useful in understanding this resistance—(1) the anti-oppression *counter-frames* of Americans of color, and (2) the *home-culture frames* they have drawn on for their everyday lives and to develop anti-oppression counter-frames. Opposing the dominant white frame, Americans of color have frequently developed significant counter-frames, which have helped them to understand and resist systemic racism. Early counter-frames, such as those of Native Americans and African Americans, were initially developed for survival purposes, and over time they have added critical elements that strengthen understanding systemic racism and strategies necessary for racism resistance. These counter-frames of people of color often contain ideals and images of *real* freedom, equality, and justice envisioned for all people. Moreover, these resistance counter-frames have drawn heavily on elements from the home-cultures of those oppressed. For instance, since the first century of enslavement, African Americans have maintained a strong home-culture frame with features stemming both from the African background and from experiences in North America.[36]

Research Methodologies and Strategies
Systemic racism theory has developed substantially out of and is grounded in much empirical research, including in-depth interviewing, ethnographic fieldwork, content analysis of diaries and other sources, and comparative-historical analyses. Systemic racism research is also often multi-methodological, combining some of these qualitative research approaches with survey techniques and statistical analyses.

Generally concerned with historically informed analysis, systemic racism theory argues for understanding the foundational and systemic realities of societies and their human relations. For example, US society cannot be understood properly without substantial knowledge of its deeply racist economic, political, and cultural foundations. Along with a multi-methodological approach and an explanatory approach that addresses the foundational and systemic realities of racial matters, systemic racism theory and research provide a counter-mainstream social science that is critical of a society's powerful white elite, an elite that generally dictates what counts as legitimate social science knowledge and who counts as the truly important social scientists. Foregrounding, critically analyzing, and dismantling racist power structures in academia and in society are major concerns of systemic racism theorists and researchers.

Systemic racism theory exposes the *sobering* realities of asymmetrical racial group relations and the profound human disorders and social pathologies stemming from entrenched racial oppression. A leading critical sociologist of racial matters, John Stanfield, has underscored the "absurd assumptions and false optimism of American sociology of race relations" and of the US social sciences generally avoiding addressing the oppressive realities of systemic racism. Researching and writing about race critically and "soberly is still grounds in this society for not getting a job, for not keeping a job, for being labeled a troublemaker." Unsurprisingly, thus, many social scientists and other academics have built their careers by emphasizing race relations paradigms "that did more to make everybody feel comfortable and optimistic than deal with the sobering aspects of race in post-World War II and now twenty-first century America."[37]

Indeed, today, few social scientists and other academics tackle the major aspects of systemic racism, including its several centuries of dramatic perseverance. The United States persists as a systemically racist society in which comprehensive racial progress, real racial democracy, and true racial group pluralism remain distant rhetorical ideals of a "feel good" ideology, including in much social science. Moreover, the social sciences remain "historically invested in white supremacy norms and values providing the professionalization experiences and canons which all must adhere."[38] Indeed, it was not a social scientist who did the first in-depth study on how the extreme racialization of the US prison-industrial complex has emerged after the 1960s civil rights movement and developed extensively to replace the legal oppression of the Jim Crow era. The brilliant critical race theorist and law professor Michelle Alexander wrote the first such detailed analysis, *The New Jim Crow*, a book that presents the sobering claim that features of Jim Crow segregation persist today in that prison-industrial complex. Central to contemporary systemic racism is this hyper-incarceration of black and brown people since the 1960s.[39] This hyper-incarceration, other large-scale discrimination in the justice system, policing that unethically profiles people of color, and very excessive police violence directed at people of color are just a few aspects of today's systemic racism that reproduce aspects of Jim Crow. Along with avoiding social science investigations of systemic racism in the justice system, mainstream social scientists have mostly evaded serious study of the *root causes* of major and persisting housing, educational, and other racial segregation.

Indeed, if they are going to be relevant in helping create a truly just and democratic society, mainstream social sciences must become much more *race-critical* and research thoroughly this society's unsettling racial realities. For instance, a central concept in systemic racism theory focusing on negative social realities is *racial oppression*, a term most mainstream social scientists never employ. Specifically, systemic racism theory identifies the US racial oppressor group as whites, and the racially oppressed groups as peoples of color. Racial oppression is not an abstract, impersonal agent-free operation, as is implied in much mainstream theorizing, for some racial groups are agents of oppression and some are targets. Further, this racial oppression is defined as foundational to, and deeply ingrained in, major US institutions and as operational throughout all societal levels. In its daily operations such oppression is extensively burdensome and hierarchically materialistic, constantly exploitative in numerous socioeconomic realms and creating unjust enrichment for whites and unjust impoverishment for Americans of color. Racial oppression is clearly integral to the creation and maintenance of the dominant societal hierarchy that stratifies racial groups with its asymmetrical allocation of individual and group longevity, power, and privilege. Thus, a truly critical social science analysis of US racial matters must encompasses a full awareness of and research about this *foundational* and *systemic* racial oppression, and of whites' role in the creation and recreation of such systemically racist societies.[40]

Unlike most mainstream social science analyses of racial matters, which remain primarily focused on micro-level (individuals) and meso-level (groups) racial analyses, systemic racism theory researches and attempts to explain the various societal levels of racial oppression. Especially important in systemic racism analyses is recurring attention to macro-level racial matters, particularly the larger institutional and systemic racism contexts of these micro- and macro-level realities. While focusing on the often overlooked macro-level contexts, systemic racism researchers also examine the necessary micro- and meso-levels of racial matters at which specific human framing and behavior are demonstrated. For example, systemic racism analysis frequently addresses individual and group racial identities and smaller-scale racial group interactions that are regularly shaped by the macro racial context of well-institutionalized racism, including its "fuel," the omnipresent white racial framing that creates *imposed* racial identities.[41] By emphasizing the intimate and recurring connections among micro-, meso-, and macro-level racial phenomena—especially the interaction between human agency and social structures involved in the *reproduction* of society's systemic racism—systemic racism theory is linked to and partially influenced by several social science traditions, including the micro-level concerns of symbolic interactionism and the macro-level concerns of structural-functionalism and conflict theory.

Lastly, although the systemic racism theory and analysis accented in this book primarily examines US racial matters, this critical approach does provide a framework for discussing *global systemic racism*—that is, the systemic racism generated and sustained by Western imperialism rooted in colonialism. From a systemic racism perspective, for centuries white racial oppression has been both local (e.g., US Jim Crow, South African apartheid) and global (e.g., European and US imperialism in

Africa, the Americas, and Asia). As scholars such as Eric Williams, Sven Becket, and Edward Baptist have demonstrated, the connections between these local and global dimensions of white racial oppression are very clear over centuries of Western slavery and colonization and in their offspring, capitalism. US slavery and Western colonialism have long represented a white-run capitalist global system of racial exploitation almost always targeting people of color, one that was the basis for what has been become known as "modernization," "global development," and "advanced civilization."[42]

We now illustrate a few of the major conceptual concerns and advances of systemic racism theory and analysis since the 1960s.

Centrality of White Racism Analysis

A central concern of systemic racism theorists and researchers entails the in-depth study and analysis of white societal power and privilege at the heart of society's systemic racism. As we demonstrated in Chapter 9, one important contribution of critical black thought over the centuries has been a steadfast concern with describing and analyzing well the tangible, exploitative, and experientially brutal operations and structures of *institutionalized white racism*, while mainstream white social theorists and analysts have generally turned a blind eye to this fundamental and systemic feature of societal reality. Numerous early critical black social theorists cogently described the metamorphosis of systemically racist social systems through different historical phases of US and global colonialism and imperialism. As already discussed, during the 1960s rights movements, activist-intellectual Stokely Carmichael (Kwame Ture) and political scientist Charles Hamilton wrote the pathbreaking book *Black Power* and thereby helped to bridge past black critical work with present-day black critical studies. With the use of rich empirical data, they generated a well-developed theory of institutional white racism, as contrasted with individual white racism, arguably the first well-developed and methodically rich theoretical analysis of systemic white racism. They explicitly analyzed elements of the "white social structure" and "white power" and the ways "institutional racism" operates throughout major US institutions.[43]

Our own understanding and delineation of systemic racism has for decades been greatly influenced by the pathbreaking insights in Carmichael and Hamilton's analysis and similar critical black analyses since the 1960s.[44] Thus, systemic racism theory highlights the systemic racism created by whites as the central motor of US and global racial matters, one that should be the primary focus of serious analysis of many contemporary societies. Institutional racism means that white racial oppression cuts across major institutions, whereas systemic racism, more broadly, encompasses racism throughout all institutions and the entire social system.[45] Most mainstream social scientists rarely consider such macro-level attributes of white racism in their analyses of US racial matters, but instead often focus on measures of individuals' racial attitudes or government census data, focusing on racial-group percentages and other statistical patterns. While these social science pursuits are important, systemic racism theorists and researchers have gone farther and integrated institutional racism theory into field research and advanced the use of critical concepts in empirical studies, concepts such as the white racial frame, the counter-frames of people of color, race/class/gender intersectionality, and the social reproduction of racial inequality over generations.

Like earlier critical black thought, systemic racism theory centralizes the analysis of white-generated and white-maintained racism, facilitating the move from vague constructions of *race theory* to *racism theory* of *white oppression* based on researching concrete, empirically documented, and historically rooted societal realities. As noted previously, Eduardo Bonilla-Silva's call for a structural theory of racism and conceptualization of a racialized social system are closely related to meanings and pursuits of institutional racism and systemic racism theorizing.[46]

In addition, several women scholars of color have explicitly emphasized the importance of whites' routine implementation of what they explicitly term "gendered racism." We have previously underscored the innovative work of Patricia Hill Collins. Additionally, since the 1990s, sociologist Philomena Essed has introduced the concept termed *gendered racism* in theorizing interviews with black women in the United States and Europe. Explaining how black women's everyday experience with white discriminators is often gendered-racist, she accents how whites' structural racism and sexism intimately intertwine. She also shows how black women develop distinctive systems of knowledge for fighting whites' gendered racism.[47] Recently, Adia Harvey Wingfield has contributed significantly to further development of this aspect of systemic racism theory with rich new empirical data on, and the explicit concept of, "systemic gendered racism." For example, studying black women entrepreneurs who started beauty salons, she found they faced systemic gendered-racist framing and discrimination, especially from white lenders and potential white clients. Wingfield has further enhanced the concepts of a home-culture frame and a black anti-racist counter-frame in documenting the racism-resistance of these women in creating safe spaces for other black women to counter negative impacts of whites' systemic gendered racism.[48]

Essential to an accurate portrayal of structural, institutional, systemic racism is a clear recognition of the central white role in creating and overseeing systemically racist societies, an important facet of Bonilla-Silva's, Collins', Essed's, and Wingfield's recent work and the central message of Carmichael and Hamilton's pathbreaking book.

Foregrounding and Analyzing Ordinary and Elite Whites

Despite increasingly strong scholarship in critical "whiteness studies" among a modest number of scholars,[49] mainstream social scientists have historically evaded critical analyses of whites—and especially elite white men—as the central agents of racial oppression in societies such as the United States. Indeed, whiteness researchers focusing centrally on whites' racist perceptions and practices often experience some academic marginalization and have frequently faced problems in getting their research published by mainstream journals and presses.[50] This is highly problematic from the perspective of gathering much neglected societal knowledge, especially considering that whites have been the most powerful, resource laden, and socially well-positioned racial group. Given that whites generally control Western societies and, to a large degree, greatly influence international political-economic relations, a comprehensive analysis of systemic racism cannot bypass a full examination of whites, especially the white (mostly male) power elite that today possesses inordinate amounts of power and vast resources.[51]

Certainly, "whites" and "whiteness" are complex, philosophically problematic racialized concepts. Yet, these conceptual understandings continue to be employed in the social world as identity markers and a means for racial group division and organization according to a white-framed racial hierarchy, one imposed on society by self-described whites. Today, certainly, multiraciality, self-chosen racial identities, and race/class/gender intersectionalities of human beings present serious challenges to this dominant white racial framing and its hoary notions of whites and whiteness. Nevertheless, whites as a group still currently have the power to set themselves apart from other racial groups and to subjugate other racial groups.

Because we already have illustrated our understanding of whites' role in systemic racism previously in this book and analyses published elsewhere, we will just recap a few other major points about whites and systemic racism theory here.[52] Systemic racism theory emphasizes that self-defined whites of European descent are the creators, overseers, and maintainers of numerous contemporary societies with highly racialized social institutions. This perspective centralizes the role of whites, especially elite white men, in this creation and perpetuation of systemic racism in these societies and perceives whites as the racial group atop a well-structured group hierarchy developed over centuries of systemic oppression. This oppression has taken the historical form of colonialism and slavery, and recently new forms of racial domination targeting an array of subordinated racial groups. For centuries, asymmetrical (i.e., unjust and unequal) power relations between people of color and whites who control and monopolize major political-economic capital and other resources have been the norm. In the modern development of Western societies, this hierarchical group organization has changed slowly, but often little in its broad social contours and major operations. For example, one still observes today the persisting negative effects of white European "settler colonialism"[53] on most Native American societies (especially "reservations"), effects frequently similar to those of centuries past. Institutional and systemic racism, although not articulated significantly in most mainstream analyses, are invaluable concepts that are necessary to fully understand the harsh realities of contemporary racial oppression.

Possibly, one major reason that numerous contemporary theorists of racial matters largely avoid a central discussion of institutional and systemic racism, including these concepts' development in the black critical tradition, is because these concepts necessarily implicate and call out whites, especially the white male elite, as those who still routinely control societal institutions that imbed and reproduce society's extensive racial discrimination and dramatic inequalities. On an everyday basis, elite and ordinary whites are the architects, builders, and maintenance workers of institutional and systemic racism. Yet, for many social scientists researching racial issues, whites are not viewed as principal progenitors of foundational and systemic racism, nor viewed as a racial group that is much more racist in its framing of society than other groups.

Most mainstream social scientists investigating racial matters never dig deeply into whites' highly institutionalized oppression of people of color; they typically do not focus upon the important ways that whites have subjugated people of color in a racial hierarchy that forcefully grants whites unjustly disproportionate power, status, and privilege. Consider the issues that a truly serious contemporary social science of "race" should be investigating forcefully and frequently. First, there is the long history of white relationships to Americans of color, a relationship of racial oppression that is foundational and systemic. This enduring relationship has routinely included myriad white exploitative and discriminatory practices that have regularly resulted in unjustly gained white resources, power, and privilege. Over several centuries, these unjustly gained material and other resource inequalities have been routinely maintained by well-institutionalized reproduction mechanisms and processes. Additionally, there is the very extensive white racial frame that rationalizes and implements persisting white oppression, a framing that includes not only conventionally studied racial stereotypes and prejudices, but also racialized narratives, images, ideologies, and emotions.[54]

In most cases, mainstream social scientists fail to substantially question the dominant white-framed perspectives of the social world and human beings. One observes this, for example, in the continuing, widespread, and usually uncritical use of white-designed intelligence-measuring tests to examine an array of racial issues. These tests are actually only skills tests demonstrably influenced by the skills-learning backgrounds of those who take them. Another example can be seen in the mainstream social sciences' avoidance of serious studies of white power structures. In contrast, critical scholars of racial matters have highlighted these power structures and the perspectives and practices of different subgroups of whites in their research.[55]

Yet, although all whites are part of the dominant oppressor racial group and benefit from that placement, that does not mean they all display negative framing of and action against subordinated racial groups in similar ways. Today, as in the past, numerous whites do not deny their position in the racial hierarchy, nor the racial privileges and power they possess, and some work to offset that unearned privilege and power and battle racially oppressive institutions. Still, even whites who are serious crusaders against racial injustice cannot escape the many privileges and societal power that comes from being identified and positioned as white. Additionally, as a matter of empirical fact, most whites are generally content with their position in the dominant hierarchy and with the norms of everyday racism. Indeed, many become disturbed, some violently, when their racial position and the racial status quo are seriously threatened by resistance from people of color and other societal change.[56]

An important issue for serious studies of US and global racial matters is a full awareness that, while most whites work together, directly or indirectly, to uphold systemic racism, some have much more racial power and privilege. At the top of most major institutions sits the white elite, those with very disproportionate and substantial capital, resources, and power, who make most of society's important decisions. In ongoing research, several sociologists have demonstrated the distinctively greater power of elite white men in shaping major US and global institutions that are central to systemic racism in the past and present.⁵⁷ Additionally, Sean Elias' fieldwork on the Aspen (Colorado) elite investigates attitudes, behaviors, and beliefs of the mostly white US and global power elite and how such power elite enclaves such as Aspen represent and reproduce racial and class hierarchies.⁵⁸ These systemic racism studies have shown how even the uppermost ranks of white America are divided between a small number of elite whites who substantially control many ideas and actions of a much larger number of whites immediately below them in status but who occupy upper-level positions in business, political, military, religious, cultural, and educational organizations. These mostly upper-middle-class white men, assisted by growing numbers of white women and modest numbers of people of color, are the primary mediators and assistants who carry out the more important actions necessary to maintain society's systemic racism. Moreover, below this uppermost rank of whites, the white middle-class majority and white working class also benefit from the institutional arrangements favoring whites generally in a systemically racist society.

The mainstream social sciences have almost entirely avoided serious race-critical analyses of the white elite, including the wealthy donors and their funding and charitable organizations that shape everything from politics to civic organizations and the universities where most social scientists work. Activists, researchers, and other analysts who seriously challenge the elite's societal framing and agendas are often cut off from various types of essential research, educational, or political-economic capital, including major private funding that increasingly helps to sustain many institutions and organizations serving the public welfare. Unsurprisingly, thus, mainstream social scientists working on racial matters are generally reduced to safely studying the racial attitudes and behaviors of ordinary whites.

Moreover, with mainstream social sciences' focus on the social pathologies of Americans of color, little attention has been paid to highly consequential white social pathologies. Considering whites' great power in affecting the lives of all other groups and society generally, systemic racism theorists understand that white social pathologies demand a central focus in serious analyses of historical and contemporary racial matters. Not surprisingly, systemic racism may be viewed as the greatest white social pathology because it permeates every walk of life. As we have noted previously, systemic racism corrupts the economy, governments, and much of civil society. Its dominant white racial framing affects the social psychology of virtually all citizens and distorts social reality to the point that false racial consciousness often reigns. In addition, systemic racism is infused throughout Western imperialism in the past and present. The severe social pathologies associated with this colonialism and imperialism are too numerous to list, but include many white-generated wars, "settler" colonialism, Westernized puppet governments, and vast exploitation of the resources of people of color on several continents.

Most social scientists would agree that the top corporate and allied political leaders are largely responsible for ruling contemporary societies. In the United States, the longtime merging of top business and political leaders into one overwhelmingly white elite—from George Washington's day to the present—demonstrates this anti-democratic reality. This is conspicuously demonstrated in the "revolving door" between the halls of government power in Washington, DC, and the executive offices of large banks and multinational corporations. We provide detailed analyses of this ruling elite elsewhere, but can briefly note just who they are in terms of racial composition.[59] For example, in 2015 the *Fortune* 500's top corporate executives (CEOs) were more than 95 percent white. Only four (0.8 percent) were black, ten were Asian (2 percent), and ten were Latino/a (2 percent). Additionally, most were men. The corporate elite is still predominantly white men. Next, consider the 2015 composition of the US Senate, arguably the world's most powerful political body. It too was overwhelmingly white in composition (94 percent). Only two senators (2 percent) were black, only one (1 percent) was Asian American; and only three (3 percent) were Latino. In addition, three-quarters of the senators were white men. In the same year, the US House of Representatives was also 80 percent white and 80 percent male.[60] When considering that the overwhelming majority of those at the top of the US government and a similarly large proportion of those in charge of major US and global corporations are white, it becomes difficult to argue against the vivid social reality of the continued racial power of elite whites (mostly men) in shaping both US and international political-economic arrangements.

A Brief Review: The Systemic Racism Critique of "Race" Theory
We can conclude this discussion of systemic racism theory by briefly referring the reader back to our systemic racism critiques of mainstream "race" theory. Generally speaking, this contemporary race theory fails to offer the conceptual tools and theoretical perspectives needed for in-depth, comprehensive race-critical analyses of an array of racial matters in the United States and globally. Indeed, one can argue that mainstream race theory is presently in "crisis."[61] For example, optimistic theories touting varieties of colorblindness and post-raciality dominate some social science research, as we demonstrated in Chapter 3. In addition, some prominent social scientists have decentered analyses of racial matters in favor of new theoretical formulations, class-based analyses, ethnicity or nationalism studies, or analyses of cultural boundaries and formations, the focus of critiques in Chapters 4 and 5. While these various efforts have led to important theoretical considerations and insights about the ways that class, ethnicity, nationality, culture, and other factors shape individuals and groups in society, they have offered little insightful theorizing about the critical matters of historical and contemporary systemic racism, for the latter raises a rather different set of important issues for social scientists to seriously consider. While many of these aforementioned thinkers have good ideas that complement systemic racism theory and other critical theories of racial matters, it is unsettling how they and other social scientists persistently attempt to explain matters of foundational and systemic white racism through the limited lenses of class, ethnicity, nationality, or culture paradigms and abstract theorizing.

We trace the fallacies of biosocial and assimilation explanations of human beings and society in Chapters 6 and 7. Biosocial theories of racial matters, which predate the birth of modern social science in the nineteenth century, today seem popular. Under diverse labels, sociogenomics, sociobiology, and biosocial analysis reflect putrid old wine in a flashy new bottle. That is, many of the early ethnocentric views of white racial superiority and the inferiority of people of color are covertly packaged now as the latest biologized social "science."

Moreover, since the early Chicago sociologist Robert Park created his "race relations cycle," assimilation theories have persisted as dominant theoretical narratives of racial matters in social science. For the most part, mainstream social scientists view assimilation uncritically as a positive social process (e.g., becoming "American") and a way of explaining racial group divisions and solutions to societal problems (e.g., people of color must assimilate to dominant white culture). Plagued with white-framed understandings that reproduce the dominant racial hierarchy and with an absence of critical analyses of systemic racism, most assimilation theorizing in effect represents a somewhat disguised theoretical justification of the racial status quo.[62]

Even some of the more progressive contemporary racial theorizing is often lacking in key respects, as our critique of racial formation theory in Chapter 8 reveals. These theorists seem to be wary of a substantial and specified discussion of the role of white agency, most importantly elite white agents, in the creation and constant maintenance of the white oppression targeting people of color. In addition, much excellent work on racial identities, including intersectionalist concerns with linkages to gender and class, fails to systematically address the macro-structural realities of racial oppression that largely contextualize most identity formations, especially the constant battle between socially imposed identities and individual self-chosen identities. Micro-level analyses of identity are incomplete without contextualization in macro-level social realities. Numerous excellent empirical studies of these racial matters exist, but remain weakly interpreted without a theoretical grounding that explains how larger macro forces and structures of systemic racism—including the commonplace, centuries-old white racial framing—still regularly shape the range of racial phenomena under study.

Notes

1 Mustafa Emirbayer and Matthew Desmond, *The Racial Order* (Chicago: University of Chicago Press, 2015), p. 1. See our Chapter 4 for a critique of their Eurocentric approach.

2 Thomas Piketty, *Capital in the Twenty-First Century* (Cambridge, MA: Harvard University Press, 2014); Mark S. Mizruchi, "The American Corporate Elite and the Financial Crisis of 2008," in Michael Lounsbury and Paul Hirsch (eds.), *Markets on Trial: The Economic Sociology of the US Financial Crises* (Bingley: Emerald Group Publishing, 2010).

3 Catharine MacKinnon, *Toward a Feminist Theory of the State* (Cambridge, MA: Harvard University Press, 2001); bell hooks, *Feminist Theory: From Margin to Center* (Boston: South End Press, 2000); Dorothy Smith, *The Conceptual Practices of Power: A Feminist Sociology of Knowledge* (Toronto: University of Toronto Press, 1990); Patricia Hill Collins, *Black Feminist Thought: Knowledge, Consciousness, and the Politics of Empowerment* (Boston: Unwin Hyman, 1990); Angela Davis, *Women, Race, and Class* (New York: Vintage Books, 1983).

4 Angela Davis, "Reflections on the Black Woman's Role in the Community of Slaves," *Black Scholar*, 3 (1971): 2–15.

5 Yanick St. Jean and Joe Feagin, *Double Burden: Black Women and Everyday Racism* (New York: M.E. Sharpe, 1998).

6 bell hooks, *Black Looks: Race and Representation* (Boston: South End Press, 1992).

7 Elizabeth Higginbotham, *Too Much to Ask: Black Women in the Era of Integration* (Chapel Hill: University of North Carolina Press, 2001); Louwanda Evans, *Cabin Pressure: African American Pilots, Flight Attendants, and Emotional Labor* (Lanham, MD: Rowman & Littlefield, 2013); Joe Feagin and José Cobas, *Latinos Facing Racism: Discrimination, Resistance and Endurance* (New York: Paradigm/Routledge, 2014); Brittany Slatton, *Mythologizing Black Women: Unveiling White Men's Racist and Sexist Deep Frame* (Paradigm/Routledge, 2014).

8 Collins, *Black Feminist Thought*, p. 67.

9 Patricia Hill Collins, "Learning From the Outsider Within: The Sociological Significance of Black Feminist Thought," *Social Problems*, 33 (1986): 14–32.

10 Patricia Hill Collins, *Fighting Words: Black Women and the Search for Justice* (Minneapolis: University of Minnesota Press, 1998), pp. xi–xii.

11 Ibid., pp. 96, 199. See Joe Feagin, Hernán Vera, and Kimberley Ducey, *Liberation Sociology*, 3rd edn (Boulder, CO: Paradigm, 2015), pp. 216–22.

12 Collins, "Learning from the Outsider Within," p. 22.

13 W.E.B. Du Bois, *The Suppression of the African Slave Trade* (Baton Rouge, LA: Louisiana State University Press, 1969 [1896]); W.E.B. Du Bois, *Black Reconstruction in America, 1860–1880* (New York: Free Press, 1992 [1935]); W.E.B. Du Bois, *Black Folk: Then and Now* (Millwood, NY: Kraus-Thomson, 1975 [1939]).

14 John Hope Franklin, with Evelyn Brooks Higginbotham, *From Slavery to Freedom: A History of African Americans* (New York: McGraw-Hill, 2010 [1947]).

15 C. Vann Woodward, *The Strange Career of Jim Crow* (New York: Oxford University Press, 1974 [1957]); C.L.R. James, *American Civilization* (Cambridge, MA: Blackwell, 1993); Kenneth M. Stampp, *The Era of Reconstruction, 1865–1877* (New York: Vintage, 1965); Winthrop D. Jordan, *The White Man's Burden: Historical Origins of Racism in the United States* (New York: Oxford University Press, 1974); Eric Williams, *Capitalism and Slavery* (Chapel Hill: University of North Carolina Press, 1994 [1970]); John G. Jackson, *Introduction to African Civilizations* (New York: Carol Publishing Group, 1990 [1970]); Lawrence Levine, *Black Culture and Black Consciousness: Afro-American Folk Thought From Slavery to Freedom* (New York: Oxford University Press, 1977); Edward W. Said, *Orientalism* (New York: Vintage, 1978).

16 Davis, *Women, Race and Class*; Aldon D. Morris, *The Origins of the Civil Rights Movement: Black Communities Organizing for Change* (New York: The Free Press, 1984); Chancellor Williams, *The Destruction of Black Civilization, Great Issues of a Race from*

4500 BC to 2000 AD (Chicago: Third World Press, 1996 [1987]); Martin Bernal, *Black Athena: The Afroasiatic Roots of Classical Civilization, Volumes I, II, and III* (New Brunswick, NJ: Rutgers University Press, 2003 [1987]); Paul G. Lauren, *Power and Prejudice: The Politics and Diplomacy of Racial Discrimination* (Boulder, CO: Westview Press, 1996); John H. Clark, *Critical Lessons in Slavery and the Slavetrade* (Richmond, VA: Native Sun Publishing, 1996); Lerone Bennett Jr., *Forced into Glory: Abraham Lincoln's White Dream* (Chicago: Johnson Publishing, 2000).

17 Ronald Takaki, *Iron Cages: Race and Culture in Nineteenth Century America* (New York: Oxford University Press, 2000); Juan Gonzalez, *Harvest of Empire: A History of Latinos in America* (New York: Penguin, 2001); Ramón Gutiérrez, *When Jesus Came, The Corn Mothers Went Away: Marriage, Sexuality, and Power in New Mexico, 1500–1846* (Stanford, CA: Stanford University Press, 1991); George M. Frederickson, *The Black Image in the White Mind: The Debate on Afro-American Character and Destiny, 1817–1914* (Hanover, NH: Wesleyan University Press, 1987); Ira Katznelson, *When Affirmative Action Was White: An Untold History of Racial Inequality in Twentieth-Century America* (New York: W.W. Norton, 2005); Molefi Asante, *The History of Africa: The Quest for Eternal Harmony* (New York: Routledge, 2007).

18 Nell Painter, *The History of White People* (New York: W.W. Norton, 2011); Jenny Irons, *Reconstituting Whiteness: The Mississippi State Sovereignty Commission* (Nashville, TN: Vanderbilt University Press, 2010); Sven Beckert, *Empire of Cotton: A Global History* (New York: Knopf, 2014); Roxanne Dunbar-Ortiz, *An Indigenous People' History of the United States* (Boston: Beacon Press, 2014); Edward Baptist, *The Half Has Never been Told: Slavery and the Making of American Capitalism* (New York: Basic Books, 2014).

19 Stokely Carmichael (Kwame Ture), with Ekwueme Michael Thelwell, *Ready for Revolution: The Life and Struggles of Stokely Carmichael* (New York: Scribner, 2003).

20 See Joe Feagin, Hernán Vera, and Kimberley Ducey, *Liberation Sociology*, 3rd edn (Boulder, CO: Paradigm, 2015); Joe Feagin, Sean Elias, and Jennifer Mueller, "Social Justice and Critical Public Sociology," in Vincent Jeffries (ed.), *Handbook of Public Sociology*, (Lanham, MD: Roman & Littlefield, 2009); Sean Elias, "W.E.B. Du Bois, Race, and Human Rights," *Societies Without Borders* 4(3) (2009): 273–94.

21 See, for example, blog sites that engage critical racial analysis using data, such as Joe Feagin and Jessie Daniels's *Racism Review*, http://racismreview.com; and Chauncey DeVaga's *We are Respectable Negroes* blog, www.chaunceydevega.com.

22 See Martin Heidegger, *Question Concerning Technology and Other Essays*, trans. William Lovett (New York: HarperCollins, 1977 [1954]; Michel Foucault, *The Order of Things: An Archaeology of the Human Sciences* (New York: Vintage, 1973); Jacques Derrida, *Of Grammatology*, trans. Gayatri C. Spivak (Baltimore, MD: Johns Hopkins University Press, 1974).

23 Franz Fanon, *The Wretched of the Earth*, trans. Constance Farrington (New York: Grove Press, 1963); Aimé Césaire, *Discourse on Colonialism*, trans. Joan Pinkham (New York: Monthly Review Press, 2001); Edward Said, *Orientalism* (New York: Vintage, 1979); Albert Memmi, *The Colonizer and the Colonized*, trans. Howard Greenfield (Boston: Beacon Press, 1991); Raewyn Connell, *Southern Theory: The Global Dynamics of Knowledge in Social Sciences* (Cambridge: Polity, 2007).

24 See Eduardo Bonilla-Silva, "Rethinking Racism: Toward a Structural Interpretation," *American Sociological Review*, 62(3) (1997): 465–80; Michael Omi and Howard Winant, *Racial Formation in the United States*, 3rd edn (New York: Routledge, 2015).

25 See Leslie H. Picca and Joe Feagin, *Two-Faced Racism: Whites in the Backstage and Frontstage* (New York: Routledge, 2007); Slatton, *Mythologizing Black Women*. Similarly, we understand the significance of "laissez-faire racism" analyzed by Lawrence Bobo

et al., but do not view this as the new norm of racism, just one current manifestation of systemic racism. See Lawrence Bobo and Ryan A. Smith, "From Jim Crow Racism to Laissez Faire Racism: The Transformation of Racial Attitudes," in *Beyond Pluralism: The Conception of Groups and Group Identities in America* (Urbana, IL: University of Illinois Press, 1988), pp. 182–220.
26 See Picca and Feagin, *Two Faced Racism*; Feagin, *The White Racial Frame*.
27 Joe R. Feagin and Sean Elias, "Rethinking Racial Formation Theory: A Systemic Racism Critique," *Ethnic and Racial Studies*, 36(6) (2013): 955.
28 Joe R. Feagin and Harlan Hahn, *Ghetto Revolts: The Politics of Violence in American Cities* (New York: Macmillan, 1973); Joe R. Feagin and Clairece Y. Feagin, *Discrimination American Style: Institutional Racism and Sexism* (Englewood Cliffs, NJ: Prentice-Hall, 1978); Joe R. Feagin and Hernán Vera, *White Racism: The Basics* (New York: Routledge, 1995); Joe R. Feagin, *Systemic Racism: A Theory of Oppression* (New York: Routledge, 2006); Joe R. Feagin, *Racist America: Roots, Current Realities, and Future Reparations*, 3rd edn (New York: Routledge, 2014); Joe R. Feagin, *The White Racial Frame: Centuries of Racial Framing and Counter-Framing*, 2nd edn (New York: Routledge, 2013); Joe R. Feagin, *How Blacks Built America: Labor, Culture, Freedom, and Democracy* (New York: Routledge, 2016).
29 See, among many others, Joe Feagin and Nijole N. Benokraitis, "Institutional Racism: A Perspective in Search of Clarity and Research" in C.V. Willie (ed.), *Black/Brown/White Relations* (New Brunswick, NJ: Transaction Books, 1976), pp. 122–45; Joe R. Feagin, *Racial and Ethnic Relations* (Englewood Cliffs, NJ: Prentice-Hall, 1978); Joe R. Feagin and Clairece B. Feagin, *Discrimination American Style* (Englewood Cliffs, NJ: Prentice-Hall, 1978); Joe R. Feagin and Melvin P. Sikes, *Living With Racism: The Black Middle Class Experience* (Boston: Beacon Press, 1994); Yanick St. Jean and Joe R. Feagin, *Double Burden: Black Women and Everyday Racism* (Armonk, NY: M.E. Sharpe, Inc., 1999); Joe R. Feagin, Hernán Vera, and Pinar Batur, *White Racism: The Basics* (New York: Routledge, 2001); Adia Harvey Wingfield and Joe R. Feagin, *Yes We Can?: White Racial Framing and the 2008 Presidential Campaign*, 2nd edn (New York: Routledge, 2012); Joe R. Feagin and José A. Cobas, *Latinos Facing Racism: Discrimination, Resistance, and Endurance* (Boulder, CO: Paradigm, 2013); Leslie Picca and Joe Feagin, *Two-Faced Racism*; Rosalind S. Chou and Joe R. Feagin, *The Myth of the Model Minority: Asians Facing Racism*, 2nd edn. (Boulder, CO: Paradigm, 2014); Ruth Thompson-Miller, Joe R. Feagin, and Leslie H. Picca, *Jim Crow's Legacy: The Lasting Impact of Segregation* (Lanham, MD: Roman and Littlefield, 2014); Evans, *Cabin Pressure*; Slatton, *Mythologizing Black Women*; Kristen M. Lavelle, *Whitewashing the South: White Memories of Segregation and Civil Rights* (Lanham, MD: Roman & Littlefield, 2014); Kamesha Spates, *What Don't Kill Us Makes Us Stronger: African American Women and Suicide* (Boulder, CO: Paradigm, 2014). On global issues, see Pinar Batur and Joe Feagin (eds.), *The Global Color Line: Racial and Ethnic Inequality and Struggle from a Global Perspective* (Greenwich, CT: JAI Press, 1999).
30 For more detail, see Feagin, *Systemic Racism* and Feagin, *Racist America*.
31 See Debra Van Ausdale and Joe R. Feagin, *The First R: How Children Learn Race and Racism* (Lanham, MD: Roman & Littlefield, 2001); Derrick Bell, *Race, Racism and the Law* (New York: Aspen Publishers 2008 [1973]); Derrick Bell, *And We Are Not Saved: The Elusive Quest for Racial Justice* (New York: Basic Books, 1989); Derrick Bell, *Silent Covenants: Brown V. Board of Education and the Unfulfilled Hopes for Racial Reform* (New York: Oxford University Press, 2004); Abraham L. Davis and Barbara L. Graham, *The Supreme Court, Race, and Civil Rights* (Thousand Oaks, CA: Sage, 1995); Kimberlé Crenshaw, Neil Gotanda, Gary Peller, and Kendell Thomas (eds.), *Critical Race Theory: The Key Writings that Formed the Movement* (New York: The New Press, 1995); Ian H. López,

White By Law: The Legal Construction of Race (New York: New York University Press, 2007 [1997]); Richard Delgado and Jean Stefancic, *Critical Race Theory: An Introduction* (New York: New York University Press, 2001); Joe R. Feagin, "Documenting the Costs of Slavery, Segregation, and Contemporary Discrimination: Are Reparations in Order for African Americans?" *Harvard Black Letter Law Journal*, 20 (2004); Wendy Moore, *Reproducing Racism: White Space, Elite Law Schools, and Racial Inequality* (Lanham, MD: Roman & Littlefield, 2007); Feagin and Sikes, *Living With Racism*; Louwanda Evans, *Cabin Pressure*; Sean Elias, *Black and White Sociology: Segregation of the Disciple* (Doctoral Dissertation, Sociology Department, Texas A&M University, 2009).

32 See Feagin, *The White Racial Frame*; Feagin and Elias, "Rethinking Racial Formation Theory," pp. 936–7.
33 See, for example, Benedict Anderson, *Imagined Communities* (London: Verso, 1983).
34 For example, Fox Cable News' ongoing obsession with discussing racial matters is noteworthy, from racially stereotyping President Obama and a hyper-focus on black pathologies to anti-Latino immigration rhetoric and avoidance of examining the white role in breeding systemic racism.
35 Picca and Feagin, *Two Faced Racism*, pp. 5–6.
36 See Feagin, *The White Racial Frame*, pp. 20–2.
37 John Stanfield II, "The Gospel of Feel-Good Sociology: Race Relations as Pseudoscience and the Decline in Relevance of American Academic Sociology in the Twenty-First Century," in Tukufu Zuberi and Eduardo Bonilla-Silva (eds.), *White Logic, White Methods: Racism and Methodology* (Lanham, MD: Roman and Littlefield, 2008), pp. 272–3, 275. Also see Elias, "Black and White Sociology," p. 2.
38 John Stanfield II, *Black Reflexive Sociology: Epistemology, Theory, and Methodology* (Walnut Creek, CA: Left Coast Press, 2011), p. 9.
39 Michelle Alexander, *The New Jim Crow: Mass Incarceration in the Age of Colorblindness* (New York: The New Press, 2012).
40 See Feagin and Elias, "Rethinking Racial Formation Theory," p. 936. See also Feagin, *Systemic Racism*; Feagin et al., *White Racism*.
41 See Marisa E. Sanchez, *Impacts of Racial Composition and Space on Racial/Ethnic Identity Development for Mexican Origin College Students*, unpublished PhD dissertation, Texas A&M University, 2015.
42 See Beckert, *Empire of Cotton*; Baptist, *The Half Has Never been Told*.
43 Stokely Carmichael (Kwame Ture) and Charles Hamilton, *Black Power: The Politics of Liberation* (New York: Vintage, 1994 [1967]), Kindle loc. 217, 255, 263.
44 For the early impact on Feagin's work, see Feagin and Benokraitis, "Institutional Racism"; Joe R. Feagin, "Indirect Institutionalized Discrimination: A Topological Analysis," *American Politics Quarterly*, 5 (1977): 177–200; Feagin and Feagin, *Discrimination American Style*.
45 For recent explication, see Shirley Better, *Institutional Racism: A Primer on Theory and Strategies for Social Change* (Lanham, MD: Roman and Littlefield, 2008).
46 Tukufu Zuberi and Eduardo Bonilla-Silva discuss this academic hostility in "Toward a Definition of White Logic and White Methods," in Tukufu Zuberi and Eduardo Bonilla-Silva (eds.), *White Logic, White Methods: Racism and Methodology* (Lanham, MD: Roman and Littlefield, 2008), pp. 3–27.
47 Philomena Essed, *Understanding Everyday Racism* (Newbury Park, CA: Sage, 1991).
48 Adia Harvey Wingfield, *Doing Business With Beauty: Black Women, Hair Salons, and the Racial Enclave Economy* (Lanham, MD: Rowman and Littlefield, 2008), p. 92.
49 See, for example, Benjamin Bowser and Raymond Hunt (eds.), *Impacts of Racism on White Americans* (Thousand Oaks, CA: Sage, 1996); Linda F. Williams, *The Constraint*

of Race: Legacies of White Skin Privilege in America (University Park, PA: Pennsylvania State University Press, 2003); Joe Feagin and Eileen O'Brien, *White Men on Race: Power, Privilege, and the Shaping of Cultural Consciousness* (Boston: Beacon Press, 2003); Matthew W. Hughey, *White Bound: Nationalists, Antiracists, and the Shared Meanings of Race* (Stanford, CA: Stanford University Press, 2012); Charles A. Gallagher and France W. Twine (eds.), *Retheorizing Race and Whiteness in the 21st Century: Changes and Challenges* (New York: Routledge, 2013), which reprints a 2008 symposium in *Ethnic and Racial Studies*.

50 *Living with Racism*, co-authored by Joe Feagin and Melvin Sikes, a leading African American social scientist, examines white racism faced by 209 African American respondents. This now well-noted work was sequentially contracted with Basic Books and Yale University Press, but eventually blocked by powerful whites at both presses who appeared to have problems believing the accurate accounts of racism given by the black respondents. It was finally published by Beacon Press.

51 Feagin and Elias, "Rethinking Racial Formation Theory," p. 939. In addition to economic, political, and social power, elites possess power over knowledge. See Shamus Khan, "The Sociology of the Elites," *Annual Review of Sociology*, 38 (2012): 370–1.

52 Our "Rethinking Racial Formation Theory" devotes five pages to white agents' centrality in societal racism. Also see Feagin, *Systemic Racism*; Feagin, *Racist America*.

53 For discussion on "settler colonialism," see Evelyn N. Glenn, "Settler Colonialism as Structure: A Framework for Comparative Studies of US Race and Gender Formation," in *Sociology of Race and Ethnicity*, 1(1) (2015): 52–72.

54 Feagin and Elias, "Rethinking Racial Formation Theory," p. 937.

55 See, for example, John H. Stanfield, II, *Philanthropy and Jim Crow in American Social Science* (Westport, CT: Green wood Press, 1985).

56 Take, as one example, the extreme violence in June 2015. A self-described white supremacist murdered nine black Americans at church. The killer was reportedly inspired by the belief that whites were losing societal power and "blacks were taking over." See Nick Corasaniti, Richard Pérez-Peña, and Lezette Alvarez, "Church Massacre Suspect Held as Charleston Grieves," *New York Times*, June 18, 2015, www.nytimes.com/2015/06/19/us/charleston-church-shooting.html?_r=0 (accessed September 2, 2015). See also Joe R. Feagin, *Racist America: Roots, Current Realities, and Future Reparations*, 3rd edn (New York: Routledge, 2014).

57 Joe Feagin and Kimberley Ducey, *Elite White Men Ruling: Who, What, When, Where, and How* (New York: Routledge, forthcoming).

58 See Sean Elias, "Investigating the Aspen Elite," *Contexts: Understanding People in Their Social Worlds*, 7(4) (2008): 62–4, and, *The Aspen Elite* (New York: Routledge, forthcoming).

59 See Feagin and Ducey, *Elite White Men Ruling*; Elias, "Investigating the Aspen Elite."

60 Jillian Berman, "Soon, Not Even 1% of Fortune 500 Companies Will Have Black CEOs," *Huffington Post* January 29, 2015, www.huffingtonpost.com/2015/01/29/black-ceos-fortune-500_n_6572074.html (accessed September 2, 2015); Jens Manuel Krogstad, "114th Congress is Most Diverse Ever," www.pewresearch.org/fact-tank/2015/01/12/114th-congress-is-most-diverse-ever (accessed September 2, 2015).

61 See Alvin Gouldner, *The Coming Crisis in American Sociology* (New York, Basic Books, 1980); Stanfield, "The Gospel of Feel-Good Sociology."

62 See Feagin and Cobas, *Latinos Facing Discrimination*.

CONCLUSION

PERSISTING SYSTEMIC RACISM, THE EMPIRICAL REALITY

On an hourly basis, disquieting US manifestations of systemic racism—for example, many police shootings of unarmed black men, women, and children; widespread anti-immigrant discrimination; and major mismanagement of Native American affairs—are conspicuous in the contemporary United States. Local, state, and federal governments still enforce well-institutionalized racist laws, policies, regulations, and cultural practices. Major and unjust socioeconomic and other resource inequalities between whites and most groups of color persist across the country. The US political economy constantly perpetuates essential elements of past systemic racism into the present day, and its major institutions generally remain controlled by many white agents of racial discrimination. Negative social psychological realities shaped by racial matters span the society, such as white psychological instabilities and pathologies witnessed in white rage and murderous inclinations directed at black Americans and other Americans of color perceived as "taking over our country." Millions of negative racist comments online and offline about President Barack Obama by many whites have demonstrated that anti-black framing and dehumanization are still prevalent, as is the extensive negative framing of people of color. Systemic racialized violence by local officials, including police brutality, has become part of everyday life for most counties, towns, and cities. Since World War II, recurring wars against people of color overseas are standard operating procedure for a still imperialist and militarily aggressive United States. Much of the population, steeped in years of white framing and well accustomed to the operations of systemic racism, has become apathetic or feels helpless in regard to such racialized realities as the massive US prison-industrial complex and secretive US detention centers abroad where US operatives torture non-Westerners, usually to maintain control of the international economy and local or global politics.

Over recent decades, the debacle of US immigration policy and enforcement, especially in regard to undocumented immigrants of color, provides another example of systemic racism emanating from a white-run government. Not just the conservative white population but also government officials across parties have often demonstrated a racialized resistance to immigrants, most currently from Latin America and Asia. These often undocumented workers, like millions of working-class European immigrants around 1900, seek to substantially improve their living conditions, employment opportunities, and human rights. Research shows that for the most part they and their descendants enrich US society by accepting low-wage jobs from US employers, who often take advantage of their undocumented status.[1] The immigrants' experience with white hostility and discrimination in various institutions demonstrates the hypocrisy of persistent claims of US democracy and social justice. Indeed, across the country, white capitalists and their white clienteles benefit greatly from Latino and Asian undocumented immigrant laborers, even as the government does not grant them citizenship rights and benefits, including fair wages and working conditions. Earlier poor European immigrants seeking similar opportunities were able to become citizens with rights, and indeed to become "white."

Moreover, some immigrant groups of color, whether undocumented or officially legal, still get labeled by powerful whites in strongly stereotyped ways, such as the white-created label of "model minority" applied to Asian immigrants and their descendants. Contrary to the stereotype, they continue to experience overt, covert, and subtle racial discrimination by whites and marginalization in workplaces and the political arena.[2] Along with these issues of immigration and group marginalization regularly shaped by systemic racism, US global relations and political-economic competition with other leading countries, such as China and India, and with the nation-state powers emerging in Africa, Asia, and Latin America are shaped and hampered by US whites' investment in persisting white-racist framing of people of color at home and abroad, as well as in imperialistic US military actions targeting people of color overseas.

Faced with these and many other problems associated with systemic racism, social scientists who wish to seriously and deeply investigate major racial matters have much theoretical and empirical work to do in the decades ahead. In our view, many need to be much better equipped than now with sufficient conceptual gear and more critical frames of mind. Let us end with several suggestions for such social scientists. We start by briefly pointing to some sites where critical racial thought is very much alive.

Theoretical analysis of systemic racism requires honest, straightforward discussion of racial matters, intellectual honesty that can jeopardize one's academic standing and perceived intellectual status. The formal and informal rules of US academia do frequently discourage critical theorizing and research about systemic racism. Striving to become an unadulterated critic of racism will likely result in some professional disadvantage or marginalization. Yet, for the sake of one's sense of self-worth, of expanded human knowledge, and ultimately of human survival, risking this professional disadvantage or marginalization is necessary; this suggests more noble human attributes than careerist advancement. Toward this end, we must remove doubts, especially among younger scientists, about challenging the dominant conceptual paradigms and intellectual figures in the contemporary social sciences, because the integrity and human relevance of the social sciences are still much in question.

We implore scholars of racial matters to pursue several primary tasks. First, invest significant energy in dismantling the white-framed perspectives of racial matters that still dominate most areas of the mainstream social sciences. Second, pursue and reflect on the long-marginalized insights of critical black social thought and of the critical-race thought of all people who actively resist the established racial hierarchy and white racial framing central to systemic racism. This will require a new or renewed emphasis on reading and utilizing the works of many critical theorists of color, the often forgotten men and women who have for centuries critically analyzed in sophisticated detail US and global racism.

Additionally, we suggest that contemporary scholars of racial matters should implement their systemic racism or other race-critical theoretical perspectives in many empirical areas of mainstream social science. Learning to detect the presence of white racial framing in society, as well as throughout the social sciences, is essential to social science and societal progress. By doing so, white-framed discourses concerning such issues as African Americans and crime, Latin Americans and immigration, Middle Eastern Americans and terrorism, Asian Americans and exotic sexuality, and numerous other topics can be more forthrightly problematized and critically evaluated in both scholarly and public discourses. Better implementation of the key insights of systemic racism theory in social science will be a major struggle, just as dismantling systemic racism in society remains a large-scale and long-term uphill struggle.

Amid the present harsh realities of systemically racist societies greatly shaped and rationalized by white racial framing, there do exist some sparks of hope. Some positive societal changes are occurring, such as the current local and national social movements aimed at repairing the broken and highly racialized criminal justice system and the similarly broken and highly racialized government immigration system. Major issues currently being addressed by hundreds of thousands of social activists include unlawful racist police profiling and violence in many local areas, unenforced laws against racial discrimination, hyper-discrimination against undocumented immigrants, and major educational and other resource inequalities between whites and people of color.

Similarly, some positive changes are currently occurring in social scientific analyses and research dissemination in regard to racial matters, including in the mainstream social sciences. We have seen the development of new social science journals addressing issues of concern for systemic racism theory and other critical-race theories, including the Association of Black Sociologists' *Issues in Race and Society: An Interdisciplinary Global Journal* and the American Sociological Association's Section on Racial and Ethnic Minorities' *Sociology of Race and Ethnicity*. *Issues in Race and Society* offers an outlet for historically marginalized scholars of color whose ideas have frequently been pathbreaking in critical thinking about US racism. Although *Sociology of Race and Ethnicity* is connected to a mainstream social science organization, its Section on Racial and Ethnic Minorities has a large percentage of race-critical researchers, and this journal aims to address US and global racial matters critically. We are also encouraged by the strength and growth of the Association of Black Sociologists, and of the Latina/o and Asia/Asian American sections of the American Sociological Association. African American, Latino/a American, Asian American, Middle Eastern American, and Indigenous American sociologists have organized important research networks in the discipline and thereby demonstrate that the larger ASA does not fulfill their research and networking needs. US social science associations are still substantially inflicted with (usually liberal) white-framed perspectives and practices that often demand this type of assertive countering by researchers of color, whose perspectives are frequently silenced.[3]

Along with contemporary journals and organizations, several other important outlets exist for theorizing systemic racism and explicating manifestations of the white racial frame. First, there is a wealth of information about racial matters available on the expanding social media, specifically Internet expert blog sites such as *Racism Review* developed by Joe Feagin and Jessie Daniels and *We Are Respectable Negroes* administered by Chauncey DeVega.[4] As of 2015, a few major cable news stations are increasing their critical coverage of racial matters and giving voice to critical thinkers of color such as social scientists Melissa Harris-Perry and Michael Eric Dyson on MSNBC. Harris-Perry, Dyson, and their often diverse guests have explicitly discussed issues of institutional, structural, and systemic racism, including the racism running through the criminal justice system, mainstream news media, educational systems, Wall Street, and the halls of Congress. Additionally, a number of less well-known newspapers, magazines, and journals regularly investigate issues surrounding institutional racism.[5] There are also progressive radio stations that address systemic racism and other forms of societal oppression, including listener-supported Pacifica radio stations across the country.

Nonetheless, despite these positive signs of progressive racial counter-framing, and examples of movements and public spaces devoted to addressing white racism, the dominant white racial framing remains pronounced, and the battle against persisting systemic racism often seems Sisyphean at present. Thus, a major task of systemic racism theorists and other critical theorists of racial matters continues to involve regularly explicating systemic racism and its white racial frame to larger public audiences, and then devising methods for dismantling this longstanding form of oppression and its well-developed, enabling institutional vehicles in society.

We and others have produced social scientific research that critically explores and deconstructs the structural and operational features of systemic racism, but have not addressed nearly enough Rutledge Dennis's challenge to probe more deeply "how racist systems may be altered and changed."[6] As we see it, one necessary, indeed imperative approach to altering white-framed racist societies is to change the way that a majority of people think in those societies. As noted, a major aim of systemic racism theory is to deconstruct the commonplace white-framed racial understandings and practices in social science and to integrate the marginalized perspectives on racism long expressed by analysts of color into mainstream social scientific dialogues where they should have a significant research impact and inspire or support progressive public policy reforms on racial issues.[7] As we see it, without an understanding and use of the insights of systemic racism theory or other race-critical theory, government, business, and civic organizations' policies will continue to greatly harm people of color and routinely perpetuate the unjust enrichments of whites. A speedy and critical replacement of mainstream theories of "race" in social science and in the larger society is a necessary first step in transforming systemically racist societies and the major institutions from which social policies and racial matters emerge.

In summary, systemic racism theory unveils and provides essential conceptual tools and theoretical perspectives that assist in the deconstruction and demolition of society's systemic racism and its central white racial framing, the latter discovered in social science and the larger society. Systemic racism theory offers an alternative way of thinking about racial issues that contrasts, often dramatically, with many current mainstream social scientific perspectives. Unlike this mainstream theorizing, systemic racism theory presents direct, unwaveringly critical explanations of numerous racial matters, including examining taboo topics such as the white elite's constant abuse of its racialized power, current racial-group conflicts sparked by the extensive racial framing of whites in authority, and the white social pathologies that are foundational in a systemically racist society. Systemic racism theorists attempt to provide an unvarnished, in-depth view of systemic racism and the white frames that sustain it and ignite serious debate and theorizing about that well-institutionalized reality. They also seek to motivate critical empirical scholarship on that racist reality, the latter being a vast and underdeveloped yet budding research field.

We certainly realize that systemic racism theory is contextual and sometimes inexact, with associated shortcomings. Our hope is that social scientists working on racial matters and others interested in critically analyzing contemporary social issues shaped by race will engage, further build, or rework systemic racism theory for the better and, more importantly, use it to disrupt and dismantle systemically racist social systems.

Systemic racism theory is in many ways a ground-up theory, holding true to its foundation in critical black thought and involving much field research and other empirical research on past and present racial oppression. For centuries, those on the ground and on the frontlines, not in the halls of academia, have frequently formulated the sharpest perceptions of the social world and human relations, including accenting and documenting the dimensions and significance of well-institutionalized racism created long ago by whites. This vast bridge in knowledge about racial matters between understandings from the ground up and views from the "heights" of academia reveal a distance that astute critical social scientists must work hard to overcome.

Notes

1 See, for example, Zulema Valdez, *The New Entrepreneurs: How Race, Class and Shape American Enterprise* (Stanford,CA: Stanford University Press, 2011).
2 See Rosalind S. Chou and Joe R. Feagin, *The Myth of the Model Minority: Asian Americans Facing Racism*, 2nd edn (Boulder, CO: Paradigm, 2015).
3 See Sean Elias, *Drawing the Sociological Color Line* (forthcoming).
4 *Racism Review* site: www.racismreview.com/blog; *We Are Respectable Negroes'* site: www.chaunceydevega.com.
5 For example, *The Nation* and *In These Times*.
6 Rutledge Dennis, "Convergences and Divergences in Race Theorizing: A Critical Assessment of Racial Formation Theory and Systemic Racism Theory," Symposium on Rethinking Racial Formation Theory in *Ethnic and Racial Studies*, 36(6) (2013): 982–8.
7 See this example in which leading researchers on health care inequalities have recently made extensive use of systemic racism theory: Jo C. Phelan and Bruce G. Link, "Is Racism a Fundamental Cause of Inequalities in Health?" *Annual Review of Sociology*, 41 (2015): 1–20. See also Joe R. Feagin and Zinobia Bennefield, "Systemic Racism and US Health Care," *Social Science & Medicine*, 103 (2014): 7–14.

INDEX

abstract liberalism 72
academic status 74
acculturation 161, 172–3
affirmative action 62–5, 193
African American studies 57, 240 *see* Black Studies
African Americans 46, 49–51, 62–4, 85, 89–90, 96, 103–6, 109, 142, 152–3, 157–8, 194, 199, 203, 218, 226–8, 252–3, 260, 262, 284; studying sociology 226–35
Alba, Richard 162–71
Alexander, Michelle 241, 255, 264
Allen, Richard 215
American Civil War 28, 222
American exceptionalism 151
American Sociological Association (ASA) 59, 140–1, 213, 285
Americanism and Americanization 150–2, 159, 171–2
analytic groupism 88
Angelou, Maya 91
Anta Diop, Cheikh 242
Appiah, Anthony 119–20
Arinori, Mori 24
Asante, Molefi K. 254
Asian Americans 48, 162, 166, 169, 194, 282, 284
assimilation processes 26–7, 38–52, 94, 121–2, 150–5, 164–8, 171–2, 222–4, 238; barriers to 166–7; economic 164; related to health 171–2; segmented 166; social costs of 171; straight-line 164
assimilation theories 158–63, 169, 171, 174–8, 274–5; deconstruction of 174–7; deficiencies in 160, 169, 175–8; general features of 158–9; in mainstream social science 158–9; reformulation and revitalization of 162–3; social 175
Association of Black Sociologists (ABS) 59, 213, 242, 284–5
Atlanta Sociological Laboratory 231
attitudinal racism 256, 260
Australia 24
autobiographies of black thinkers 90–1, 219-20

Back, Les 113–14
Baldwin, James 234, 236
Banneker, Benjamin 221
Baptist, Edward 254, 266
Becket, Sven 254, 266
Bell, Derrick 241, 255
Ben-Jochannan, Yosef 242
Bennett, Lerone 240–1, 254
Ben-Tovim, Gideon 111
Bernal, Martin 254
Beyer, Amber 134–5
biological determinism 93–4
"biological turn" in social science 140
biology: and racism 120; and social science 141–5
biosocial theories of race 130–47, 186, 275
Birmingham Centre for Contemporary Cultural Studies (CCCS) 110–13, 116
Birth of a Nation (film, 1915) 259
Black Americans *see* African Americans
black power 59, 235–8, 266–7
"black radical tradition" 182
"Black Renaissance" (1920s and 1930s) 226, 239 *see* Negro (Harlem) Renaissance

black studies 57, 184–5, 225 *see* African American studies
Blackwell, James 236
Blauner, Robert 114
Blumenbach, Johann 19
Blyden, Edward 223
Boas, Franz 31
Bode, Thomas 134–5
Bolnick, Deborah 135
Bonacich, Edna 114
Bonilla-Silva, Eduardo 60, 71–3, 79–80, 92, 241–2, 255–6, 267–8
Bourdieu, Pierre 86–7, 248
Brantlinger, Patrick 58
Brooks, Mo 1, 152
Brown, Sterling 226
Brown, William Wells 218, 223, 253
Brubaker, Rogers 80–4, 91
Bryant, Karl 140, 142–3
Bunche, Ralph 226

Calhoun, Craig 59
capitalism 24, 29–30, 109–12, 116–17, 146, 153–4, 167, 196, 198, 224
Carmichael, Stokely 59, 236–8, 254, 266–8
Carnegie, Andrew 24
Carter, Wilmoth 228
Cayton, Horace 227
Césaire, Aimé 235, 255
Chamberlain, Houston 23–4
Chicago school of sociologists 18, 227–8
Chivers, Walter 228
Christianity 21, 224
Chua, Amy 154–7
Civil Rights Act 2, 65
Clarke, John Henrik 254
class-based analyses of race 102–18, 249–50
Cole, Stephen 59
Collins, Patricia Hill 241, 250–2, 268
colonialism and colonization 19, 26, 30, 37, 115, 133, 210–11, 214, 236–7, 265–6, 269, 273
color-coded racial categories 184–5
"color line" 8–9, 63, 95, 213, 223
"colorblindness" 2–4, 12, 50, 60–75, 102, 107, 147, 197, 224, 255–6, 274; *critical* 69
Comte, Auguste 18–25, 30, 42, 221
Comtemporary Sociology (journal) 130, 138
Congo 24
Conley, Dalton 130, 138–41
Connell, Raewyn 255
Connor, Walker 123–6

Contexts (journal) 130, 140–1, 143
Cooper, Anna J. 225, 228, 253
Cornish, Samuel 220
counter-framing of racial matters 7, 12, 199, 201, 209–10, 260–1, 267–8
Cox, Oliver C. 45–6, 114–15, 211, 225–7, 231
Crenshaw, Kimberlé 241
criminal justice system 61–4, 190, 194–5, 284
critical black theory 12–13, 161, 201–26, 238–9, 243, 248, 266–7, 283, 287; before the Civil War 214–22; following the Civil War 222–6; key features of 201–13; renaissance in the 1970s 239
critical theory in general 9, 58, 60, 70, 109, 113, 249–50, 265; overview of 239–43
Crummell, Alexander 218, 223–5
Cullen, Countee 226
cultural commonalities 155
cultural construction of race 134–5
cultural evolution 131–3
cultural pluralism 52, 160–1
cultural racism 72, 113
cultural studies 118–20
"cultural turn" in race theory 31

Daniels, Jessie 285
Davis, Allison 228
Davis, Angela 241, 250–1, 254
Dawes, Christopher 138
deCODE genetics (company) 146
Delany, Martin 218, 222–3, 253
Delgado, Richard 241
Democratic Party 62, 64
Dennis, Rutledge 91, 219, 241, 286
Derrida, Jacques 58, 255
Desmond, Matthew 85–91, 248
DeVega, Chauncey 285
Dewey, John 87
discrimination, racial 62–3, 70, 108, 155, 157, 167, 178, 195, 238, 282, 284
DNA 147
Douglass, Frederick 218–23, 231, 254
Doyle, Bertram 227
Drake, St. Clair 98, 227
Dreyfus, Alfred 31
D'Souza, Dinesh 70–1
Du Bois, W.E.B. 59, 82, 86–91, 114–15, 119–20, 161, 196, 211, 217, 219, 224–33, 237, 240, 253–4

INDEX

Dunbar, Paul 226
Dunbar-Ortiz, Roxanne 254
Durkheim, Émile 18, 21, 28–32, 67, 86–7
Duster, Troy 135, 146
Dyson, Michael Eric 285

Elias, Sean 272
elite groups 117, 171, 176–7, 183–4, 190, 193–8, 202, 252, 271–4; in the corporate world 273–4
Emirbayer, Mustafa 85–91, 248
Engels, Friedrich 30
epigenetics 144
Essed, Philomena 94, 267–8
ethnic boundaries 83–5, 120
ethnic economies 167
ethnicity 39, 47–50, 79–81, 83–5, 121–3, 163, 182; as distinct from race 93–8, 133
"ethnicity turn" 256
"ethnies" 124
ethnocentrism 137, 275
eugenics 137
Eurocentrism 5–9, 12–13, 20–5, 31–2, 37–44, 67, 87, 113, 115, 132, 169, 174, 186, 199, 224
Evans, Louwanda 251
evolution, cultural and genetic 131–3
evolutionism 145
exploitation, racial 109–10, 125, 175, 184, 195–6, 266, 270, 273

Fanon, Frantz 235, 255
Fauset, Jessie 226
Feagin, Clairece 257
Feagin, Joe 13, 71, 193, 257, 261, 285
feminism 112, 216, 249–51
Fitzhugh, George 22–3, 221–2
Fletcher, Jason 138
Foner, Nancy 121
Foner, Philip 114
formation theory 181–91, 199–203, 255–6, 275 see racial formation theory; limitations of 190–1; and systemic racism 183–9
Forten, James 215–17
Fortune, T. Thomas 226
Foucault, Michel 58, 255
Frankfurt school of social theorists 214
Franklin, John Hope 253
Frazier, E. Franklin 161, 227
Frederickson, George 254

Freedom's Journal 220
Fujimura, Joan 135–7

Gabriel, John 111
Gadamer, Hans-Georg 58
Gans, Herbert 121, 164
Garnet, Henry Highland 218, 223, 253
Garrison, William Lloyd 220
Garvey, Marcus 231–3, 238
Gates, Henry Louis 91
gender role differences 142
gendered racism 267
genetic reductionism 141
genetics 131–43, 146
Genovese, Eugene 114
Germany 33
"ghettos" 104, 106
Giddens, Anthony 57–8
Giddings, Franklin 23–4
Gilroy, Paul 70, 112
Glazer, Nathan 49–51, 158–62, 166
Goldberg, David Theo 113
Gomillion, Charles 228
Gonzalez, Juan 254
Gordon, Milton 47–50, 121, 158, 163–5, 169
Gottfredson, Linda 186
Gouldner, Alvin 59
Grant, Madison 97
Grimké, Charlotte 223
Gumplowicz, Ludwig 23–4
Gutiérrez, Ramón 254

Habermas, Jürgen 58
Hahn, Harlan 257
Haiti 28
Hall, Prince 215
Hall, Stuart 111, 115–17
Hamilton, Charles 59, 236–8, 266–8
Haney-López, Ian 241
Hannity, Sean 152
Harris, Cheryl I. 241
Harris-Perry, Melissa 285
Hatch, Anthony 147
Haynes, George 228
health care 190
Heidegger, Martin 255
heritability 135, 137–8
hermeneutics 58
Hernstein, Richard 27
hierarchy, racial 8–9, 19–21, 47, 82–3, 94–7, 184–7, 270

Higginbotham, Elizabeth 251
Himes, Joseph 228
Holder, Eric 63–4, 190
Hollinger, David 70–1
hooks, bell 250–1
Horowitz, Donald 120
Horowitz, Irving 59
HoSang, Daniel 135, 137
Hsu, Stephen 137
Hubbard, Ruth 146
Hughes, Henry 22–3, 221–2
Hughes, Langston 226
human beings: as distinct from biological bodies 143; as unique social animals 145
"human capital immigrants" 167
Hume, David 19
Huntington, Samuel 97
Hurston, Zora Neale 226
Hurwitz, Jon 64
hyper-incarceration 264
hyper-scientism 145

immigrant groups, differences between 165–8, 172
immigrant studies 52, 121–2
immigration policy 24–6, 43, 165, 282
imperialism 24, 26, 29, 31, 37, 42, 133, 153–4, 265, 273, 283
incorporation of immigrants 168
India 30
inner city neighborhoods 104
"insider" doctrine in research 87
institutional analysis 86
institutional procedures 170
institutional racism 7, 12, 59, 64–5, 73, 92, 103, 236–8, 266–70, 286
integration, racial 238
intelligence, study of 40
intelligence (IQ) testing 27–8, 139, 186–7, 271
intermarriage 3, 24, 26, 166
intersectionality analysis 225–6, 250–4, 275
Irons, Jenny 254
Issues in Race and Society (journal) 285
Italian Americans 162

Jackson, John G. 253
Jacobs, Harriet 219, 221, 225
James, C.L.R. 235, 253
Janowitz, Morris 236
Japanese Americans 48–9
Jay Z 62

Jenkins, Richard 120
Jewish Americans 51
'Jim Crow' regime 2–3, 50, 64, 197, 200–1, 222–4, 264
Jindal, Piyush (Bobby) 153
jingoism 151, 176
Jodan, Michael 62–3
Johnson, Charles 227
Johnson, Helene 226
Jones, Absalom 215
Jones, Butler 228
Jordan, Winthrop 253
journals 284–5

Kant, Immanuel 19
Katznelson, Ira 254
Kaufman, Jay 135, 146
kin selection 132
King, Martin Luther 2, 234–5
Kwan, Kian 164

Ladner, Joyce 60, 235–6, 239
Lancaster, Roger 140–1
Larsen, Nella 226
Latin American immigrants to the US 64, 121, 162, 166, 194, 282, 284
Lauren, Paul Gordon 254
Lenski, Gerhard 145
Levine, Lawrence 253
Lewontin, Richard 135
liberal perspectives in research 105–6
Lieberson, Stanley 121
Locke, Alain 226
Long, Elizabeth 58–9
Loveman, Mara 78–81, 91–2, 120–1
Lyman, Stanford 242–3

McKay, Claude 226
McKee, James 242–3
MacKinnon, Catharine 250
macro-level racial phenomena 265
Maddow, Rachel 151
Malcolm X 234–6
Manheim, Karl 87
Marks, Jonathan 135
Martineau, Harriet 22
Marx, Karl 18, 28–30, 87, 115–16, 248–50
Marxism 110–17
Maryanski, Alexandra 145
materialism 157
Matthews, Chris 151–2

"melting pot" metaphor 44, 47, 121–2, 152
Memmi, Albert 255
meso-level racial phenomena 265
Mexican immigrants to the US 3, 166
micro-level racial phenomena 265
middle-class black communities 106–8, 156–7, 177
"migrant labor" model of racial issues 111
Miles, Robert 111–12
Miller, Kelly 228
Mills, Charles 240
Mizruchi, Mark 250
"model minority" label 282
Morning, Ann 135–6, 240
Morris, Aldon 109, 254
Moses, Wilson 233
Moynihan, Daniel 49–51, 158
Moynihan Report (1965) 104
"mulattos" 40–1
multiculturalism 52, 63, 160–2
multidimensional analysis of racism 111
multiracial and multiethnic nations 126
Murray, Charles 27
Muslim Americans 152–3
Myrdal, Gunnar 44–6, 158, 228

"nation," definition of 123
National Association for the Advancement of Colored People (NAACP) 229
nationalism 33, 121–6
Native Americans 3, 24, 48–9, 194, 262, 269
"naturalization" of racial issues 72
nature–nurture debate 142
Nee, Victor 162–71
"negroes" 40–1, 44, 51, 221
Negro (Harlem) Renaissance *see* 'Black Renaissance'
Nelson, Alondra 141–2
"new ethnicity" 122
"new racism" 113
newspapers for black Americans 220
"nicotine receptor gene" 139
Niedenzu, Heinz-Jürgen 145
Nigerian Americans 156–7
Nkrumah, Kwame 235
North Star (newspaper) 220

Obama, Barack 1, 64, 152–3, 177, 185, 190, 195, 281
Omi, Michael 61, 181–203, 255–6
oppression, racial 200, 237–8

organicist model of society 20–5, 30, 221
Ossario, Pilar 135
Outlaw, Lucius 240

Pacifica radio station 286
Padmore, George 235
Painter, Nell I. 254
pamphleteering by black social thinkers 215–18
Park, Robert 18, 31, 38–44, 67–8, 119, 158, 161, 165, 174–5, 228, 274
Parrott, Russell 215, 217
Pattillo, Mary 86
Peffley, Mark 64
Peller, Gary 241
Pennington, James 219
"people of color," definition of 8
phenotype characteristics 134
Phizacklea, Annie 111
Piketty, Thomas 250
Pioneer Fund 137, 196
pluralist view of racism 188
Poland 33
policy mistakes arising from genetic research 140
political institutions 193
polyethnic nations 124
post-modernism 113
post-raciality 1–4, 12, 61–75, 102, 107, 274
power relations: asymmetry in 197; racialized 6, 182; within social science 5
power structures 271
public policy, research input into 139–40
Purvis, Robert 218

race: as distinct from ethnicity 93–8, 133; as distinct from racism 202–3; socially defined 136; as an umbrella concept 118
"race card" 66
race theory 212, 248–9, 274; divisions in 59–61
racial concepts 78–83
racial formation theory *see* formation theory
racial groups 94–7
racial relations cycle 41–3, 174–5, 274
racialization, concept of 191
racism: *backstage* 66; minimization of 72; *white* and *non-white* versions of 188
racism theory (as distinct from race theory) 212, 214
Rajagopalan, Ramya 135
Randolph, A. Philip 226

reflexivity of researchers 85–90
Reid, Ira 228
"relative autonomy" model of racial issues 110–11, 116
Republican Party 62, 64
"reverse racism" 66
Roberts, John 62, 70
Rockefeller, John D. 24
Rodriquez, Richard 185
Romney, Mitt 64
Rossi, Peter 59
Rubenfeld, Jed 154–7
Rumbaut, Rubén 171–4
Russwurm, John 220

Said, Edward 253, 255
St. Jean, Yanick 251
Sanderson, Stephen 145
segregation, racial 3, 24–5, 65–6, 108, 201, 223, 264
Selvig, Daniel 134–5
Sesardic, Neven 137
"settler" countries 96, 269
Shadd, Mary Ann 215–16
Shiao, Jiannbin Lee 134–7
Shibutani, Tamotsu 164
Sica, Alan 59
Slatton, Brittany 251
slavery 2, 6, 19, 22–3, 26–9, 37, 108, 115, 197, 210, 214–15, 218–22, 236, 266, 269
Smith, Anthony 123–6
Smith, Dorothy 250
smoking and smoking tax 139–40
Snowden, Frank 98
"social closure" concept 79
social conflicts 175
social construction of race 136–8, 191
social Darwinism 23–4
social justice 30–1, 218, 228–9
social theory 248, 252; *see also* critical social theory
societal adaptation theory 168
societal racism 114–15, 119
sociobiology 131, 139–40, 275
socio-genomics 138, 144–7, 275
socio-historical analyses 253–4
Sociological Theory (journal) 130, 134–5
sociology 20–7, 38–9, 47, 59, 67, 74, 213; African American students of 226–35; of knowledge 58
Solomos, John 102–3, 110–18
South Africa 24

Sowell, Thomas 70
Spencer, Herbert 18, 21–7, 42
Springer, Kristen 140, 142–3
Srole, Leo 164
Stampp, Kenneth 253
Stanfield, John 85, 240, 263
Staples, Robert 60, 236
"state," definition of 123
state formation 192–202
status, societal 170–1
Steele, Shelby 70
Steinberg, Stephen 42, 46, 157–8, 242–3
Steinmetz, George 243
stereotypes, racial 185–8
Stewart, Maria 215–16, 221–2, 225
Stoddard, Lothrop 97
successful individuals, criteria for 155
"survival of the fittest" 23
systemic racism 5–13, 17–18, 47–8, 66–9, 73, 88, 92, 107–9, 116–18, 125–6, 146–7, 159, 162–3, 173–4, 177–8, 182–91, 199–203, 209–10, 248–75, 281–7; definition of 258; global 265; and racial formation theory 183–9; research on 91–2

Takaki, Ronald 254
Tarde, Gabriel 23–4
Thernstrom, Stephan and Abigail 70–1
Thomas, W.I. 23–4, 74
Time magazine 130–1
de Tocqueville, Alexis 21–2, 221
Toomer, Jean 226
"traits" of racial groups 27
Trotter, Monroe 226
Turner, Henry M. 223
Turner, Jonathan 145
Turner, Stephen 59
Tuskagee Institute 38
23andMe (company) 146

"underclass" communities 103–6
United States Congress and government institutions 62, 64, 193–8, 273–4
Universal Negro Improvement Association (UNIA) 232

van den Berghe, Pierre L. 131–4
Vanderbilt, Cornelius 24
Vann Woodward, C. 219–20, 253
van Sertima, Ivan 242
Veblen, Thorstein 250

Vera, Hernán 257
vetting of immigrants 170
Voting Rights Act (1965) 193

Wacker, Fred 45
Wacquant, Loïc 92
Wade, Nicholas 130–1
Walker, David 215, 217–18, 221
Wall Street Journal 186
Wallman, Sandra 120
Ward, Lester 23–4
Warner, W. Lloyd 93, 164
warranteeism 22
Washington, Booker T. 38–9, 231–3
Waters, Mary 122
Weber, Max 18, 28, 32–4, 67, 79, 96, 248
welfare recipients 51
Wells-Burnett, Ida B. 228–33, 253
West, Ed 97
white racial framing of society 4–7, 11–12, 18, 25, 28, 31–2, 37–9, 50, 65–7, 73–5, 80, 83, 90, 115, 121, 134, 136, 156, 158–9, 174, 177–8, 182–4, 187, 189, 199–200, 203–4, 211, 214, 237, 254–61, 265–70, 273–5, 283–7; centrality of 266–74
white social pathologies 272–3
white supremacists 22, 25–7, 31, 41–2, 92, 188–9, 199, 201, 210, 215, 222
whiteness 183–5, 269; levels of 183–4; politics of 114; as "property" 241; as an unspoken standard 239
whiteness studies 225
whites 186–9, 258, 261, 266–274; definition of 8; power and priveleges of 212, 271
Wicks, Elizabeth 215–16
Williams, Chancellor 254
Williams, Eric 235, 253, 266
Williams, George Washington 223, 253
Williams, Raymond 118
Willie, Charles 177
Wilson, E.O. 131
Wilson, William J. 102–9, 118, 177
Wimmer, Andreas 83–5, 91
Winant, Howard 61, 181–203, 255–6
Winfrey, Oprah 62–3
Wingfield, Ada Harvey 268
Woodson, Carter G. 226, 253
working-class immigrants 167
Wright, Richard 226
Wu, Frank 185

Yancy, George 240

Zuberi, Tukufu 241–2

Taylor & Francis eBooks

Helping you to choose the right eBooks for your Library

Add Routledge titles to your library's digital collection today. Taylor and Francis ebooks contains over 50,000 titles in the Humanities, Social Sciences, Behavioural Sciences, Built Environment and Law.

Choose from a range of subject packages or create your own!

Benefits for you
- » Free MARC records
- » COUNTER-compliant usage statistics
- » Flexible purchase and pricing options
- » All titles DRM-free.

Benefits for your user
- » Off-site, anytime access via Athens or referring URL
- » Print or copy pages or chapters
- » Full content search
- » Bookmark, highlight and annotate text
- » Access to thousands of pages of quality research at the click of a button.

REQUEST YOUR FREE INSTITUTIONAL TRIAL TODAY

Free Trials Available
We offer free trials to qualifying academic, corporate and government customers.

eCollections – Choose from over 30 subject eCollections, including:

Archaeology	Language Learning
Architecture	Law
Asian Studies	Literature
Business & Management	Media & Communication
Classical Studies	Middle East Studies
Construction	Music
Creative & Media Arts	Philosophy
Criminology & Criminal Justice	Planning
Economics	Politics
Education	Psychology & Mental Health
Energy	Religion
Engineering	Security
English Language & Linguistics	Social Work
Environment & Sustainability	Sociology
Geography	Sport
Health Studies	Theatre & Performance
History	Tourism, Hospitality & Events

For more information, pricing enquiries or to order a free trial, please contact your local sales team:
www.tandfebooks.com/page/sales

 **Routledge** | The home of
Taylor & Francis Group | Routledge books

www.tandfebooks.com